Taqwiat-Ul-Iman

Taqwiat-Ul-Iman

By

Hazrat Ismail Shaheed

Translated & Edited by

Badar Azimabadi

ADAM PUBLISHERS & DISTRIBUTORS

New Delhi - 110002

Adam Publishers & Distributors
(Exporters & Importers)
1542, Pataudi House, Darya Ganj,
New Delhi-110002
Ph.: (O) 23282550, 23284740,
Fax.: 23267510
E-mail: apd@bol.net.in,
syedsajid_ali@rediffmail.com
website: www.adambooks.com

Edition- **2013**
ISBN : 81-7435-032-2
Price :

Printed & Bound in India
Published by :
S. Sajid Ali, for
Adam Publishers & Distributors
1542, Pataudi House, Darya Ganj,
New Delhi-110002, India

Contents

Taqwiat-Ul-Iman

Tadhkirul Ikhwan

(Remaining Part of Taqwiat-Ul-Iman)

Preface

Thousands of thanks are due to you O Lord, that you conferred on me your Favours and Blessings; showed me the right path of your religion and made me learn your real *Tauheed* (Oneness); included me in the Ummah of Your Messenger, Muhammad (peace and blessings of Allah be upon him); made me fond of learning to follow his path; instilled in my heart the love of those who show us His Way. O Lord! send Your Blessings to Your Beloved Prophet, his family members, Companions and his deputies and those who follow him.

It is to be borne in mind that all men are the slaves of Allah and the main function of a slave is to serve. Hence one who does not serve is not a slave at all; and the real service is to keep Faith intact. If Faith of anyone is disturbed anyway, none of his service is acceptable; anyone whose Faith is straight, even a little of his service may suffice. Hence everyone of us should make all out efforts to keep Faith right and intact and should prefer to obtain this. People these days adopt different ways in Faith. Some follow the rites and customs of their fathers; others follow their religious guides blindly and adopt the figments of their mind. The right way is to follow the path of Allah and His Messenger (peace and blessings of Allah be upon him) without using their own power of reasoning. The plea that it is almost impossible to understand the Word of Allah and His Messenger directly, without the help of a religious scholar or guide or a saint. This is perfectly untrue. Allah, the Almighty has observed in Surah Al-Baqara of His Book in unequivocal word:

وَلَقَدْ اَنْزَلْنَا اِلَيْكَ آيَاتٍ بَيِّنَاتٍ وَمَا يَكْفُرُ بِهَا اِلاَّ الْفَاسِقُوْنَ :

> "We have sent down to thee Manifest Signs (*ayah*); and none rejects them but those who are perverse."

That is to say, it is not difficult to understand but to follow it, because One dislikes to obey, and hence disobeys. Not much learning and knowledge is required to follow the Words of Allah and His Messenger. The Messengers were sent to show the right path to the Ignorants and guide the misguided persons. Thus Allah, the Almighty says in Surah Al-Juma of the Holy Qur'an:

هُوَ الَّذِىْ بَعَثَ فِى الاُمِّيِّنَ رَسُوْلاً مِنْهُمْ يَتْلُوْا عَلَيْهِمْ آيَاتِهِ وَيُزَكِّيْهِمْ وَيُعَلِّمُهُمُ الْكِتَابَ وَالْحِكْمَةَ وَاِنْ كَانُوْا مِنْ قَبْلُ لَفِى ضَلاَلٍ مُّبِيْنٍ-

> "It is He Who has sent amongst the Unlettered a messenger from among themselves, to rehearse to them His Signs, to purify them, and to instruct them in the Book."

That is, it is a great Favour of Allah that He sent such a Messenger who warned the misguided people, purified the impure, gave knowledge to Ignorants, reason to unwise and showed right path to the deviated ones. Now if one, even after hearing this *ayah,* says that what the Messenger says cannot be understood directly without the help of a religious scholar is one who negates this *ayah.*

One should, therefore, follow the dictates of Allah and His Messenger and keep their Faith accordingly. There are two constituents of Faith: to consider Allah as Allah and Messenger as Messenger. Considering Allah as Allah means none should be associated as partner to Him; while considering Messenger as Messenger means none should be followed other than he. The first element is *Tauheed* (Oneness of God) which is against *shirk* (polytheism). Second is the follow the *Sunnah*, the opposite of which is *bid'at* (innovation).Hence everyone should hold *Tauheed* and *Sunnah* fastly and save himself from *shirk* and *bid'at*, because these two factors disturb the real *Faith*, while other defects disturb the functions, only a person well versed in *Tauheed* and *Sunnah* is worthy of being a teacher and guide. Hence a few *ayahs* and *ahadith* containing matters regarding *Tauheed* and *Sunnahs* have been collected in this book.

Chapter - I

Oneness and Plurality of God

فِي ذِكرِ التَّوحِيد وَالشّرك

Polytheism is spreading fast among people. The concept of Oneness of God is now hard to find. But, generally, people do not fully understand the real meaning of the unity and plurality of God in spite of claiming themselves to be 'Believer'. In most cases they are found to be immersed in polytheism. So, at first it is essential to fully understand the real meaning of unity and Plurality of God. And the virtues and evils of both of them must be understood in the light of the Qur'an and the Hadiths. Most people call out saints, spiritual guides, prophets, patriarch, religious leaders, martyrs, angels, fairies etc. in difficult moments of life, in junctures and in sufferings and ask for their favour in times of crisis. They make a vow, make offerings for getting some needs fulfilled and attribute their sons to them for evading some distress, calamities and misfortunes. Some people name their sons as Abdun-nabi while others call their sons by the names of Ali Baksh, Husain Bux, Peer Bux, Madar Bux, Salar Bux, Ghulam Mohiuddin, Ghulam Moinuddin and so on so forth. And to keep them living long, they either make their sons have a tie of hair behind in the name of someone or make them put on 'baddhi' in the name of someone or make them wear dresses in the name of someone or put in chains in the name of someone and sacrifice animals in the name of someone. Some of them cry for help and mercy and cry out for justice in sorrows and sufferings while others swear in someone's name during their talks and speeches. In short, what the Hindus do with their deities and idols, these so-called Muslims do with Prophets, saints, holymen, spiritual guides, religious leaders, martyrs, angels and fairies etc. and in spite of all these they claim to be Muslims. What a wonder! Allah, the Almighty has very truthfully said in Surah Yusuf:

وَمَا يُؤمِنُ اَكْثَرُهُمْ بِاللّٰهِ اِلاَّ وَهُمْ مُشْرِكُوْنَ ـ

"The greater part of them believe in Allah but they associate others with Him."

(Q.12:106).

That is, most of the people are immersed in polytheism in spite of their claim to have faith in One Allah. So if a warner tells them that they are indulged in polytheism in spite of claiming faith in One Allah and mix up unity with plurality, they reply that they are not indulged in polytheism; rather, they put their faith in prophets and saints. One may be said to be a polytheist only when one equalises prophets, saints, spiritual guides and martyrs with Allah. But we do not have such a faith. We, rather, consider them as the slaves of Allah and His creation. It is Allah who has bestowed on them power of possessing and using objects of nature. They possess and use objects of the universe with the sole consent and permission of the Divine Power. Calling them means calling Allah, the Almighty. Seeking their help means seeking help from Him alone. They are dear to Allah so they may do whatever they like. They are their intercessors and pleaders in the court of Allah. They are supposed to find Allah by approaching them and get access to Allah by being near to them. Moreover, they think that they come near to Allah by calling them; and the more they show respect to them, the more they are near to Allah. They utter such senseless things. The reason behind all these is that they exercise their own reason keeping aside Words of Allah and His Apostle. They follow false stories and take wrong and baseless rites and rituals to be authentic. Had they gone deep into the Words of Allah and His Messenger, they would have come to know that the unbelievers used to say such things before the Prophet of Allah (peace and blessings of Allah be upon him). Allah, the Almighty did not pay heed to them, became enraged and declared them as liar. Allah, the Almighty says in Surah Yunus of the Holy Qur'an:

وَيَعْبُدُوْنَ مِنْ دُوْنِ اللهِ مَا لَا يَضُرُّهُمْ وَلَا يَنْفَعُهُمْ وَيَقُوْلُوْنَ
هٰؤُلَآءِ شُفَعَاءُنَا عِنْدَ اللهِ قُلْ أَتُنَبِّئُوْنَ اللهَ بِمَا لَا يَعْلَمُ
فِى السَّمٰوَاتِ وَلَا فِى الْأَرْضِ سُبْحَانَهُ وَتَعَالٰى عَمَّا
يُشْرِكُوْنَ :

> "They worship besides Allah that which can neither harm nor help them, and say: 'These will be our intercessors with Allah.'
>
> Say: 'Do you presume to tell Allah of what He knows to be neither in the heavens nor in the earth? Glory be to Him! Exalted be He above what they associate with Him !'
>
> (Q.10:18)

Allah, the Almighty conferred no power on those whom they call for help. They can neither harm them nor they can give them any profit. Those who claim that they are their intercessors with Allah, should know that Allah never told such things. Are they aware of the fact more than Allah that they know what Allah do not? This verse reveals that there is no intercessor from earth to sky who may be called for help or may give profit or loss. The intercession of the Prophets and friends of Allah depends on the Will of Allah; calling or not calling them makes no difference. And one should keep in mind that one is polytheist even if he worships them as their intercessors with Allah. Allah, the Almighty says in Surah Zumar of the Holy Qur'an:

وَالَّذِيْنَ اتَّخَذُوْا مِنْ دُوْنِهِ اَولِيَاءَ مَانَعْبُدُهُمْ اِلاَّ لِيُقَرِّبُوْنَا اِلَـى اللهِ زُلْفٰى ط اِنَّ اللهَ يَحْكُمُ بَيْنَهُمْ فِى مَاهُمْ فِيْـهِ يَخْتَلِفُـوْنَ ط اِنَّ اللهَ لاَيَهْدِىْ مَنْ هُوَ كَاذِبٌ كَفارٌ -

> "As for those who chose other guardians besides Him, (saying): `We serve them only that they may bring us nearer to Allah; Allah Himself will judge between them concerning their differences. He does not guide the untruthful unbeliever".
>
> (Q.39:3)

The reality that Allah, the Almighty is nearest to His slaves has been falsified by them and keeping aside this fact, they coined something new considered them their helpers. They failed to recognise the blessing of Allah by which He directly bestows on His slaves, grants their desires and ward off their calamities and misfortunes. They offered no thanks to Allah for His alround blessings and benedictions; they, rather, wanted all these from other than Allah. Nevertheless, they seek proximity with Allah, although the course adopted by them is reverse. Certainly, Allah will not show right path to them and they will not come close to Allah in this way. The more they go along this path, they will be away from Him.

It can be inferred from this verse that one who seeks anybody's help other than Allah, he is also a polytheist, a liar and a thankless person. Allah, the Almighty says in Surah Mominoon of the Holy Qur'an:

قُلْ مَنْ بِيَدِهِ مَلَكُوْتُ كُلِّ شَىْءٍ وَهُوَ يُجِيْرُ وَلَا يُجَارُ عَلَيْهِ
اِنْ كُنْتُمْ تَعْلَمُوْنَ : سَيَقُوْلُوْنَ لِلّٰهِ فَاَنّٰى تُسْحَرُوْنَ :

> "Say: 'In whose hands is the sovereignty of all things, protecting all, while against Him there is no protection? Tell me if you know the truth: 'In Allah's', Say: 'How then can you be so bewitched?'
>
> (Q.23:89)

Even if the unbelievers are asked who administers the universe and to whom none is a challenger, they will certainly say, this is the glory of Allah alone. Thus it is totally senseless to adore others.

The above verse makes it clear that Allah, the Almighty has delegated none the power to share in His administration of the universe. Hence nobody can help anybody else. It is also something well-known that even the unbelievers during the days of the Prophet of Allah would not equalise their idols with Allah; they, rather, consider them to be the creation and slaves of Allah. They never put them as rival to Allah, but their act of infidelity and polytheism was just to calling them for help, for vowing for them, for offering something to them and taking them to be their pleader and intercessor. Thus, anyone who acts like this is equal to Abu Jahl in polytheism, inspite of considering them slaves and creation of Allah. One should, therefore, keep in mind that it is not only an act of polytheism to consider anyone else equal or rival to Allah. Polytheism is rather, to adore anybody else in the same manner what Allah deserves alone without any associate; for example, bowing before them, sacrificing animals in their names, vowing for them, calling them for help in times of troubles and sufferings, thinking them to be omnipresent and considering them to share the Power of Allah in the administration of universe. Thus it is all the same whether one adored in this way is inferior to Allah in stature or the slave and creation of Allah. It makes no difference whether these objects of worship are prophets and friends of Allah, or jinns and Satan, ghosts and fairies, one turns a polytheist if he or she adore them. Hence, Allah, the Almighty becomes enraged with the Jews and the Christians as He has done in case of the idol worshipers, although they dealt with prophets and friends of Allah. Allah the Almighty says in Surah Bara'at (Tauba) of the Holy Qur'an:

اِتَّخِذُوْا اَحْبَارَهُمْ وَرُهْبَانَهُمْ اَرْبَاباً مِّنْ دُوْنِ اللّٰهِ وَالْمَسِيْحَ
ابْنَ مَرْيَمَ وَمَا اُمِرُوْا اِلَّا لِيَعْبُدُوْا اِلٰهاً وَّاحِداً لَا اِلٰهَ اِلَّا
هُوَ سُبْحَانَهُ عَمَّا يُشْرِكُوْنَ:

> "They take their rabbis and monks as Lords besides Allah, and also al-Masih, son of Maryam, though they were ordered to serve one God only. There is no god but He. Exalted be He above those whom they associate with Him!"
>
> (Q. 9:31)

Thus they consider Allah to be the big Master and the Molvis and Saints to be the small ones. But they have not been enjoined to do so. Hence they become victim of polytheism. He is unique and none, big or small, is His associate. All, big and small, are His slaves and nothing else; all are needy and humble. Allah, the Almighty says in Surah Maryam of the Holy Qur'an:

اِنْ كُلُّ مَنْ فِى السَّمٰوَاتِ وَالْاَرْضِ اِلَّا اٰتِى الرَّحْمٰنِ عَبْداً
لَقَدْ اَحْصٰهُمْ وَعَدَّهُمْ عَدًّا وَّكُلُّهُمْ آتِيْهِ يَوْمَ الْقِيَامَةِ فَرْداً:٥

> "There is none in the heavens or on earth but shall return to Him in utter submission. He has kept strict count of all

(His creatures) and numbered them; and one by one they shall approach Him on the Day of Resurrection."

(Q.19: 93-94-95)

It means no man or angel is above the status of a slave and has no power of his own but lies in the possession of Allah. He has power over every thing and delegates His power to none. Hundreds of verses in the Qur'an carry these topics and whosoever fully understands the real meaning of a few such verses, becomes aware of the contents of Unity and Polytheism. Now it is a matter of inquiry and deep understanding what Allah, the Exalted has appropriated for Himself that nobody is allowed to share them. These are many, but a few things deserve mention and these should be tested on the touchstone of the Qur'an and the Hadiths, so that these become clear to all those who want to understand these things. Thus it is Allah who is omnipresent and has the power to have knowledge of all objects whether near or distant, open or hidden, in darkness or in bright day light, in heavens or lands, on the top of mountains or in the deep sea. This is the grandeur of Allah and of no others. Thus if one praises anybody else day and night, calls him from far and near, cries for help and justice, attacks the enemies in his name, recites the whole Qur'an in his name or keeps himself busy in his name or conceives his face and think that by taking his name by tongue or heart or by thinking of his face or of his grave he gets informed and he knows all his ins and outs and whatever happens to him like his sickness and recovery, expansion of wealth and destitute, life and death, weal and woe, all is known to him all the time and hears whatever comes out of his mouth, and he is aware of all his whims and thoughts; all these things make him polytheist and all such things are but polytheism. This is called partnership in the knowledge of Allah. Such a creed makes one Polytheist, whether he keeps such a creed with prophets or friends of Allah or with spiritual guide or a martyr or with spiritual leader or his son, with a ghost and fairy and whether he thinks that those powers are their own or are assigned to them by Allah; in short, all these creeds create polytheism in him.

Secondly, by thinking that they administer the universe according to their will and issue their order and kill and bring back to life by their own desire, expand livelihood and bring about destitute, make one fall sick and bring about recovery to anyone, confer victory and cause defeat, bestow fortune and cause misfortune, fulfil desire and needs, evade calamities, help in sufferings, reach in distress; these are all within the power of Allah and beyond the power of prophets, friends of Allah, spiritual guides, martyrs, ghosts and fairies. Thus anybody who proves power of administration in anyone else except Allah, puts his needs and desires before him and make offerings in this hope, makes a vow and calls him in times of distress and calamities, turns a polytheist. This is called partnership in the administration of Allah. Hence, whether he thinks that they have their own power or such a power is assigned by Allah; in all cases these are acts of polytheism.

Thirdly, Allah has specified for Himself some acts of adoration which are called prayers; for example, 'Sajdah' (prostration) and Ruku (bowing head and body in prayer), keep standing with hands joined, spending money in His name, observing fast in His name, making journey from far off places towards His House, moving in such a form and shape that one is taken to be a pilgrim, calling one's Lord and Master in the way, avoiding nonsense talks, keeping away from hunting and circumambulating of Ka'aba in this manner, lying in prostration towards the House of Allah, carrying animals of sacrifice towards it, taking vow there, putting veil on it, supplicating at its threshold, asking for a favour in this world and the Hereafter, kissing a stone, rubbing face and chest against its wall, invoking Allah by holding its cover, lighting its surroundings, keeping at its service as an attendant as sweeping it, lighting it, spreading carpet, providing drinking water and water for ablution and bathing, drinking water of its well thinking it to be pure and sacred, washing body with this water, distributing it among themselves, carrying it for the absentees, treading with backward steps while going back, showing respect to the forests around i.e. keepıng from hunting, from cutting trees, from uprooting grass, from grazing animals etc; all these Allah, the Almighty has enjoined upon the slaves for His adoration. Hence anyone adoring any prophet or spiritual guide or ghost or fairy or any real or unreal grave or any place or any 'chilla' (the forty days of Lent in which the religious people retire to their cells or to mosques and engage themselves in fasting and divine worship) or any house or 'tabarruk' (a portion of presents or what is left of food presented to great men) or a bier or standard or observing fast in its name or keep standing with hands joined or offering animals of sacrifice or making journey from far off places for such houses, or getting them lighted, putting cover on them or offering sheet for them, erecting sticks in their names, treading with backward steps at the time of departure, kissing their graves, fanning 'morchal' (fan of peacock feathers for driving away flies), erecting canopy over it, kissing its threshold, entreating with folded hands, taking vow, sitting in attendance, showing respect to the forests around and other such things, is to be labelled as a polytheist. This is called 'partnership in prayer' i.e. adoring anyone thinking him liable to be adored of his own or thinking that Allah is pleased with such an act of adoration and He showers His blessings with such acts and wards off calamities and misfortunes, he is liable to be convicted as a polytheist.

Fourthly, Allah, the Exalted has taught His slaves to remember Him in all activities of life and keep on adoring Him so that Faith remain intact and all the tasks of their day to day life remain blessed. These activities consist of vowing in the name of Allah in times of calamities and misfortunes, calling Him for help in difficult times and beginning every task in His name, sacrificing animals in His name on having a child and naming him Abdullah, Abdul Rahman, Khuda Bux, Allah Diya, Ummatullah, Allah Di etc. and setting aside in His name a portion from the produce of hand and garden, keeping a portion of wealth and ornaments as an offering to Allah, showing respects to the animals led towards His House ie. neither riding on them nor putting any load on them; and submitting to His orders while eating, drinking and wearing something ie. doing what is permitted and refraining from what is prohibited from Allah; thinking all the calamities from Allah, like famine and abundance, health and sickness, victory and defeat, fortune and misfortune, weal and woe etc. saying that the task to be performed depends on the Will of Allah i.e. to name Him in a manner that shows greatest regard and authority i.e. to say He is the Lord, Master and Creator; to swear in His name if need be; such things are enjoined by Allah for His adoration. Thus anyone who adores prophets and friends of Allah; religious guides and martyrs, ghosts and fairies in a way that he makes offering in times of distress, calls for help in calamities, takes their names in place of 'Bismillah', makes offerings on having a child, names his children as Abdun-Nabi, Imam Bux, Peer Bux; sets aside some portions of the produce from land and garden in their names, makes offering in their names what is obtained from harvest before putting it in his personal use; specifies a portion of wealth and some animals from the flock in their name and then shows respects to those animals, does not drive them away from fodder and water, does not hit with wooden stick and stones; and does not practise any rites with regard to eating, drinking and dressing that such person must not eat a particular thing and wear a particular dress; 'Sahnak' of Hadrat Bibi must not be eaten by a male, a slave girl or a maid servant or a woman married twice, provisions of Shah Abdul Haque must not be eaten by a smoker of pipe. Moreover, the person who refers to what good or evil caused to anyone saying that so and so has become mad owing to the curse of so and so; so and so has turned destitute because of being rejected by so and so, and so and so has achieved victory and fortunes after being favoured by so and so; famine has been caused by such and such star; such and such task could be accomplished because of being started at such a day or time or such and such object can be had if Allah or the prophet or the spiritual guide wills so or addresses him with the title of 'the worshipped', the Benefactor, the Carefree, God of the gods, Lord of the territory, the Emperor; and if swearing is needed, he swears by the Prophet or by Ali or by his spiritual guide or religious leader or swears by their graves; polytheism is caused in each case.

This is called 'Partnership in habits' i.e. adoring others in the same manner one adores Allah habitually. All these four types of polytheism are openly mentioned in the Qur'an and Hadiths. Hence this chapter has been divided in five parts. Part one deals with the evil of Polytheism and virtues of Unity; part two deals with the evil of the partnership in knowledge; part third mentions the evil of the partnership in administration; part fourth mentions the evil of the partnership in Prayer and; part fifth mentions the evil of the partnership in habits.

PART - ONE

In Defence of ‘Shirk’ (Polytheism)

فِی الْاِجْتِنَابِ عَنِ الْاِشْرَاکِ

Allah, the Almighty says:

اِنَّ اللّٰه لَایَغفِرُ اَن یُّشرَکَ به وَیَغفِرُ مَا دُونَ ذٰلِکَ لِمَن یَّشَاءُ
وَمَن یُّشرِك بِاللّٰهِ فَقَد ضَلَّ ضَلَالاً بعیداً ۔ (نساء)

“Allah will not forgive setting up partner with Him. He will forgive whom He will, all other sins. He that sets up partners with Allah has strayed far from the truth.”
(Q.4:116)

Deviating from the way of Allah is also not making any difference between lawful and unlawful, becoming immersed in theft and debauchery, abandoning ‘namaz’ (prayer) and ‘rozah’ (fasting), usurping the rights of wife and children, showing disrespect to parents. But one who indulges in ploytheism is the most deviated and perverted person and hence Allah, the Almighty will never pardon him although He may pardon other sins.

The above verse makes it clear that polytheism will never be pardoned and the polytheist will receive punishment fixed for it. Now if he is a polytheist of the high degree when a person turns an unbeliever, he will always remain in the hell; he will never come out of it nor will get any comfort therein. Moreover, acts nearing polytheism will invite punishment according to what is fixed by Allah and for the rest of the sins Allah's will will be the deciding factor. It is also clear by now that there is no sin graver than ploytheism. For example, if the subjects of a king indulge in acts of crime like theft, robbery, getting asleep at the time of keeping a watch, ignoring the court hours, retreating from the battlefield, criminal negligence in depositing money with the royal treasury etc. Although each of this criminal act has a punishment from the king, but it all depends on the king whether he inflicts any punishment on the criminal or leave him scot free. But if his subjects rise in rebellion against the king and declare any noble or a minister or a headman or a mean person as king and offer crown and throne to him or call him shadow of God or pay their respects to him or fix a day of feast and festivity for him and make some offering for him these are the greatest offences against the king, and the offenders must be severely punished. If the king ignores such offences, he is at fault. Wise men will surely declare such a king as shameless. Hence one should fear Lord of the territories and the most high-minded and powerful for how can He pardon such a degree of polytheism? How severe a punishment He will inflict on them? May Allah show His Mercy to all the Muslims and save them from the scourge of polytheism. Amin

Allah, the Almighty says in Surah Luqman of the Holy Qur'an:

وَإِذْ قَالَ لُقْمَانُ لِابْنِهِ وَهُوَ يَعِظُهُ يَا بُنَيَّ لَاتُشْرِكْ بِاللّٰهِ إِنَّ

الشِّرْكَ لَظُلْمٌ عَظِيمٌ -

"And (remember) when Luqman said to his son when admonishing him: "My son, associate none with Allah, for

to associate others with Him is a tremendous wrong."
(Q.31:13)

Allah, the Almighty had given great wisdom to Luqman and hence he thought it to be an act of great injustice that the right of one is handed over to someone else. Thus, if one transfers the right of Allah to any one among His creatures, it is tantamount to transfer the right of the highest and the greatest to the lowest and the meanest, 'as if one puts the crown of a king on the head of a cobler' What a greater injustice would be than this? One should keep in mind that every creature, big or small, is baser than a cobler before the glory of Allah.

The above verse makes it abundantly clear that as from the point of view of 'Shara' (the divine code of life), polytheism is the greatest sin, similarly from the standpoint of reason, polytheism is the greatest fault, for showing disrespects to the great souls is a fault. Since none is greater than Allah, and polytheism is utter disgrace to Him.

Allah, the Almighty says in Surah Anbiya of the Holy Qur'an:

وَمَا اَرسَلنَا مِن قَبلِكَ مِن رَّسُولٍ اِلَّا نُوحِيِ اِلَيهِ اَنَّهُ لَا اِلٰـهَ
اِلاَّ اَنَا فَاعبُدُونَ -

"We sent no apostle before you to whom We did not send this inspiration: 'There is no god but Me. Therefore, 'Serve Me."

(Q.21:25)

Hence all the Prophets came with the same decree from Allah that one should obey Allah alone and none but one Allah. The above verse makes it clear that all the divine codes of all ages ordain practising oneness of Allah and forbids polytheism. This is the only way of salvation and except this all other ways are wrong.

Abu Hurairah (Radiallah-o-anho) reports the Holy Prophet

(peace be upon him) to have said: "

انَا اغنى الشركَاء عن الشرك من عمل عملا اشرك

فيه معى غيرى تركته وشريكه وانا منه برىء -

> Allah, the Almighty has said: 'I am very careless about partnership attached to Me and about one who performs such an act, and I leave him and his act of attaching partnership aside and I am displeased with one who acts like that."
>
> (Muslim as mentioned in Mishkat)

That is, I do not do like those who divide among themselves what they have in common. I do not take my share from those who perform something for Me and do the same for others. I am rather disgusted with such persons. This Hadith makes it clear that one who performs something for Allah as well as for someone other than Allah too, is one who commits polytheism. It is also derived from this Hadith that any act of worship performed by a polytheist is not approved by Allah and He is disgusted with such an act. Allah, the Almighty says in Surah A'raf of the Holy Qur'an:

واذ اخذ ربك من بنى آدم من ظهورهم ذريتهم قال

جمعهم فجعلهم ازواجًا ثم صورهم فاستنطقهم

فتكلموا ثم اخذ عليهم العهد والميثاق والعهد هم على

انفسهم الست بربكم قا لو بلى ط قال فا نى ا شهد

عليكم السموت السبع والارضين السبع واشهِد عليكم

ابا كم آ د م شهدنا ان تقولوايوم ا لقيمة انا كنا عن

هذا غفلين لم نعلم بهذا اعلموا انه لا اله غيرى

ولارب غيری ولاتشركوابی شيئاً انی سارسل اليكم
رسلی يذكرونكم عهدی وميثاقی وانزل اليكم كتبی
قالوا شهدنا بانك ربنا والهنا لا رب لنا غيرك ولااله
لنا غيرك -

> "When your Lord brought forth descendants from the loins of Adam's children, and made them testify against themselves, (He said): Am I not your Lord?' They replied: "We bear witness that you are." (This He did) lest you should say on the Day of Resurrection: "We had no knowledge of that, or: "Our forefathers set up partners with Allah; but will you destroy us, their descendants, on account of what followers of falsehood did?"
>
> (Q.7:172-173).

That is, Allah, the Almighty says in the above Surah Araf that when your Lord brought forth descendants from the loins of Adam and made them testify that was he not their Lord? They replied that they bore witness that He is. This He did so that they might not say on the Day of Resurrection that they had no knowledge of that or you might say that it were their forefathers who had set up partners with Allah, so will they be destroyed on account of what the followers of falsehood did. This is the translation of the verse of the Qur'an. Abi bin Ka'ab (R.A.) says in the commentary of the verse that Allah, the Almighty brought all the progeny of Adam together at a place and formed them into groups, for example, separate groups of the prophets, of the friends of Allah, of the martyrs, of the virtuous persons, of the obedient persons, of the debauch etc. In the same way groups of the unbelievers were also formed separately, as those of the Jews and the Christians, and of the Magi and the Hindus and so on and so forth. Thereafter, they were given a shape, i.e. there were given the same form and shape as they were to be given later in the world, some were made handsome and beautiful while others were made ugly; some were made dumb, others were made blind of one eye and still on others were made totally blind and so on and so forth. After that they were given power of speech and following this Allah, the Almighty said, "Am I not your Lord?" All of them confessed, "You are certainly our Lord." Thereafter, He made them to make covenent that there is no Lord and Master except Me and none should be obeyed other than Me. All of them confessed it accordingly. Allah, the Almighty then made the sky, the earth and Adam witness to it and said, "Prophets will be coming with Books to remind this covenent." Thus all the individuals confessed unity of Allah separately and rejected polytheism outright. Hence, in matters of polytheism nobody should be followed, neither spiritual guide, nor the teacher, nor the forefathers, nor a king or a ruler, nor a molvi, nor a saint or an elderly person. And whosoever thinks that he has forgotten all after arriving in this world and how a thing forgotten can be authentic enough to be followed; this is something utterly wrong. It is because many things go out of mind but one trusts it after being told by trusted persons; for example, no body retains in memory his or her birth from the womb of the mother but believes it after being told by some reliable persons, and accepts his or her mother as real mother and none other than her. Thus, if he does not pay the rights to one's mother and instead serve anybody else like his mother, he will be reproached by others. But he can not reply that he did not remember his birth at all and hence cannot accept that anybody to be his mother. As a result of this he will be called stupid and rude. Thus if a person is led to believe something simply by being told by the masses, what to speak of Prophets! How one cannot believe something after being informed by the Prophets.

The above Hadith denotes that the ordination of practising 'Tauheed' (Unity of Allah) and of prohibiting 'shirk' (setting up partner with Allah) was issued right in the world of Spirits and all the Prophets have been emphasizing this and; all the Books have been revealed to make it clear to the slaves of Allah. Thus the sayings of one lakh twenty-four thousand prophets and the teachings of one hundred four Books from Allah centre round the point that 'Tauheed' should be strengthened and kept intact and shun the evil of 'shirk'. Consider none to be the ruler who administers any thing; none is there to be approached for any help or for fulfilling any need or desire.

Imam Ahmed reports from Ma'adh bin Jabal (Radiallah-o-anho) that the Holy Prophet (pleace be upon him) said:

لاتشرك بالله شيئاً وان قتلت وحرقت -

> "Set up no partner with Allah even if you are killed or burnt alive."
>
> (Mishkat)

That is, worship none but Allah, the Almighty and fear not that any jinn or ghost would inflict any trouble. Hence the Muslim should keep patience at the trouble caused by jinn and ghost as they should not corrupt their 'Deen' (religion) for fear of open calamities. They should keep in mind that all acts are performed on the part of Allah because He has power over everything. But, however, He inflicts trouble on any of His slaves in order to test his loyality and causes miseries to even virtuous person at the hands of a wicked person. He wants to draw a line of demarcation between a perfect and an imperfect, the Believer and the Unbeliever. So as the piousmen are troubled by the transgressors and the Believers by the Unbelievers at the Will of Allah, and they have to keep patience and do not allow their 'Deen' to be perverted, in the same way, sometimes a pious man receives trouble from jinn and devils at the will of Allah; hence one should keep patience at all such troubles and these evil spirits must not be obeyed.

The above-mentioned Hadith reveals that if one feels disgusted with polytheism and ceases to worship others; considers bowing and offerings made to them an evil act and makes all-out efforts to ward off evil rites without caring for loss of wealth or children or; if one keeps patience at the troubles caused to him by any devil in the name of any spiritual guide or a martyr and does not budge an inch from his position thinking that Allah intends to put his 'deen' on test, and Allah seizes one after giving him long rope and gets the oppressed free from their hands; in the same manner, He will save the virtuous from the trouble caused by the wicked jinns.

Bukhari and Muslim report that Ibn Masud (Radiallaho Anho) said that a person asked the Prophet (peace be upon him) that which sin is the most heinous near Allah. The Prophet (peace be upon him) said:

ان تدعو لله ندا وهوخلقك

"To call one other than Allah in distress while He created you". (Mishkat)

As it is thought that Allah is omnipresent and All-powerfel, so they call Him for help in times of distress; others must not be called in this way. It is a grave sin. Firstly, it is itself totally wrong that anybody else has the power to fulfil the needs or he is omnipresent; Secondly, when Allah is our Creator and He has created us; we also should call Him for help in all business of law; as the slave of one king does not have any such relation with any other king; what to speak of baser elements.

Tirmidhi reports from Anas (Radiallah-o-anho) that the Prophet (peace be upon him) said:

قال الله تعالى يَا اِبنِ ادَمَ اِنَّكَ لو لقيتنى بِقرابِ

الأرضِ خطايا ثُمَّ لقيتنى لاتشرك بى شيئًا لأتيتكَ

بِقرابها مغفرةً -

> "Allah, the Almighty says: "O children of Adam ! Certainly, if you appear before Me with plenty of sins except polytheism, I shall confer plenty of blessings on you."
>
> (Mishkat)

That is, if a person commits sins in the same proportion as Pharaoh and 'Haman' including the Satan have committed but in case he is clear of all acts of polytheism, Allah the Almighty will bless him in proportion to the sins committed by him.

It is obvious from this Hadith that as all sins are pardoned with the blessings of 'Tauheed', all good acts are declared worthless only because of 'shirk'. And this is perfectly true. It is because when a person is clean of 'shirk', does not consider anybody Maste other than Allah and thinks that he has no place of refuge from Him nor he can ever escape Him, none has power to overtake Him; nobody can extend any support in His presence; none can intercede for anybody else; all his sins are supposed to have been committed out of human nature or by way of lapses. Moreover, such a person would feel ashamed at his sins and find his life insipid; and Allah will send His blessings for such a person. So as his sins increase in number, Allah's blessings also increase in the same proportion. Thus, anybody whose sense of Unity of Allah is perfect, his sin performs what prayers of others cannot work. A transgressing unitarian is thousand times better than a pious polytheist, as a criminal subject is thousand times better than a rebel sycophant. One is ashamed of his sin and the other one is proud of his deception.

PART - TWO

About Partnership In Knowledge

فِی رَدِّ الْاِشْرَاكِ فِی الْعِلْمِ

This part of the chapter carries those Verses of the Holy Qur'an and the Hadiths which establish association of Allah, the Almighty in His Knowledge.

Says Allah, the Almighty in Surah Al-Ana'm of the Holy Qur'an:

وَعِنْدَه مفاتِيحُ الغَيبِ لَا يَعلَمُهَا اِلَّا هُوَ ط

"He has the keys of the unseen: none knows them but He."
(Q: 6:59)

That is, Allah, the Almighty conferred upon His slaves objects as an aid to know and understand for example, eyes to see, ears to hear, nose to smell, tongue to taste, hands to feel, wisdom to understand and they have been given power to use them at will. They open their eyes when they want to see something and close them when they do not want to see anything; they put in the mouth what they want to taste and do not do so if they don't want. He has given keys to His slaves for knowing things; they may unlock anything at will and don't do so at will. Thus it depends upon their will and pleasure to do or not to do anything anytime. But to have knowledge of hidden things is beyond their power. It is within the Power of Allah alone; no prophet and friend of Allah, no jinn and angel, no spiritual guide and martyr, religious leader or their sons, ghosts and fairies have been given any such power. They cannot know anything hidden of their own. Allah, the Almighty gives to know as much as He wants them to know. Thus it neither depends on their will nor on their desire. It has so often happened with the Prophet (peace and blessings of Allah be upon him) that he wanted to know something but the same could not be known by him unless Allah, the Almighty wanted it to happen. Thus when the hypocrites accused Hadrat Ayesha (Radiallah-o-anha) and the Holy Prophet (peace and blessings of Allah be upon him) became sad, nothing came to his knowledge in spite of extensive investigation. This state of affairs remained so for several days. But when Allah, the Almighty so desired He revealed that the hypocrites were liars and Ayesha Siddiqa (Radiallah-o-anha) was chaste. One should, therefore, keep in mind that the key to the treasure of the hidden things lie in the hands of Allah, the Almighty. He never handed it over to anybody else. None is the treasurer except Allah, who can confer upon others this treasure as much as He likes. Nobody has the power to stop Him from doing so.

It is clear from the above verse that whosoever claims to have knowledge of the hidden things and of having knowledge of the future happenings, he is a great liar, because he claims to have divine power. Moreover, one who attaches such a power to any prophet and friend of Allah or jinn and angel, religious leader or sons of religious leaders or spiritual guide and martyr or astrologer and foreteller or charms- maker and soothsayer or Brahmin or ghost and fairy, is bound to become a polytheist. However, if it sometimes happens that anything told by an astrologer or soothsayer or Brahmin comes true, it does not mean that the person concerned has got any such power. It is totally wrong. If anything foretold by any of them comes true, it is only by fluke, because many more predictions on their part prove utterly wrong. The same is true with 'Istikharah' (looking into the Holy Book for a good augury); 'Kashf' (a divine inspiration) and; 'fal' from the Qur'an (i.e. to foretell by reference to holy books). But, however, there is no possibility of any mistake so far as 'Wahi' (Divine revelation) is concerned, but this is beyond their power. Allah, the Almighty says in Surah Naml of the Holy Qur'an:

قُل لَّا يَعلَمُ مَن فِي السَّمٰوٰتِ وَالاَرضِ الغَيبَ اِلَّا اللّٰهُ وَمَا
يَشعُرُونَ اَيَّانَ يُبعَثُونَ ط

> "Say: 'No one in the heavens or the earth has knowledge of what is hidden except Allah. Nor shall they ever know they will be raised to life."
>
> (Q. 27:65)

Allah, the Almighty told the Holy Prophet (peace and blessings of Allah be upon him) to say the people that nobody knows the hidden things except Allah neither the angels nor the man nor the jinn nor anything else i.e. to have knowledge of the hidden things is not within the power of anybody else; the point is that all the virtuous persons know that one day will be the Doomsday, but nobody knows when it will happen. If this could be possible, they must have known this too.

Allah, the Almighty says in Surah Luqman of the Qur'an:

اِنَّ اللّٰهَ عِندَهٗ عِلمُ السَّاعَةِ ط وَيُنَزِّلُ الغَيثَ ج وَيَعلَمُ مَا فِى
الاَرحَامِ وَمَا تَدرِى نَفسٌ مَاذَا تَكسِبُ غَدًا وَّمَا تَدرِى
نَفسٌ بِاَىِّ اَرضٍ تَمُوتُ اِنَّ اللّٰهَ عَلِيمٌ خَبِيرٌ ○ط

"Allah alone has knowledge of the Hour of Doom. He

> sends down the rain and knows what is in the wombs. No mortal knows what he will earn tomorrow; no mortal knows in what land he will die. Surely Allah is Knowing, Aware."

That is, Allah, the Almighty knows alone what is hidden and nobody has the power to know it. Thus even the occurrence of the Hour of Doom, which is so much well-known and so certain, cannot be ascertained by anybody so far as the exact time is concerned; then how can one know about the ordinary happenings of life; for example, victory or defeat of somebody, falling sick or getting recovery, for these things are neither so noted as the occurrence of the Day of Judgment nor so certain. Similarly, nobody knows about the time of raining, although the season is well-known and it most often rains in this season and all the Prophets, friends of Allah and kings and wise men have a desire for it; so if there could be a way to know it, it would have been known before hand. How can they know about life and death, offsprings, wealth and poverty, victory and defeat etc. Similarly, nobody knows what is there in the womb of the mother one or two, male or female, valid or invalid, beautiful or ugly. Although, men of wisdom write about the causes of all these, how can they know the hidden characteristics of men like their thoughts, intentions, faith, hypocricy etc? And while one does not know about one's tomorrow, how can he know about other's future? If one does not know one's place of demise, how can he know about that of others? In fine, nobody can have knowledge of future except Allah, the Almighty.

This verse makes it clear beyond doubt that all those who claim to have knowledge of the hidden things; some persons claim to have the power of 'Kashf' (a divine inspiration); some teach the practice of 'Istikharah' (looking into the holy book for a good augury); some takes out almanac; some cast dice of divination while others keep running with file of omen — these are all liars and imposters, and hence one should keep away from being entrapped by them. But one who says this much that he comes to know something from Allah, but he has no power to know anything at will and by his own choice and power it may perhaps, be possible on such a person may be a hypocrite.

Says Allah, the Almighty in Surah Ahqaf of the Qur'an:

وَمَنْ أَضَلُّ مِمَّن يَدْعُوا مِن دُونِ اللَّهِ مَن لَّا يَسْتَجِيبُ لَهُ
إِلَىٰ يَوْمِ الْقِيَٰمَةِ وَهُمْ عَن دُعَآئِهِمْ غَٰفِلُونَ ٥

> "Who is in greater error than he who invokes besides Allah those who will never hear him till the Day of Resurrection — who are, indeed, unconscious of his prayers?"
> (Q. 46:5)

That is, those who practise polytheism are fools because they, leaving Allah, the Almighty, call those who hear not their call. Moreover, they have no power over anything, so they cannot respond even if they are called till the Day of Resurrection.

This verse makes it clear that as some people call some saints from far off places and say this much:

"O, so and so invoke Allah to fulfil my need"; and then think that they practised no polytheism because they did not ask them directly to fulfil their needs but instead, they only made them to invoke Allah. But this is utterly wrong, for so far as only begging of help from Allah is concerned, this is not an act of polytheism, but the channel through which the call is made is certainly an act of polytheism because the callers think that the one called hears their call from far and near and only then they call like this. But Allah, the Almighty has declared in this verse that all those other than Allah are quite oblivious to the callers.

Allah, the Almighty says in Surah A'raf of the Qur'an:

قُل لَّا أَمْلِكُ لِنَفْسِي نَفْعًا وَلَا ضَرًّا إِلَّا مَا شَاءَ اللَّهُ وَلَوْ كُنتُ
أَعْلَمُ الْغَيْبَ لَاسْتَكْثَرْتُ مِنَ الْخَيْرِ وَمَا مَسَّنِيَ السُّوءُ

اِن اَ نَااِلاَّ نَذِيرٌ وَّ بَشِيرٌ لِقَومٍ يُّومِنُونَ –

"Say: 'I have not the power to acquire benefits or to avert evil from myself, except by the will of Allah. Had I possessed knowledge of what is hidden, I would have availed myself of much that is good, and no harm would have touched me. But I am no more than one who gives warning and good news to true believers."

(Q. 7:188)

That is, the chief of all prophets and friends of Allah is the Last Prophet (peace and blessings of Allah be upon him) and people have observed his miracles alone and have learnt from him all matters mysterious and; all saints have achieved greatness only through him. Hence Allah, the Almighty has asked the Apostle to tell the people clearly his own state and condition and he did accordingly. The Prophet of Allah made it abundantly clear that he had neither any power nor any knowledge of the hidden things. He had such a power that he had nothing to do with the gain and loss of his life too; what to speak of others. Had he had any knowledge of the hidden things he would have tried to know the result of everything before hand; he would undertake a task in case it looked good and refrained from doing it if it looked bad in regard to result. In short, he had no power and knowledge of the hidden things nor claimed any Divine power. He claimed only prophethood and the task of prophethood is only to learn against evil doings and give good news in regard to virtuous deeds. Even this brings about profit to only those who have trust in heart and to put trust into a heart is beyond his power; it lies only within the power of Allah, the Almighty.

It is clear from the above verse that the reason behind the greatness of the prophets and the friends of Allah is that they signify the way of Allah and since they are fully aware of the good and bad actions, they teach people about them and Allah, the Almighty make their teachings effective. Many people tread upon the right path following their teachings. And it is not a matter of greatness that Allah give them the power to administer the universe, to bring death to anyone they like or give them offsprings or remove their difficulties or fulfil their desires or confer victory and difficulty or make them wealthy and pauper or appoint someone king or chief or minister or take away kingdom or chiefdom or ministership; put faith in anyone's heart or take out faith from anyone's heart or make anyone fall sick or get anyone back to recovery; all big or small are equally humble and helpless. It is also not a matter of greatness if Allah, the Almighty give anyone knowledge of the hidden or know what lies in the heart of anyone or know about the hidden as to whether one is living or dead or which city one is living in and in what condition or know the future as and when one needs or know whether one will get an issue or not or one will get profit in business or not or one will get victory or defeat in a certain battle; all the slaves of Allah, big or small, are equally unaware of all these things. Similarly some great men say something from their wisdom or conjecture and these sometimes come true by fluke; but what is sent by Allah, the Almighty in the form of revelation or inspiration is something wonderful and this is beyond their power.

Bukhari reports from Rabia bint Muawwaz bin Afra'a:

جاء النبی صلی الله علیه وسلم تدخل حین بنی علی
فجلس علی فراشی کمجلسك منی فجعلت جویریات
لنا یضربن با لدف ویندبن من قتل من ابائی یوم بدراذ
قالت احدیٰهن وفینا نبی یعلم ما فی غدٍ فقال دعی هذه
وقولی بالذی کنت تقولین –

"On my marriage, the Holy Prophet (peace and blessings of Allah be upon him) came and sat on a cushion before me as you are sitting before me. In the meanwhile, some lasses started playing drums eulogizing those martyred in the battle of Badr and saying further; 'among us there is an Apostle who knows what is going to happen tomorrow.' Thereupon, the Apostle asked them to stop saying like this and say instead what was saying before."

Rabia was a lady from Ansar. The Messengar of Allah took part in her marriage and sat near her. Some lasses started singing something. *Eulogizing* the Apostle they said that Allah, the Almighty has given him such a status that he knows the future. This the Apostle forbade and asked them not to say anything like that but sing as before.

It is clear from this Hadith that one should not keep such a faith about Prophets, friends of Allah, religious guides or martyrs that they have knowledge of the hidden things. One should not, rather, have such a belief about the Prophet of Allah too that any such thing be said about him. And it is utterly wrong for the poets to eulogize Prophets, friends of Allah, saint's, spiritual guides or teachers in a way that equalizes him with the attributes of Allah, the Almighty and utter that verses contain such exaggerations. When the Apostle of Allah forbade lasses to sing any such thing how can a man of sense and wisdom be allowed for such an exercise in exaggeration?

Bukhari reports from Hadrat Ayesha (radiallaho-anha) to have said:

من اخبرك ان محمدا صلى الله عليه وسلم ليعلم الخمس التى قال الله تعالى ، ان الله عنده علم الساعة فقد اعظم الفرية

"Those of you assign the Apostle of Allah to be knowing five things mentioned by Allah create storm of the highest degree."

These five things are being mentioned at the end of Surah Luqman the commentary of which has already passed in part one of this chapter. All the hidden things form part of these five basic things. Hence anyone who says that the Messenger of Allah did know those five i.e. all the hidden things is a great liar. Nobody has knowledge of the hidden things except Allah, the Almighty.

Bukhari reports from Ummil Ala that the Apostle of Allah

و الله لا ادری و انا رسول الله مایفعل بی و لابکم

> "By Allah I know nothing, although I am the Messenger of Allah, what will happen to me and to you."

That is, nobody knows how Allah, the Almighty will deal with anybody in this world or in the grave or in the Hereafter. No Prophet and no friend of Allah knows about one's own condition or about anybody else. However, only those persons can foretell anything whom Allah, the Almighty informs beforehand. But to know more than what Allah has informed by revelation or inspiration is beyond their power.

PART - THREE

About the Evils of Partnership in Administration of Allah

فِي رَدِّ الْإِشْرَاكِ فِي التَّصَرُّفْ

Allah, the Almighty says in Surah Mominun of the Qur'an:

قُلْ مَنْ بِيَدِهِ مَلَكُوتُ كُلِّ شَيْءٍ وَهُوَ يُجِيرُ وَلَا يُجَارُ عَلَيْهِ إِنْ كُنْتُمْ تَعْلَمُونَ سَيَقُولُونَ لِلَّهِ قُلْ فَأَنَّى تُسْحَرُونَ:

"Say: 'In whose hands is the sovereignty of all things, protecting all, while against Him there is no protection? Tell me, if you know the truth.' 'In Allah's', they will reply."

Say: 'How then can you be so bewitched?'

(Q.23:88-89)

That is, whenever anybody is asked who has the sole power to keep control over every thing and to do what he likes and none is there to prevent him from doing so and none can give protection to one convicted by him; "It is Allah who has such a power!"; all will say in one voice. Hence one should consider that in such a case it is a derangement of mind if one wants to get his needs and desires fulfilled by any other quarter.

This verse makes it quite clear that even the Unbelievers of the times of the Holy Prophet (peace and blessings of Allah be upon) would confess that there is none equal to Allah and none has the power and capacity to vie with Him. But they considered their idols as their advocate; and hence they became Unbelievers. Thus even now one who consider any creature to be having partnership in the administration of Allah and take him to be his advocate, he is liable to commit polytheism; although he does not consider him equal to Allah and a power equal to Him.

Says Allah, the Almighty in Surah Jinn:

قُل اِنِّي لَا اَمْلِكُ لَكُم ضَرًا وَّلَا رَشَدًا قُل اِنِّي لَن يُّجِيرَنِي

مِنَ اللّٰهِ اَحَدٌوَّ لَن اَجِدَ مِن دُونِهِ مُلتَحَدًا:

> Say: 'I have no control over any good or evil that befalls you.'
>
> Say: 'None can protect me from Allah, nor can I find any refuge besides Him.'
>
> (Q.72: 21-22)

That is, Allah, the Almighty asked His Apostle to tell the people that he (Apostle) had no power to have any control over their gain or loss. Moreover, by believing me and joining my 'Ummah' you must not take pride in becoming strong and stable, thinking that your advocate was able and your intercessor is highly loved, and hence you do whatever you like having in mind that he (Apostle) would save you from the wrath. This is utterly wrong because I myself fear and none is there to protect me other than Allah, how can I save others?

It is clear from the verse that the common people who forget Allah, the Almighty, relying on the help and support of the religious guide and martyrs and refrain from showing respects to His ordinations, are utterly deviated and perverted, because the religious guide of the religious guides feared Allah day and night and did not consider anybody other than Allah to save him; what to speak of others.

Says Allah, the Almighty, in Surah Al-Nahal of the Qur'an:

وَيَعْبُدُونَ مِن دُونِ اللّٰهِ مَا لَا يَمْلِكُ لَهُمْ رِزْقًا مِنَ السَّمٰوٰتِ
وَالْاَرْضِ شَيْئًا وَّلَا يَسْتَطِيعُونَ :

> "And they worship those other than Allah, who have no power to provide them livelihood neither from the heavens nor from the earth and have no power whatsoever."
> (Q. 16:73)

That is, they show respects to those who have no power at all; they can neither make any provisions for them nor make it rain from sky, nor can grow anything from earth and they do not have power of any kind.

This verse falsifies the wrong concept adopted by the masses that the Prophets, friends of Allah, religious leaders and martyrs have administrative capacity no doubt, but they are content with the fate decided by Allah and do not rise against the working of Nature out of respect for the Creator, otherwise they have the power to create disorder in the planning of Nature. This notion is perfectly wrong; they have no power over anything nor can they interfere with the working of the Nature.

Allah, the Almighty says in Surah Yunus of the Qur'an:

وَلَا تَدْعُ مِن دُونِ اللّٰهِ مَا لَا يَنفَعُكَ وَلَا يَضُرُّكَ فَاِنْ فَعَلْتَ
فَاِنَّكَ اِذًا مِّنَ الظّٰلِمِينَ :

> "Do not pray besides Allah to anything which can neither help nor harm you, for if you do, you will become a wrongdoer."
>
> (Q.10:106)

That is sheer injustice that any such thing be called for help leaving Allah, the Most Powerful, which can neither confer any gain nor inflict any loss. To transfer the status of such a great power to such mean persons is nothing short of utter injustice.

Allah, the Almighty says in Surah Saba of the Qur'an:

قُلِ ادعُوا الَّذِينَ زَعَمتُم مِن دُونِ اللّٰهِ لَايَملِكُونَ مِثقَالَ ذَرَّةٍ فِى السَّمٰوٰتِ وَلَافِى الَارضِ وَمَا لَهُم فِيهِمَا مِن شِركٍ وَّمَا لَه مِنهُم مِن ظَهِيرٍ – وَلَا تَنفَعُ الشَّفَاعَةُ عِندَهٗ اِلَّالِمَن اَذِنَ لَهٗ حَتّٰى اِذَا فُزِّعَ عَن قُلُوبِهِم قَالُو مَاذَا قَالَ رَبُّكُم قَالُوا الحَقَّ وَهُوَ العَلِىُّ الكَبِيرُ:

> Say: 'Call on those whom you claim to be besides Allah. They do not control an atom's weight in heaven or earth, nor have they any share in either. Nor has Allah any helpers among them.'
>
> No intercession with Allah avails except for him who has received His sanction. When fear is banished from their hearts, they shall ask each other: "What has your Lord ordained? 'The truth', they shall answer. He is the Most High, the Supreme One."
>
> (Q. 34. 22-23)

That is, anyone who seeks help from anybody and calls him in difficulty and he fulfils his needs, it is possible only when he is himself the master or his associate or can exercise his pressure on him; for example, a king agrees with the nobles under their pressure, for they are his wings and constituent parts of his kingdom; their displeasure may put the rule to disorder. Similarly, one makes intercession with the master and he accepts their intercession under some pressure with pleasure or displeasure; as a king cannot reject the intercession of his queens or daughters. But those who call Allah for help and fulfil their needs are neither master of even a particle in the sky and the earth nor they share anything with Allah, the Almighty, nor they are constituent parts of the dominion of Allah, nor its wings that He agree with them under pressure. On the other hand, it is a system of His rule that as He issues a decree, His managers get embarrassed and don't have the courage even to ask anything about the order.They cannot do but carry out the orders; what to speak of making any advocacy and extending any support to them. Here, one significant thing is to be kept in mind. The Prophets and the friends of Allah on whose intercession they are proud of and forget even Allah, the Almighty due to their misunderstanding of the real meaning of the word, they should know the fact that 'shifa'at' means 'sifarish' (intercession), and intercession is of various kinds; for example, if the burglary of a person is proved in the court of the worldly king and the convict is saved through the intercession of a minister or a noble, then it is one thing that the king pardons the convict out of pressure from an influential person of his court, for it is easier for the king to pardon the thief than to invite the anger of a noble, for his displeasure may create many problems for the kingdom. This is called intercession of high position. That is, the king accepted the intercession out of regard for the high status of the noble. But this type of intercession cannot be submitted to Allah. And he is the perfect polytheist who considers any Prophet or friend of Allah or religious guide or martyr or angel or any spiritual guide intercessor in the Honour of Allah, the Almighty. Such a person is highly ignorant because he does not understand the real meaning of Allah and failed to understand the value of the Lord of the territory. His greatness is that He can bring into being crores of prophets, friends, jinns and angels equal to Jibrail (Gabriel) and Muhammad (peace and blessings of Allah be upon him), and put to disorder the entire world from earth to sky and create a new world in its place just by saying Kun' (be). His will is enough for creating anything. He need not collect materials for building anything. If all the predecessors and followers, men and jinn belong the category of Jibrail and the Prophet of Kingdom of the Lord of the territories will get no lustre and splendour, and if all of them join the company of Satan and Dajjal (anti-Christ), its lustre will not recede. His is the greatest of the greats and king of the kings. Nobody can either do any good or wrong to Him.

In another case, a king may pardon a thief under the pressure of an intercession from his offsprings or wives or some beloved, this is called intercession of love. That is, the king acknowledges his or her intercession because of his love for the intercessors. Here, the king thinks that pardoning a thief is easier for him than to invite the wrath of his beloved. But these sorts of intercessions have no place in the Court of Allah. And anybody who considers someone an intercessor of the same stature is the polytheist and an ignorant one of the same colour as has been referred to before. Even if that Lord of the territory bless someone abundantly, and entitle him as the Beloved or the Friend or the Speaker or the Spirit of God or the Merciful Prophet or the Holy spirit or the Angel Jibrail, but, however, the Lord and the slave is after all a slave and nobody can overstep the status of slavery and go beyond this limit. As every soul is delighted with the blessings of Allah so also it shudders with His horror.

Thirdly, committing of theft is proved but the thief is not accustomed to it and he has not adopted it by way of profession. However, he committed theft out of bad luck and thereupon he is shameful and fears the consequences day and night; pays regard to the laws enforced by the king and professes his crime and finds himself liable to be punished and does not seek refuge with any minister or noble escaping the king nor bank upon anybody's support but keeps looking towards the king for his right decision.

In such a case the king feels pity but does not pardon the convict keeping in view the laws of the kingdom so that the laws may not lose its dignity in the eyes of the subjects. Now if any minister or noble, keeping in view the will of the king, intercedes with him on behalf of the convict, the king, although intending to pardon the convict, pardons him apparently to add to the respect of that noble or minister. Thus the noble or minister does not intercede for the thief because of having any relation with the convict. He did so only after knowing the will of the king, for he is the noble of the king and not that of the thief. One who extends any support to a thief himself turns a thief. This is called intercession with permission. Thus it happens so with the will and pleasure of the king. Such an intercession is possible in Honour of Allah too. And the intercession of a Prophet or a friend of Allah which finds mention in the Qur'an and Hadith means the same. Hence all the individuals should call Allah alone, fear Him alone, entreat Him alone, keep confessing his sins before Him, consider Him his only Lord and Helper, consider none his saviour other than Allah and rely none for favour. He is the Forgiver and Merciful. He will remove all the difficulties and troubles and will forgive all the sins by His Mercy. He may appoint anybody an intercessor for anyone by His command. Hence one should entrust even this need to Him like all others. He may appoint anyone an intercessor for anybody. Thus one should not rely upon anyone's favour and support to call anybody for help and forget the real Master and Lord considering anyone to be his helper. One who puts the code of Allah to disgrace and consider anybody as his helper and supporter and attach importance to the relation established with his so- called helper, invites wrath and annoyance of the Prophet and the friend of Allah and they never intercede for such persons. They, rather, become angry with them and oppose them instead. Their very greatness lay in the fact that they considered Allah, the Almighty, ahead of their wives and daughters, pupils and disciples, friends and acquaintances. Thus when such great men found anybody practising against the command of Allah, they also opposed him. Thus who are these callers in whose support these friends of Allah will come into conflict with the Will of Allah.

Their real greatness lies in the fact that they love someone for Allah and oppose anyone for Allah. Hence one who has the pleasure of Allah as the only ideal of life, will push further towards the Hell whom Allah has decided so.

Tirmidhi reports from Ibn Abbas (Radiallah-o-anho) :

كنت خلف رسول الله صل الله عليه وسلم يوما فقال
يا غلام احفظ الله يحفظك احفظ الله تجده تجاهك
واذا سألت فاسئل الله واذا استعنت فاستعن بالله
واعلم ان الامة لواجتمعت على ان ينفعوك بشىء لم
ينفعوك الابشىء قد كتبه الله لك ولو اجتمعوا على
ان يضروك الا بشىء قد كتب الله عليك رفعت
الاقلام وجفت الصحف

> "Once I was alongwith the Holy Prophet (peace and blessings of Allah be upon him) that he observed: 'O boy! remember Allah so that He remember you; remember Allah and you will find Him before you; whenever you beg, beg from Allah alone; when you seek any help, seek from Allah alone; keep in mind that all the persons put together cannot extend you any help but what Allah has already written for you and, all the persons put together cannot do any harm to you but what Allah has already written for you and there after the pen is lifted and the paper is dried up."

That is, Allah is the King of the Kings but, however, He is not arrogant like others that he pays no heed to his subjects in spite of invocations. It is because of this, his subjects find out means from his nobles so that their invocation is acknowledged. No advocacy from anybody is required there; He remembers those who remember Him whether one intercedes with Him or not. And, although He is Most High and Exalted, but it is not that His Court is inaccessible like those of other worldly kings where they have no approach, and even ministers and nobles pass orders for them and subjects have to obey their orders and appear before their courts. He is, rather, very close to His slaves. Even an ordinary slave of Him who attends to Him from the depth of his heart, will find Him at hand. There is no screen besides his own negligence and anyone who is away from Allah is only due to his own carelessness. He is nearer to His slaves. Thus anyone who calls any Prophet or spiritual guide to bring him near to Allah does not understand that the Prophets and spiritual guides are away from him while Allah is nearest to him. Thus it happens that any of the subjects is sitting alone with his king and the king is all attentive to him, but meanwhile, the person starts calling some minister or noble who is far away from there and entreat him to submit before the king anything on his (caller's) behalf, he is surely either blind or insane. Thus one should beg everything from Allah alone and seek His help in all troubles and sufferings. One should keep in mind that the decrees of fate cannot be obliterated. Hence all the big and small elements of the whole world put together can neither do good nor inflict harm to anybody. Nothing can be added to what has already been written. This Hadith makes it clear what is said by the common people that friends of Allah have been conferred upon such power that they could change the fate too; can give offsprings to one who is deprived of it; prolongate one's age after it is over; these are all wrong notions. One should know that Allah, the Almighty sometimes accepts the supplication of any of His slave and so often those of the Prophets and His friends. But even supplication is made under divine guidance and its acceptance too is from Him. But both making supplication and getting it accepted are from Allah, the Almighty, and have already been decreed. Nothing can go out of destiny and nothing can happen out of one's own power. Each slave of Allah whether big or small, Prophet or friend of Allah has no power except that he begs Allah and invoke Him alone. Moreover, He is omnipotent and it is up to Him whether He accepts anything by way of His Grace or rejects it by way of His Wisdom.

Ibn Majah reports from Amr bin Al-As (Radiallaho-anho):

قال رسول الله صلى الله عليه وسلم ان لقلب ابن ادم
لكل واد شعبة فمن اتبع قلبه الشعب كلها لم يبال الله
باى واد اهلكه ومن توكل على الله كفاه الشعب –

> "The Messenger of Allah has said, 'Certainly, every heart wanders along various fields; then, if one whose heart runs towards all the fields may be ruined in any forest uncared by Allah. But one who relies on Allah, he gets all the ways open and safe for him."

That is, when a person requires something or some difficulty arises, an idea creeps into his heart that so and so Prophet should be called out; so and so religious guide, spiritual guide and martyr should be entreated, so and so fairy be beseeched, so and so astrologer or soothsayer be consulted and so and so priest be asked to foretell by reference to holy book. Thus, if they follow these fellows, Allah turns His eyes from them and does not count them among His true slaves. The path of guidance and instruction is left out of their hands. They run after such notions and this exercise continues for the whole of life.

Thereafter, some of them turn atheist, while others become heretic and polytheist. Those who rely on Allah alone and refrain from running after any notion, Allah counts such persons among His chosen slaves and opens the path of guidance for them; confers peace of heart and tranquillity on them. Everyone gets what has already been decreed for him. One who trusts Allah gets his needs fulfilled by the Grace of Allah, the Almighty.

Tirmidhi reports from Anas (Radiallaho anho):

قال رسول الله صل الله عليه وسلم ليسئل احدكم ربه حاجته كلها حتى يسئل الملح وحتى يسئله شسع نعله اذا نقطع -

> "The Holy Prophet (peace and blessings of Allah be upon him) said: 'Everyone should beg all things needed right from his Lord, even the lace of his shoe in case it is broken."

It is totally wrong to consider Allah, the Almighty, like worldly kings that they perform big tasks and the small ones they assign to their workers and servants; as a result of this they have to entreat these menial workers and servants even for petty things. But, Allah, the Almighty, does not run His administration in this way; rather He is so omnipotent that He can perform crores of big and small tasks in a jiffy. None has the power in His kingdom to interfere and hence even the smallest objects should be begged from Him, for nobody can give either big or small things.

Bukhari and Muslim report from Abu Hurairah (Radiallaho anho):

لما نزلت : وانذر عشيرتك الاقربين

دعا النبى صلى الله عليه وسلم قرابته فعم وخص افقال يا بنى كعب بن لوى انقذوا انفسكم من النار فانى لا اغنى عنكم من الله شيئا يا بنى مرة بن كعب انقذوا انفسكم من النار فانى لا اغنى عنكم من الله شيئا ويا بنى عبد شمس انقذوا انفسكم من النار فانى لا اغنى عنكم سن الله شيئا ويا بنى عبد مناف - انقذوا

انفسكم من النار فانى لا اغنى عنكم من الله شيئًا ويا بنى عبد المطلب انقذوا انفسكم من النار فانى لا اغنى عنكم من الله شيئًا ويا فاطمة انقذى نفسك من النار ، سلينبى ما شئت من مالى فانى لا اغنى عنك من الله شيئًا :

"When the verse 'Wa andhir ashiratakal aqrabina' (warn those who are related to you) was revealed, the Apostle of Allah called his relatives together and individually and said:

"O Bani Ka'b bin Lowi! save yourselves from the Fire, for certainly I have no power with Allah; O Bani Murrah bin Ka'b! save yourselves from the Fire for I have no power with Allah; O Bani Abd Shams! save yourselves from the Fire for I have no power with Allah; O Bani Abd Manaf! save yourselves from the Fire for I have no power with Allah; O Bani Abdul Muttalib! save yourselves from the Fire, for I have no power with Allah and; O Fatima! Save yourself from the Fire; ask me for whatever wealth and property you need, but I have no power with Allah.

That is, those who belong to any saint rely on him and get fear of Allah reduced. Hence Allah, the Almighty asked His Prophet (peace and blessings of Allah be upon him) to warn his dear and near. Thus the Apostle warned them all including his daughter Fatima who was told that the right of relationship is limited to one's possessions, hence she could take as much from his wealth as she needed but the matter with Allah is beyond his power. He cannot help anybody nor can he plead for anybody before Allah; hence affairs of the Hereafter must be put to right and everybody should take care of his safety from Hell.

This Hadith makes it clear that relationship with any saint cannot stand in good stead before Allah, the Almighty, unless one keeps his matter clear with Allah, the Almighty.

PART - FOUR

About the Evil of Partnership in Prayer of Allah

فِى ذِكْرِرَدِّ الْاِشْرَاكِ فِى الْعِبَادَةِ

Prayers are those actions which are ordained by Allah, the Almighty for His own adoration. This part of the book indicates those actions which have been mentioned in the Qur'an and Hadith for adoring Allah, so that the servants of Allah refrain from those actions leading to polytheism.

Allah, the Almighty says in Surah Hud of the Qur'an

وَلَقَد اَرسَلنَا نُوحًا اِلٰى قَومِهٖ اِنّى لَكُم نَذِيرٌ مُّبِين ط اَن لّاتَعبُدُوا اِلَّااللّٰهَ اِنّى اَخَافُ عَلَيكُم عَذَابَ يَومٍ اَلِيمٍ ط

"And We sent forth Nuh to his people. He said: Surely I am a plain warner to you. Serve none but Allah. I fear for you the torment of a woeful day."

(Q.11:25-26)

That is, confrontation between the Believers and Unbelievers has started right from the days of Hadrat Nuh (peace be upon him). The point of confrontation is that the chosen slaves of Allah has been saying that anybody else must not be adorned like Allah.

Allah, the Almighty says in Surah Fussil'at of the Qur'an:

لَاتَسجُدُوا لِلشَّمسِ وَلَالِلقَمَرِ وَاسجُدُوا لِلّٰهِ الَّذِى خَلَقَهُنَّ
اِن كُنتُم اِيَّاهُ تَعبُدُونَ

> "Do not prostrate yourselves before the sun or the moon; rather prostrate yourselves before Allah, Who created them both, if you would truly serve Him."
>
> (Q.41:37)

That is, one who wants to serve Allah alone should prostrate Him alone and not the sun and the moon. In our 'deen' (faith) it has been clearly pointed out that only Allah, the Creator has the right to be worshipped. Hence no creature deserves prostration and as a creation of Allah, the sun and the moon, the Prophet and friend of Allah are all equal. Those who plead that in earlier Faiths, some of the creatures were also adored; for example, Hadrat Adam were adored by the angels and Hadrat Yaqub adored Hadrat Yusuf (peace be upon all of them); so if they also adore some saints, there should be no harm. But this notion is utterly wrong. During the age of Adam (peace be upon him) they would marry their sisters too. Hence the advocates of such a notion should marry their sisters too. The fact is this that all the slaves should serve Allah alone and obey His injuctions from the depth of heart. They should avoid such arguments that such and such things were not practised in ancient ages so why should they be asked to obey such injunctions. These arguments lead one to become an Unbeliever. For instance, if a king issues an order for sometimes and then asks his subjects to obey a new order, then none among his subjects may argue that he will obey the previous order only and not the one promulgated later on. Such a person would be declared as rebel.

Allah, the Almighty says in Surah Jinn of the Qur'an:

وَاَنَّ المَسَاجِدَ لِلّٰهِ فَلَا تَدعُوا مَعَ اللّٰه اَحَدًا وَّاَنَّهٗ لَمَّا قَامَ
عَبدُاللّٰهِ يَدعُوهُ كَادُو يَكُونُونَ عَلَيهِ لِبَدًا o قُل اِنَّمَا اَدعُوا
رَبِّى وَلَآاُشرِكُ بِهٖ اَحَدًا –

> "The places of worship are built for Allah's worship; invoke in them no other (god) besides Him. When His servant (Muhammad) rose to pray to Him, they pressed round him in multitudes."
>
> (Q.72:20)

When a true servant of Allah calls Allah from the depth of heart, stupid fellows take him to be a saint and say he (the saint) has the power to give and take away whatever he wants and hence centre round him. In such a case the saint should make the matter clear and emphasise upon them that it is only Allah Who should be asked for help and it is He Who should be attached power of conferring gain and inflicting loss and associating such a matter with anybody else is an act of polytheism. Allah says He is sick of polytheism, hence He cannot be pleased with such heinous act.

It is amply clear from the above verse that to stand in respect, to call for help and to chart His name are some of the acts which are specified for Him.

Allah, the Almighty says in Surah Hajj of the Qur'an:

وَاَذِّن فِى النَّاسِ بِالحَجِّ يَاتُوكَ رِجَالًا وَعَلٰى كُلِّ ضَامِرٍ
يَاتِينَ مِن كُلِّ فَجٍّ عَمِيقٍ لِيَشهَدُوا مَنَافِعَ لَهُم وَيَذكُرُوا
اسمَ اللّٰهِ فِى اَيَّامٍ مَّعلُومَاتٍ عَلٰى مَا رَزَقَهُم مِّن بَهِيمَةِ

الَانعَامِ فَكُلُوا مِنهَا وَاَطعِمُوا البَـا ئِـسَ الَفقِـيرَ ثُـمَّ لِيَقضُـوا
تَفَشَهُـمْ وَاليُوفُو نُذُورَهُـم وَلَيَطَّوَّفُوا بِالبَيتِ العَتِيقِ :

"Proclaim the pilgrimage to men. They will come to you on foot and on the backs of swift camels from every distant quarter; (they will come) to avail themselves of many a benefit and to pronounce on the appointed days the name of Allah over the cattle which He has given them. Eat of their flesh yourselves, and feed the poor and the unfortunate. Then let the pilgrims accomplish their acts of cleansing, make their vows, and go round the Ancient House."

(Q.22:27-29)

That is, Allah, the Almighty has specified some places for His worship like Ka'bah, Arafat, Muzdalafah, Mina, Safa and Marwah, Place of Hadrat Ibrahim (peace be upon him), the entire Masjid-ul-Haram (the Ka'bah), rather the whole Mak'kah (Mecca) and the whole of Haram (the sacred territory of Mak'kah) and; put into their hearts eagerness for visiting these sacred places. Hence they resolve to come to these places on mount and on foot; arrive at the place with much trouble s and sufferings and in dirt and filth; sacrifice animals in His name, making their offerings to Him, go round it and worship Allah to the fill; some persons kiss the threshold while others are invoking Allah at the door; entreating Allah by holding the cover (of Ka'bah); praying Allah day and night sitting with the intention of I'tikaf (retirement to a mosque for a continuing prayer) and; seeing it by standing in respect. In fine, they perform such acts of worship and Allah is pleased with them. In this way they gain advantage in this world and the Hereafter. Hence such acts must not be performed for persons other than Allah. Similarly, performing 'chilla' (the forty days of Lent in which people engage themselves in some religious acts): resolving to make journey for these places from far off places; reaching there taking the troubles of the journey and getting immersed in dirt and dust; sacrificing animals there; making offerings there, going round any grave or abode; paying respects to the forests around it; avoiding game-hunting there, cutting trees, uprooting grass and performing other such acts keeping in mind to have some benefits from these are all acts of polytheism. One should keep away from such acts, for these acts are specified with Allah alone and no creature deserves all these.

Allah, the Almighty says in Surah Al-Ana'm of the Holy Qur'an:

اَوفِسقًا اُهِلَّ لِغَيرِ اللّٰهِ بِهٖ

> "And what has been profanely slaughttered to gods other than Allah."
>
> (Q. 6:145)

That is, the animal sacrificed in the name other than Allah is as unclean and unlawful as the swine, blood and carrion.

It is clear from the above verse that an animal kept in the name of someone except Allah is unlawful and unclean. This verse makes no mention that the animal would turn unlawful only when it is slaughtered in the name of any creature; it rather says this much that if an animal is noted with the name of any creature like 'the cow of Syed Ahmed Kabir' or "the he- goat of Shaikh Saddu" etc. it turns unlawful. Hence any animal, be it hen or camel, if slaughtered in the name of anyone else, whether he be a Prophet, a friend of Allah or ancestors, ghost or fairy, is certainly unlawful and clean and the person who acts with such a faith is bound to become a polytheist.

Allah, the Almighty says in Surah Yusuf of the Qur'an:

يَا صَاحِبَىِ السِّجنِ ءَ اَربَابٌ مُّتَفَرِّقُونَ خَيرٌ اَمِ اللّٰهُ

الوَاحِدُ القَهَّارُ ، مَاتَعبُدُونَ مِن دُونِهٖ اِلَّآاَسمَآءً سَمَّيتُمُوهَا

اَنتم وَاٰبَآءُكمُ مَّا اَنزَلَ اللّٰهُ بِهَا مِن سُلطَانٍ ، اِنِ الحُكمُ اِلَّالِلّٰهِ ، اَمَرَاَن لَّاتَعبُدُوا اِلَّا اِيَّاهُ ، ذٰلِكَ الدِّينُ القَيِّمُ وَلٰكِنَّ اَكثَرَالنَّاسِ لَايَعلَمُونَ :

> "Hadrat Yusuf (peace be upon him) said: "My two fellow-prisoners! Are sundry gods better than Allah, the One, the conquerer? Those whom you serve besides Him are nothing but names which you and your fathers have invented and for which Allah has revealed no sanction. Judgment rests with Allah only. He has commanded you to worship none but Him. That is the true faith: yet most men do not know."
>
> (Q.12: 39-40)

Firstly, it is not in favour of a slave to have more than one master. He should rather have one strong and powerful master who could fulfil all his needs and put all business of life to right. Secondly, others have no strength, power and reality. They form a notion of their own that someone has the power to make it rain or others grow grains, give children, health etc. Moreover, they name such agencies of their own and distribute tasks among them and call them for help. Thereafter, these rites and customs get currency and keep going. But all these things are based on wrong notions and they are totally baseless. There is neither anyone other than Allah nor anybody has any power to interfere with His working. One who is omipotent is none but Allah and neither he is Ali nor Muhammad. And any one whether he is Ali or Muhammad has no power whatsover. So there is none with the name of Muhammad or Ali who controls the affairs of the universe. This is just a whim. Allah, the Almighty has never commanded to form any such notion; He has, rather, forbidden to form any such idea about any of the creatures and none has anything reliable to say except Allah.

Following the command of Allah is the real Faith. Hence nobody should be followed and obeyed. But most of the people fail to go along this right path; they, rather, prefer rites attached to their religious guides to the Commands of Allah, the Almighty.

The above verse makes it clear that to follow rites and rituals associated with anybody and to consider them as authentic is really something unreal and whimsical. Hence anyone who attaches such power to the creature what is specific for Allah is undoubtedly a polytheist. It is only the Apostle of Allah who shows the way to make an access to Allah. Thus anyone who prefers the sayings of any 'Imam' (religious guide) or 'mujtahid' (religious director) or 'qutb' (lord) or 'ghaus' (saint) or 'maulvi' (a man of religious learning) or masha'ikh (holy persons) or ancestors or any king or minister or bishop or pundit to those of the Prophet of Islam and follow the sayings of 'Peer' (religious guide) and teacher to those of the Hadiths or even considers the sayings of the Apostle to be the code of Islam and thinks that the Apostle would say of his own whatever he liked, are all polytheism. Allah is the real Ruler and the Apostle is none but the Messenger of Allah. Thus one should follow him alone and in case anybody's teachings fall against those of his must be utterly rejected.

Tirmidhi reports from Muawiyya that the Prophet of Islam said:

من سره ان يتمثل له الرجال قياما فليتبوا مقعده من النار :

> "Anyone who likes others to keep standing before him like a statue should seek his place in Fire."

That is, one who wants that people keep waiting upon him without even shaking a bit, speaking a little and looking left and right, just like a statue, he is certainly a hellish. It is because he claims to have Divine power. He wants from masses what Allah wants them to observe and practise during prayer. i.e. to keep standing before Him.

It is clear from this Hadith that to keep standing before anyone out of regard is among actions which Allah, the Almighty has specified for Himself.

Tirmidhi reports from Thauban that the Holy Prophet (peace and blessings of Allah be upon him) said :

لا تقوم الساعة حتى تلحق قبائل من امتى بالمشركين

وحتى تعبد قبائل من امتى الاوثان :

> "The Hour of Doom will not occures unless some among my 'ummah' will be practising polytheism and others will start adoring some places."

That is, polytheism is of two kinds: one is to worship some figure by naming it; this is called 'Sanam' (idol) in Arabic. Another thing is to adore any place or tree or stone or wooden piece or a piece of paper after giving it a name; this is called 'Wathan' in Arabic. It includes grave, 'chillah' in the name of somebody or tomb or stick in the name of somebody of ta'ziyah (a model of the tombs of Imam Hasan and Husain carried in procession during Muharram) or standard or 'mehndi'(the henna plant) of Imam Qasim and peer Dastigir or 'Chabutra' (a platform) of Imam or the seats of teachers and 'peers'. People worship these places, make their offerings to these places, make vows for them; similarly, arch in the name of a martyr or ensign and swear by these objects. Moreover, some people give reputation to some places by some names, like place of 'Stella' or of 'Masani' or 'Bhawani' or of 'Kali' or of 'Kalka' or of 'Brahi' etc; these are all 'Wathan.' Hence the prophecy of the Prophet of Islam that some of the Muslims will turn polytheists about the Hour of Doom, refers to these states of affair. Both kinds of persons are polytheists - whether they worship idols or others such objects. Both of them are deviated from the path shown by Allah and they are the enemies of the

Messenger of Islam to.

Muslim reports from Abi Tufail (Radiallaho anho).

ان عليا رضی الله عنه اخرج صحيفة فيها لعن الله من ذبح لغير الله :

"Hadrat Ali took out a book wherein it was written that curse of Allah be upon that person who makes sacrifice (of an animal) in the name of one other than Allah."

That is, one who sacrifices animals in the name of anyone other than Allah is the Cursed one. This is one of a few Hadiths of the Apostle perserved by Hadrat Ali in a book.

The above Hadith makes it clear that to sacrifice an animal in the name of anyone other than Allah is among the form of adoration of Allah, the Almighty has specified for Himself. Hence it should be performed for Him alone and doing this in the name of anybody else is an act of polytheism.

Muslim reports from Hadrat Ayesha (Radiallaho anha) to have heard from the Prophet of Allah saying:

لا يذهب الليل والنهار حتى يعبد للات والعزى فقلت يارسول الله ان كنت لأظن حين انزل الله هُوَالَّذِى اَرسَلَ رَسُولَه بِا لهُد ى وَدِينِ الحَقِّ لِيُظهِرَه عَلَىَ الدِّينِ كُلِّه وَلَوكَرِهَ المُشرِكُون ط ان ذلك تام قال انه سيكون من ذالك ما شاء الله ثم يبعث الله ريحا طيبة فتوفى كل من كان فى قلبه مثقال حبة من خردل من ايمان فيبقى من لاخير فيه فيرجعون الى دين ابائهم

"Days and nights will not cease (i.e. the Hour of Doom will not occur) unless people begin to worship Lat and Uz`za." Thereupon I said, "O Prophet of Islam, I certainly thought that it (Islam) will remain unchanged after the revelation of the verse meaning. "It is He Who has sent forth His Apostle with guidance and the true faith to make it triumphant over all religions, however much the polytheists may dislike it (9:34). The Apostle replied that "it will certainly remain so till Allah will choose to leave it so; thereafter, Allah, the Almighty will send a wind which will make those pass away having a grain of faith, but will leave those untouched having nothing but evil and following the faith of their forefathers."

Muslim reports from Abdullah bin Umar (Radiallaho anho) that the Holy Prophet (peace and blessings of Allah be upon him) said:

يخرج الدجال فيبعث الله عيسى ابن مريم فيطلبه ويهلكه ثم يرسل الله ريحا باردة من قبل الشام فلا يبقى على وجه الارض احد فى قلبه مثقال ذرة من ايمان الاقبضته فيبقى شرار الناس فى خفة الطير واحلام السباع لايعرفون معروفًا ولاينكرون منكرًا فيتمثل لهم الشيطان فيقول الا تستحيون فيقولون فماذا تامرنا فيا مرهم بعبادة الاوثان وهم فى ذالك دار رزقهم حسن عيشهم :

"Dajjal (Anti Christ) will appear and then Allah will send 'Isa (Jesus Christ) who will find him out and kill him on the spot. Thereafter, Allah will send cold wind from Syria so that all with even a grain of Faith will die leaving wrongdoers alive like birds and beasts having no true sense of right and wrong. After that Satan will come to them in disguise and will say if they were not ashamed of themselves. Upon asking as to what he had to say to them, he would ask them to worship places and these (places) would produce subsistence for them and they would continue to roll in wealth."

That is, by the end of this world, the Believers will pass away, while the stupids will remain alive; always ready to usurp the wealth and property of others without least care for right and wrong. Thereupon Satan will tell them that to be Unbeliever is an act of great shame. This repprochement will create in them love for religion. But they will not follow the words of Allah and His Apostle; rather they will innovate their religion with their own reason and hence they will fall a prey to polytheism. And in this state also if they flourish abundantly, they will go deep into polytheism, thinking that more they adore them more their desires are fulfilled. But one should fear the stratagem of Allah. It so often happens that a person is immersed in polytheism and invokes others for fulfilling his needs, still Allah, the Almighty gives him in abundance. In such a case, he thinks he is on the right path. Hence fulfilling of desires or not is not to be relied on and in all cases the true religion of 'Tauheed' should never be renounced.

It is clear from this Hadith that even being immersed in sins and acts of shamelessness and usurping others' property etc. are something better than worshipping others because Satan teaches one to act like this.

Bukhari and Muslim report from Abu Hurairah (Radiallaho anho) that the Holy Prophet (peace and blessings of Allah be upon him) said:

لاتقوم الساعة حتى تضطرب اليات نساء دوس حول
ذى الخلصة -

"The Hour of Doom will not occur unless buttocks of the women of Daus will shake around Dhil-Khalesa."

Daus is an Arabian tribe. They worshipped an idol named Dhil-Khalesa. This idol was destroyed during the days of the Prophet of Islam. But it will again be worshipped about the occurrence of the Doomsday, and women will go round it with their hips in movement.

It is clear from this Hadith that it is an act of polytheism to go round anything except that of the House of Allah and it, certainly, is the rite of the Unbelievers. Hence it must be avoided.

PART - FIVE

Association with Allah in the Affairs of Life

فِى رَدِّ الْاِشْرَاكِ فِى الْعَادَاتْ

Under this chapter those verses of the Holy Qur'an and *ahadith* have been mentioned which denote that one must not adore anyone else as he does in case of Allah, the Almighty.

Allah, the Exalted says in Surah Nisa of the Holy Qur'an

اِن يَّدعُونَ مِن دُونِهٖ اِلَّا اِنٰثًا وَاِن يَّدعُونَ اِلَّا شَيطَانًا مَّرِيدًا
لَّعَنَهُ اللّٰهُ م وَقَالَ لَاَتَّخِذَنَّ مِن عِبَادِكَ نَصِيبًا مَّفرُوضًا وَّلَاُ
ضِلَّنَّهُم وَلَاُ مَنِّيَنَّهُم وَلَاٰمُرَنَّهُم فَلَيُبَتِّكُنَّ اٰذَانَ الاَنعَامِ
وَلَاٰمُرَنَّهُم فَلَيُغَيِّرُنَّ خَلقَ اللّٰهِ وَمَن يَّتَّخِذِ الشَّيطٰنَ وَلِيًّا مِّن
دُونِ اللّٰهِ فَقَد خَسِرَ خُسرَانًا مُّبِينًا ط يَعِدُهُم وَيُمَنِّيهِم

وَمَا يَعِدُهُمُ الشَّيْطٰنُ اِلَّا غُرُورًا ، اُولٰئِكَ مَاوٰئهُم جَهَنَّمُ
وَلَا يَجِدُونَ عَنهَا مَحِيصًا ○ ط

"They worship none but females, (and) worship none but a rebellious devil (Satan) whom Allah has cursed because he had said: 'I shall entice a certain number of Your servants and lead them astray. I shall arouse in them vain desires and order them to slit the ears of cattle. I shall order them to tamper with Allah's creation.' Indeed, he that chooses the devil rather than Allah for his protector ruins himself beyond redemption.

He makes promises and stirs up in them vain desires, and the devil makes them promises only to deceive them. Hell shall be their homes, from it they shall find no refuge."
(Q. 4:117-121)

That is, while calling anybody other than Allah, they have a concept of women. Some of them take the name of Hadrat Bibi, while other take the names of Bibi A'sia, Bibi Atewali, Lalpari, Seahpari, Satila, Masani and Kali, etc. But in fact, there is neither any such woman nor man. This is just a notion and whim and mere evil suggestion of the devil. And the one who speaks at the top of man and sometimes works wonders is none but the Satan. Thus all types of offerings reach none but to him. Hence, infact, all those things go to the devil what they offer to women. They, therefore, get nothing from their offerings, neither in this world nor in the Hereafter. It is because the Satan is the cursed one from Allah, the Almighty, how can he be of any advantage in the Hereafter. Moreover, it is well-known that the Satan is the sworn enemy of the man, so how can he be of any help to man whatsoever. He has rather told before Allah that he will make many of His servants to serve him and deviate from the right path, so that they will make offerings in the form of animals etc. and make symbols in his name such as cutting and slitting the ear, putting thread around their neck, applying myrtle to their forehead, tie 'Sehra' (a garland worn on the forehead by the bride and the bridegroom at the marriage ceremony) on the face, putting coins inside their mouth. In short. it consists of all what is done with the animals in the name of offerings to someone in view. The Satan has also said that he will make them learn how to bring about changes in the appearance of human being. Hence someone will have the plait in anyone's name, make openings in the nose and ears in anyone's name, while others will show his face clean-shaved. These are all the whims created by the Satan and quite against the Will of Allah and His Prophet (peace and blessings of Allah be upon him). Thus one who treads on the way shown by the Satan leaving the way of Allah is deceived beyond doubt. Moreover, the Satan has no power with him other than creating doubt and suspicion in the minds of men. He makes men to indulge in false promise and create thousands of desires and yearnings in them for worldly comforts. In this way they are so much embarrassed that they forget Allah and runs after others. But it happens what Allah, the Almighty, has already decreed. Following this or that other than Allah yields nothing. All these are nothing but the doubts and deceptions inculcated by the Satan. And as a result of these mis-conceptions a man turns away from Allah, the Almighty, is caught in the net of polytheism spread by Allah and becomes a hellish person. At last, it becomes almost impossible for him to come out of the grip of the Satanic acts.

Allah, the Almighty says in Surah Al-A'raf of the Holy Qur'an

هُوَ الَّذِى خَلَقَكُم مِن نَّفسٍ وَّاحِدَةٍ وَّجَعَلَ مِنهَا زَوجَهَا
لِيَسكُنَ اِلَيهَا فَلَمَّا تَغَشّٰهَا حَمَلَت حَملًا خَفِيفًا فَمَرَّت بِهٖ
فَلَمَّا اَثقَلَت دَّعَوَاللّٰهَ رَبَّهُمَا لَئِن اٰتَيتَنَا صَالِحًا لَّنَكُونَنَّ مِنَ
الشّٰكِرِينَ فَلَمَّا اٰتٰهُمَا صَالِحًا جَعَلَا لَهٗ شُرَكَآءَ فِيمَا اٰتٰهُمَا—
فَتَعٰلَى اللّٰهُ عَمَّا يُشرِكُونَ ط

"It was He who created you from single being. From that being He created his mate, so that he might find comfort in her. And when he had covered her, she conceived, and for a time her burden is light. She carried it with ease, but when it grew heavy, they both cried to Allah, their Lord: "Grant us a goodly child and we will be truly thankful."

Yet when He had granted them a goodly child, they set up other gods besides Him in return for what He had given them. Exalted be He above what they associate with Him." (7:189-190)

That is, Allah, the Almighty created the first Man and it is He Who gave him a wife and created love between husband and wife. And when there is a hope for an issue, he invokes Allah to give him a sound and healthy one. But when Allah, the Almighty, confers upon him an issue, he calls others for help and makes offerings to them; taking him (the child) to a shrine, makes him to have a plait or wear 'sacred' thread, fasten irons to his legs, make him a beggar and name him Nabi Bux, Ali Bux, Imam Bux, Peer Bux, Satila Bux, Ganga Bux, etc. But Allah, the Almighty, does not care for their offerings, for He is beyond all such anxieties, and they are themselves accursed.

Allah, the Almighty says in Surah Ana'm of the Holy Qur'an:

وَجَعَلُوا لِلَّهِ مِمَّا ذَرَأَ مِنَ الْحَرْثِ وَالْأَنْعَامِ نَصِيبًا فَقَالُوا هَٰذَا لِلَّهِ بِزَعْمِهِمْ وَهَٰذَا لِشُرَكَائِنَا فَمَا كَانَ لِشُرَكَائِهِمْ فَلَا يَصِلُ إِلَى اللَّهِ وَمَا كَانَ لِلَّهِ فَهُوَ يَصِلُ إِلَىٰ شُرَكَائِهِمْ سَاءَ مَا يَحْكُمُونَ

"They set aside for Allah a share of what He has created tilth and cattle saying: "This is for Allah 'so they pretend'

> and this for our associate gods.' The share of their associate-gods. How will they judge!"
>
> (Q. 6:136)

That is, all harvests and cattle are created by Allah alone and none else has done the least. But they make offerings to Allah as they do for others, rather in the more adoring manner.

Allah, the Almighty says in Surah Al-Ana'm of the Holy Qur'an:

وَقَالُوا هٰذِهٖ اَنعَامٌ وَحَرثٌ حِجرٌ لَّا يَطعَمُهَآ اِلَّا مَن نَّشَآءُ بِزَعمِهِم وَاَنعَامٌ حُرِّمَت ظُهُورُهَا وَاَنعَامٌ لَّا يَذكُرُونَ اسمَ اللّٰهِ عَلَيهَا افتِرَآءً عَلَيهِ سَيَجزِيهِم بِمَا كَانُوا يَفتَرُونَ ط

> "They say: 'These cattle, and these crops are forbidden. None may eat of them save those whom we permit." So they assert. And there are other cattle whose backs are forbidden, and others over which they do not pronounce the name of Allah, thus committing a sin against Him. Allah will punish them for their invented lies."
>
> (6:138)

That is, they form an idea of their own that so and so is a thing untouchable and such and such person may eat it while others can't. Similarly some particular types of animals may bear the burden of men and materials while others can't because it is vowed to someone and hence it must be paid especial regard. Some of them do not hold their animals in the name of Allah but attach them to someone other than Allah and think that Allah, the Almighty becomes happy with such an act and fulfils desires. But these all are untruth and they will be punished for that.

Allah, the Almighty says in Surah Al-Ma'ida of the Holy Qur'an:

مَاجَعَلَ اللّٰهُ مِن بَحِيرَةٍ وَّلَاسَآئِبَةٍ وَّلَا وَصِيلَةٍ وَّلَاحَامٍ وَّلٰكِنَّ الَّذِينَ كَفَرُوا يَفتَرُونَ عَلَى اللّٰهِ الكَذِبَ وَاَكثَرُهُم لَايَعقِلُونَ ٥

"Allah demands neither a *bahira*, nor a *saibah*, nor a *wasilah*, nor a *hami*. But those who disbelieve invent lies against Allah. Most of them are lacking in judgment."[1] (5:103)

That is, when they kept an animal in the name of someone, they made a slit in its ear, and call it that *bahira*; what they turned into a bull, they called that *saibah*; when they vowed that if the particular animal would deliver a male, they would offer that to so and so, and in case the animal would deliver male and female at the same time, even the male was not offered; such a female was called *wasilah* and; the animal which would deliver ten kids, was made to abstain from carrying burden and was called *hami*. But all these were not enjoined by Allah, and they had coined these rites out of their own idiocy.

It is clear from the above verse that to keep an animal in the name of someone and apply any sign to an animal and to fix up that only a cow may be attached to so and so and a she-goat to so and so; all these rites are the signs of idiocy and is, therefore, totally against Allah.

Allah, the Almighty says in Surah al-Nahl of the Holy Qur'an:

وَلَاتَقُولُوا لِمَا تَصِفُ اَلسِنَتُكُمُ الكَذِبَ هٰذَا حَلَالٌ وَّهٰذَا حَرَامٌ لِتَفتَرُوا عَلَى اللّٰهِ الكَذِبَ اِنَّ الَّذِينَ يَفتَرُونَ عَلَى اللّٰهِ الكَذِبَ لَايُفلِحُونَ ٥

> "And do not utter when you speak false: 'This is lawful, and this is forbidden', in order to invent a falsehood about Allah. Those who invent flasehoods about Allah shall never prosper."
>
> (Q. 16:116)

That is, one should not form false notion that such and such thing be done while others should be avoided. It is in the power of Allah alone to allow some work to be done and disallow others.

Thus to think that a particular task is to be done in this way or that way is just to go against the Will of Allah and one cannot get his desires fulfilled in this way. It can be concluded from the above verse that to say that betel- leaf should not be taken in the month of Muharram: red clothes should not be put on; 'sahnak' of Hadrat Bibi should not be eaten by male persons and while making offerings to her, such and such vegetable must be included, together with 'missi' (a tooth-powder) and 'mehndi' (myrtle) and this should not be eaten by a slave-girl and the women married twice and the persons of low origin and the adulterer. Moreover, they think that the 'toshah' (provision) of Shah Abdul Haq may be prepared only in the form of 'halwa' (a kind of sweet dish made of flour, ghee and sugar), and hence it should be prepared with care and the person smoking 'huqqah' (smoking pipe) should be debarred from eating it. Similarly, 'malidah' (sweatmeat made with wheat) is attached to Shah Madar, 'Sehmani' with Bu'ali Qalandar, meat and bread with people of 'Kahaf'. They have fixed some rites with marriage, while others with death. All such people are in the grip of polytheism and may be charged of breaking the Divine Laws by formulating their own laws.

Bukhari and Muslim report from Zaid bin Khalid that the Holy Prophet (peace and blessings of Allah be upon him) led the prayer of Fajr (early morning) at Hudaibiya and then turned towards us saying:

على اثر سماء كانت من الليل فلما انصرف فقال هل

تدرون ماذا قال ربكم قالوا الله ورسوله اعلم قال قال
اصبح عبادی مومن بی وکافر بی فاما من قال مطرنا
بفضل الله ورحمته فذالك مومن بی وکافر بالکواکب
واما من قال مطرنا بنوء کذاوکذا فذالك کافر بی
ومومن بالکواکب -

> "It rained last night, and do you know what did your Lord say?"
>
> "Allah and His Apostle know better," said the companions.
>
> The Apostle said, "This morning some persons will turn Believers, while others will be declared Unbelievers. Those who say that they got rain by the blessings of Allah and refused to follow the stars will be considered Believers while others who say that they got from such and such 'nachhattar' (a star) believed in stars will be declared Unbelievers."

That is, one who considers worldly affairs running under the guidance of some stars, he is Unbeliever and one adoring stars in the sight of Allah: while one who considers wordly affairs running under the guidance of Allah, the Almighty. He includes them in His selected servants and take them out of those adoring stars.

It is clear from the above *hadith* that to consider a moment good or evil, auspicious or inauspicious and have the same notion about dates and days and believe in the sayings of astronomers commits polytheism. All these things belong to stars and following the dictates of stars is the act of star-worshippers.

Mishkat reports from Ibn Abbas that the Holy Prophet (peace

and blessings of Allah be upon him) said:

من اقتبس با بًا من علومٍ النجوم بغیرما ذکر اللــه فقد
اقتبس شعبة من السحر المنجم کا هن و الکاهن ســاحر
و الساحر کافر

"One who learns anything from astronomy unless revealed by Allah Himself, learns a way of magic. An astronomer is a soothsayer, and a soothsayer is a magician and a magician is an Unbeliever".

That is, the Book of Allah has mention of stars and that they have Power of Allah in them and they show the wisdom of Allah and the beauty and splendour of the sky and devils are beaten and made to take to their heels by them. But at no place in the Qur'an we find mention of the fact that working of the universe is controlled by the stars or they have any effect whatsoever in the good and evil of this universe. So as the Brahmins know something of the unseen from the jinns and they are called 'kahin' (a soothsayer) in Arabic, the astronomer reveals something after getting it from stars. Hence both the soothsayers and astronomers tread the same path. The soothsayers establish friendship with the jinns by calling and following them. Hence both of them go along the path of paganism.

Muslim reports from Hadrat Hafsa that the Holy Prophet (peace and blessings of Allah be upon him) said:

من اتی عرافًا فسا لــه عن شــیءٍ لم تقبل لـه صلـوة
اربعین لیلةً –

"One who goes to a soothsayer and tries to know anything unseen from him has his prayers of forty days unaccepted."

That is, one who goes to a soothsayer to know about the unseen finds his prayers of forty days unaccepted. It is because he committed polytheism and polytheism puts off the light of everything. And all the astronomers, astrologers and soothsayers fall in the same category.

Abu Dawud reports from Qabisa that the Holy Prophet (peace and blessings of Allah be upon him) said:

العيافة والطرق والطيرة من الجبت –

"Flying birds for omens, pouring something for soothsaying and trying to know the omen of any object is among the rites of paganism."

Abu Dawud reports from Ibn Masood (radiallaho anho) that the Holy Prophet (peace and blessings of Allah be upon him) said:

الطيرة شرك الطيرة شرك الطيرة شرك –

"Practising augury is polytheism; practising augury is polytheism; practising augury is polytheism."

That is, the Arabs practised augury too much and have deep belief in it. The Holy Prophet (peace and blessings of Allah be upon him) told them several times to shun the evil of polytheism.

Abu Dawud reports from S'ad bin Malik that the Holy Prophet (peace and blessings of Allah be upon him) said:

لا ها مة ولاعدوى ولاطيرة وان تكن الطيرة فىشىءٍ
ففى الدار والفرس والمراة –

"Neither there is anything like 'hama' nor one is touched by the disease of someone else nor any object is inauspicious. However, if there may be any inauspiciousness in anything, it is either in a house or a horse or a woman."

That is, the ignorant Arabs had a belief that if someone is killed unavenged, an owl comes out of his or her skull and goes on complaining for the neglect: it was called 'hama'. The Prophet (peace and blessings of Allah be upon him) forbade to believe in such a thing.

It is amply clear from this that it is wrong to say that a dead person appears incorporating himself in an animal figure. Moreover, to say that the disease like scabies and leprosy are infectious disease.

We may now conclude that to avoid the person caught in smallpox is an act of paganism and hence must not be practised. It is also wrong to think that such and such task or job proved inauspicious to anyone. So if it is true with respect to anything, it is a house or a horse or a woman.

But one should bear in mind that there is no way to get known what is auspicious and what is not. Hence the Believers must not believe in such things, and when purchasing a new house or a horse and marrying a woman or buying a slave girl, one should invoke goodness and virtue from Allah, the Almighty, and seek refuge with Allah from evils of these objects. Moreover, nobody should think that such and such things proved auspicious or inauspicious for him.

Bukhari reports from Abu Hurairah (radiallaho anho) that the Holy Prophet (peace and blessings of Allah be upon him) said:

لا عدوى ولاهامة ولاصفر

> "Neither anyone is infected by anybody else's disease nor an owl comes out of the skull of a dead person nor is 'safar' anything is reality."

It was thought by Arabs of the Age of Ignorance that one who develops such a disease that he goes on eating without getting satiated, what is called 'jual kalb' by the physician, he must be having a ghost in his stomach; this is called 'Safar'. But the Holy Prophet (peace and blessings of Allah be upon him) declared it wrong, for there is nothing like it.

It is quite clear from this that to say that thirteen days of 'Safar' are inauspicious, because evil spirits descend during this period, and the name 'tera tezi' was given to it because any swiftness in this period may cause harm. Similarly, to consider any month or date or day as auspicious is among the rites of polytheism.

Ibn Majah reports from Jabir (radiallaho anho) that the Holy Prophet (peace and blessings of Allah be upon him) caught the hand of a leper and putting it in his plate said:

كل ثقة با لله وتوكلا عليه

"Eat from it relying on Allah and keeping faith in Him."

That is one should think that he has to rely on Allah,

Who can keep healthy and cause to fall sick at Will and hence he should not believe in any infection and avoid eating with anyone.

Abu Dawud reports from Jabeer (radiallaho anho) that an Arab rustic came to the Holy Prophet (peace and blessings of Allah be upon him) and said:

جهدت الانفس وجاع العيال وهلكت الاموال فاستسق

الله لنا فانا نستشفع بك على الله ونستشفع بالله عليك

> "We are passing through very hard days and our kith and kin and cattle are dying of starvation; hence ask Allah for rain because you are intercessor with Allah and He with you."

Thereupon, the Holy Prophet (peace and blessings of Allah be upon him) observed:

سبحان الله سبحان الله

ويحك انه لا يستشفع بالله على احد
شان الله اعظم من ذالك ويحك اتدرى ما الله ان
عرشه على سموته هكذا وقال باصابعه مثل القبةعليه
وانه ليئط به اطيط الرحل بالراكب

> "Allah is Unique, Allah is Unique", and went on saying like this so that faces of his companions changed and he further added:
>
> "How foolish you are that you know not what actually Allah is. Certainly His Throne is being put on the heavens like this (he indicated it with his fingers), and undoubtedly it produces sounds like that of the pack saddle when the mount is on."

That is, famine had broken out in Arabia and a rustic and uncivilized person came in and after narrating the severity of the famine asked to invoke Allah and added that his (the Apostle's) intercession with Allah and Allah's with him (the Apostle) could do the needful. Thus, having heard these words, the Holy Prophet (peace and blessings of Allah be upon him) shuddered from within and started speaking highly about Allah so much so that faces of the Companions of the Prophet of Allah present there changed out of respect and glory for the Lord. Thereafter, the Holy Prophet (peace and blessings of Allah be upon him) told the rustic Arab that the only one having control over affairs may do anything as a result of intercession from any agency. Now when anybody says that Allah is the intercessor with the Apostle, it means he considers the Apostle to be the actual controller of affairs and a sovereign power and Allah to be his intercessor; this is totally wrong. The Glory of Allah is beyond human comprehension. All the Prophets, saints and Friends of Allah are lesser than the smallest of the particles in the sight of Allah. His Greatness is far beyond all wisdom and knowledge and none among His creatures is able to describe His Glory and Splendour. He can perform crores of wonders in an instant without any adviser, minister and army, then who is there before whom He will intercede and who become a sovereign in His presence? Glory be to Him ! Muhammad, the Prophet (peace and blessings of Allah be upon him), the most superior among His creatures shuddered to hear something from the tongue of a rustic person and started eulogizing His Greatness spread from earth to sky. It creates wonder when a commoner claims that he has purchased the Lord in return for very little amount; others say if Allah appears in any guise other than that of their saint, they will never see Him. There are persons who consider the Prophet of Allah better than the Divinity. May Allah keep us under His refuge!

It is clear from the above-mentioned *hadith* that one must not ask anything from anybody other than Allah. When it is said, "O 'Shaikh Abdul Qadir ! Give me for Allah", it is wrong and such words must not be uttered. However, if one says "O 'Allah ! Give me for Shaikh Abdul Qadir', it is correct. In short, any word indicating polytheism or disrespect must not be spoken. He has Magnificence and Splendour and He is care-free. It is He Who lays hold of in a jiffy and favours one in a moment. And it is out of place to use uncivilized word for Allah and mean something else. Such an enigma may be practised at some other places, it is not necessarily to be used for Allah alone. Nobody makes fun with his king or father. Such words look suitable with friends and acquaintances.

Muslim reports from Ibn Umar (radiallaho anho) that the Holy Prophet (peace and blessings of Allah be upon him) said:

ان احب اسمآ ئکم عبداللہ وعبد الرحمن -

"The best among the names are Abdullah and Abdur Rehman."

That is, Abdullah means 'Servant of Allah' and; Abdur Rahman means 'Servant of the Most Merciful.' Abdul Quddus, Abdul Khaliq, Khuda Bux, Allah Din, Allah Dad belong to the same category.

Abu Dawud and Nisai report from Shariah that when his father appeared before the Holy Prophet (peace and blessings of Allah be upon him) with his people, he (the Apostle) heard him to be called "Abul Hakam" (the main arbiter) and said:

ان اللہ هو الحَكم واليه الحكم فلم تكنى ابالحكم -

> "Allah alone is the "the Main Arbiter" and it is He who arbitrates; why then he be called 'Abul Hakam'?

This is only then in the Power of Allah that all disputes are settled. It is He Who will appear on the Day of Judgment to settle all the disputes of the worldly life. No creature has any such power.

It is known from the above *hadith* that the word suitable to describe the glory of Allah must not be used for anybody else; for example, King of the kings, Master of the worlds etc.

Sharhe Sunnah reports from Hudhaifa (may Allah be pleased with him) that the Holy Prophet (peace and blessings of Allah be upon him) said:

لا تقولوا ماشاء اللہ وشاء محمدو
قولوا ماشاء اللہ وحده -

> "Don't speak what Allah and Muhammad like, but say what only Allah likes."

That is, any creature must not be attached with what is exclusively for Allah; however big the personality be and however near be he to Allah. Everything happens with the Will of Allah and the Messenger of Allah has nothing to do with these happenings. However, if one says in matters of religion that Allah and His

Apostle know better, there is nothing wrong, for Allah, the Almighty has revealed all the Divine matters to His Apostle and has enjoined upon all His servants to obey him.

Tirmidhi reports from Ibn Umar (radiallaho anho) that the Holy Prophet (peace and blessings of Allah be upon him) said:

من حلف بغير الله فقد اشرك

"One who swears by anyone other than Allah commits polytheism".

Muslim reports from Abdur Rahman bin Samura (may Allah be pleased with him) the Holy Prophet (peace and blessings of Allah be upon him) said :

لاتحلفوا بالطواغيت ولا با بائكم

"Swear neither by false gods not by ancestors."

Bukhari and Muslim report from Ibn Umar (Radiallaho anho) that the Holy Prophet (peace and blessings of Allah be upon him) said:

ان الله ينهكم ان تحلفوا با بآئكم من كان حالفاً فليحلف بالله او ليصمت

"Allah forbids to swear by ancestors; and whoever swears, he should swear by Allah or keep silent."

Bukhari and Muslim report from Abu Hurairah (may Allah be pleased with him) that the Holy Prophet (peace and blessings of Allah be upon him) said:

قال من حلف فقال فى حلفه با للات والعزى فليقل لااله الاالله

"One who wants to swear and swears by Lat and Uz'za by mistake must say "*La Ilaha Illallah*"

That is, the people of Arab would swear by idols in their state of paganism. Hence if such words come out of the lips of a Believer, he should utter *'La Ilaha Illallah'* without loss of time.

It is clear from the above *ahadith* that one should not swear by anyone other than Allah and in case such a thing happens and he swears like an idol worshipper, his Faith is spotted.

Abu Dawud reports from Thabit bin Zehak that:

A certain person vowed, during the life-time of the Holy Prophet (peace and blessings of Allah be upon him) to slaughter a camel at a place called Bawana. Thereafter, he came to the Prophet of Allah and informed him about his scheme. The Apostle asked him whether that was a place of worship. He replied in the negative. Was any festivel held there? He said, "No".

اوف بنذرك فانه لاوفاء لنذر فى معصية الله تعالى

> "Accomplish then your vow", said the Apostle and added, "only such a vow must not be fulfilled which brings about a sin a gainst Allah.

It means it is an act of sin to vow for anybody else other than Allah and hence such a vow must not be fulfilled.

It can be concluded from the above *hadith* that, at first, one should not vow for anyone other than Allah and if ne does so, it must not be fulfilled. It is because it is a sin, and if one is adamant on it adds to his sin. Moreover, a place where animal is sacrificed for anyone other than Allah or they worship anybody else or gather for performing any polytheistic act, one should avoid carrying such an animal which is to be sacrificed in the name of Allah. Good or evil intention makes no difference, as any similarity with the evil-doers is itself wrong.

Imam Ahmad reports from Hadrat Ayesha (may Allah be pleased with her) that once the Holy Prophet (peace and blessings of Allah be upon him) was sitting among the 'Muhajirin'

(Migraters) and the Ansar (Helpers) that a camel appeared and it prostrated before the Messenger of Allah. Thereupon, his companions said:

يارسول الله يسجد لك البهائم والشجر فنحن احق ان
نسجدلك فقال اعبدوا ربكم واكرموا اخاكم

> "When animals and trees lay in prostration before you why not me."
>
> "Worship your Lord and pay respect to your brethren", The Messenger of Allah observed.

That, all men are brethren and hence they deserve respects of one another, but since Allah is the Lord and Master of all, He should be worshipped.

It can safely be inferred from the above *hadith* that all persons like Prophets, Saints, Friends of Allah, religious heads and their sons, however closer they might be to Allah, are nothing but human beings and are, therefore, humble and like our brothers whom Allah, the Almighty conferred upon greatness; hence we should obey them for we are younger, but they should be paid respects like a man only, and not like that of Allah.

It is also clear from the above *hadith* that certain trees and animals pay regards to certain saints, as lions appear at some shrines and elephants and wolves at others, but all these must not be misunderstood for anything but they should be respected as men.

Abu Dawud reports from Qais bin S'ad:

اتيت الحيرة فرأيتهم
يَسجدون لمرزبان لهم فقلت لرسول الله صلى الله عليه
وسلم احق ان يسجد له فا تيت رسول الله صلى الله
عليه وسلم فقلت انى اتيت الحيرة فرايتهم يسجدون

لمرزبان لهم.فانت احق ان نسجدلك فقال لى ارأيت لو مررت بقبري اكنت تسجد له فقلت لا ، فقال لا تفعلوا

"Once I had been to a city named Heerah and I saw there people laying in prostration before their king. I thought the Messenger of Allah deserved the prostration most. Thereafter, I appeared before the Holy Prophet (peace and blessings of Allah be upon him) and narrated: "I had been to Heerah and there I found people prostrating before their king, but you deserve it most. The Holy Prophet (peace and blessings of Allah be upon him) said:

"Will you prostrate at my grave?"

"Not at all !" I said.

"Don't do so then", said the Apostle.

That is, one day he (the Apostle) was also to die and mingle with dust and then how does he deserve prostration; only He deserves it Who is immortal.

It is obvious from the above *hadith* that neither the living one nor the dead nor a grave, nor a place deserve prostration, for one who is living, he has to die one day. And anybody who dies does not become God; a slave is after all a slave.

Muslim reports from Abu Hurairah (may Allah be pleased with him) that the Holy Prophet (peace and blessings of Allah be upon him) said:

لا يقولن احدكم عبدى وامتى كلكم

عبيدالله وكل نساءكم اماءالله ولايقل العبد لسيده

مولاى فان مولكم الله تعالى -

> "None of you should say 'my slave or my slaves.' All of you are the slaves of Allah and your ladies are the girl-slaves of Allah. No lady should call her husband her 'master', for Allah is the Master of all."

That is, the husband should not call his slave or slave-girl his own slave and the slave girl should not call her husband her master, for Allah alone is the Master and the rest are His slaves. Nobody is either slave or master to one another.

It can be concluded from the above *hadith* that one should not call a man as his slave even if he is slave of anyone in real life and same is the case with a master. Hence it is quite improper to call anybody Abdun-nabi (slave of the Prophet), Banda-e-Ali (slave of Ali) etc. Moreover, it is sheer polytheism to say that someone is his sustainer or master of life and property or he is in the possession of anybody.

Bukhari and Muslim report that the Holy Prophet (peace and blessings of Allah be upon him) said:

لاتطرنى كما اطرت النصارى عيسى بن
مريم فا نما اناعبده فقولوا عبد الله ورسوله

> "Don't enhance me beyond a certain limit as the Christians did with Jesus, the son of Mary; I am His slave, and hence say, 'Allah's slave and His Messenger."

That is, if anyone who calls me the Messenger of Allah, it is enough because it consists of all the attributes bestowed upon me by Allah, the Almighty for nothing is greater for man than prophethood. All other ranks are below it. But a man remains a man even after Prophethood is being conferred on him. A slave is after all a slave whatever greatness he achieves. The Christians became pagans after attaching some attributes to Jusus Christ and were accursed by Allah, the Exalted. Hence, the Holy Prophet (peace and blessings of Allah be upon him) asked his *Ummah* not to follow the path of the Christians and do not eulogize the Last Prophet of Islam so that you be accursed by Allah like the Christians. But alas ! rude and disrespectful persons did not pay heed to what the Messenger of Allah said. Later on, they started saying like the Christians that Allah appeared in the guise of Jesus Christ and hence he (Christ) is both man and God. Almost the same thing was said about the Holy Prophet (peace and blessings of Allah be upon him). Some unfortunate people attribute to the Prophet of Allah that he has himself said: "I am Ahmad without mim." Similarly, they have compiled an address with such nonsensible things and named it `Khutbatul Iftikhar' and assigned it to Hadrat Ali (may Allah be pleased with him).

May Allah, the Almighty, blacken faces of these unfortunate ones. And as the Christians claim that all the affairs of the universe fall the control of Jesus, and one who follows and entreat him need not serve anybody nor any sin could meddle with his state of affairs and he rises above the concept of lawful and unlawaful. He thinks that he is at liberty to do whatever he likes, for Jesus Christ will intercede for him and save him on the Day of Resurrection. The same idea based on ignorance is being formed about the Holy Prophet (peace and blessings of Allah be upon him) and they go much below to attach the same concept with their saints and religious guides. May Allah guide them.

Abu Dawud reports from Matar'rif:

انطلقت فی وفد بنی عامر الی رسول الله صلی الله علیه وسلم فقلنا انت سیدنا فقال السید الله فقلنا وافضلنا فضلا واعظمنا طولا فقال قولوا قولکم اوبعض قولکم فلایجترئنکم الشیطن

"I, accompanied by the envoys of Bani Amir appeared before the Holy Prophet (peace and blessings of Allah be upon him) and said:

"You are our Chief".

"The Chief is Allah alone", the Apostle said.

"You are superior to us in respect and generosity",

we said.

"You can say such a thing but it is better to say a little less than this; may the Satan make you disrespectful."

That is, one should be cautious in eulogizing a respectful person and praise a man what he deserves; be brief in praising anybody and don't run in this like an unbridled horse so that you show disrespect to Allah, the Almighty.

The word 'Sardar (Chief) has two meanings:

(1) One is that he is autocratic and sovereign and obeys none or dictated by nobody. He functions at his well, as a king apparently does. But Allah alone is magnificent enough to do so and; none is there like Him.

(2) Secondly, he may be subject to any superior agency but is superior to other subjects. He carries out orders from his superiors and impose them on the subjects below in ranks, as is the case with the chief of the village or a landlord. In this respect, a Prophet is the chief of his *Ummah*: every Imam is the chief of the people of his times, every 'mujtahid' (religious director) is the chief of his followers and; every religious scholar is chief of his pupils. These chiefs learn or take orders from their superiors and impart them to their subordinates. In this meaning our Prophet (peace and blessings of Allah be upon him) is the chief of this universe. His rank is the highest in the sight of Allah; he follows the dictates of Allah most, and others have no course but to learn the injunctions of Allah from His Apostle. Thus there is no harm if he is called the chief of the universe. But in the first meaning, he is chief not even of an ant,

for he cannot dictate even an ant.

Bukhari reports from Hadrat Ayesha (may Allah be pleased with her) :

انها اشترت نمرقة فيها تصاوير

فلما راها رسول الله صلى الله عليه وسلم قام على

الباب ، فلم يدخل فعرفت فى وجهة الكراهية قالت

فقلت يا رسول الله اتوب الى الله والى رسوله ماذا اذنبت ؟

فقال رسول الله صلى الله عليه وسلم مابال هذه

النمرقة ؟ قالت قلت اشتريتها لك لتقعد عليها وتوسدها

فقال رسول الله صلى الله عليه وسلم ان اصحاب هذه

الصور يعذبون يوم القيامة و يقال لهم احيوا ما خلقتم

وقال ان البيت الذى فيه الصور لاتدخل الملائكة

"I bought a small carpet having pictures. When the Holy Prophet (peace and blessings of Allah be upon him) saw that, he stopped at the door and did not enter the house, I found the sign displeasure on his face, and I said: 'O Messenger of Aallah, I vow not to sin any more, what sin I have committed? Thereupon, the Messenger of Allah said:

"What for this small carpet is?"

"I have purchased this for you to sit and to use as a pillow", I replied.

"People having such pitcures will get entangled on the

> Day of Resurrection, they will be asked to infuse life in what you have made," the Apostle elucidated and added, "A house where there is any picture, is not visited by angels."

That is, the polytheists generally worship idols, hence angels abhor pictures and Prophets also hate them. Makers of pictures will be punished, because they provide objects of idolworship.

It is clear from the above-mentioned *hadith* that some ignorant persons adore the pictures of a Prophet or religious guides or spiritual leaders etc and keep them for blessings are but deviated and perverted and immersed in polytheism. Prophets and angels are displeased with such persons. Hence these pictures should be cast off from the house thinking them to be impure and unlawful so that both the Prophet and the angels express their pleasure and come to houses with blessings and grace.

Baihaqi reports from Abdullah Ibn Abbas (may Allah be pleased with him) that he heard the Holy Prophet (peace and blessings of Allah be upon him) saying:

اشـدا النـاس عذابـا يـوم القيامـة مـن قتـل نبيـا او قتلـه
نبـى اوقتـل احدوالديـه والمصورون وعالم لا ينتفع بعلمه

> "The most terrible punishment on the Day of Judgment will be inflicted on one who either kills a Prophet or is killed by a Prophet or kills his mother or father and on picture makers and on the religious scholar whose knowledge is fruitless."

That is, the picture maker is one among the most terrible and heinous sinners. The sin of a picture maker may be imagined from the fact that Yazid and Shimr did not kill the Prophet but his maternal grandson and the deputy of the Prophet, but the picture maker incurs sin equal in proportion to that of the killer of a Prophet; hence he is worse than Yazid and Shimr.

Bukhari and Muslim report from Abu Hurairah (may Allah be pleased with him) that he heard Holy Prophet (peace and blessings of Allah be on him) saying:

قـال الله تعـا لى ومـن اظلـم ممن ذهب يخلـق كخلقـى
فليخلقـوا زرة اوليخلقـوا حبـة اوشعيرة

> "Allah, the Almighty says: Who will be more disrespectful than one who plans to create as I create; so let him produce even a dust particle or grain or a grain of barley."

That is, a picture maker claims indirectly to have divine power, in that he plans to make things like those created by Allah. Hence such a person is highly disrespectful and picture-making is totally a false act because he cannot produce a thing equal even to a grain.

Razin reports from Anas (may Allah be pleased with him) that the Holy prophet (peace and blessings of Allah be upon him) said:

انى لااريد ان ترفعـوا فـى فـوق مـنزلتى التـى
انزلنيها الله تعالى انا محمد بن عبدالله ورسوله

> "Don't enhance my position more than what Allah has bestowed on me; hence I am the same Muhammad, son of Abdullah, the slave of Allah and His Messenger."

That is, the Holy Prophet (peace and blessings of Allah be upon him) was not like these chiefs who are pleased with excessive praise, because other chiefs have nothing to do with religion. But the Holy Prophet (peace and blessings of Allah be on him) was very kind and affectionate to his *Ummah* and exerted day and night to put the Faith. When he came to know that the people of his *Ummah* love him to the extreme and are very grateful to him he became very careful in this matter. It is a common experience that one who loves anybody, he breaks all limits in praising his beloved. But one who breaks the limits in eulogizing the Prophet, he will certainly show disrespect of Allah, the Almighty. In this way, his Faith will be undone. Thus the Apostle emphasised that he did not like exaggeration; his name is Muhammad; he is neither a creator nor a sustainer and has born fr om his father like others; slavery is a matter of pride for him. However, the point of distinction for him is that he knows the religion of Allah perfectly and fully well while others are neglectful. Hence they should learn about the religion from him. May Allah, the Almighty shower thousands of blessings upon him. May Allah, the Almighty, accept my efforts as I am very humble and destitute. And as you heve taught me thoroughly, the meaning of unity and polytheism and gave me to know real and deep meaning of 'la ilaha illallah' and took me out from among the polytheists and made us a pure and a unitarian Muslim, so also make me fully understand the real meaning of *bid'at* (innovation in religion) and *sunnat* (saying and practice of the Prophet) and the mission and spirit of the Holy Prophet (peace and blessings of Allah be upon him) and take me out from among the innovators and lead us to the path of those who follow the Will of Allah and His Apostle. So be it O' Lord of the worlds!

TADHKIRUL IKHWAN

تَذكِيْرُ الْاِخْوَانْ

Remaining Part Of

بقيه

TAQWIAT - UL - IMAN

تَقْوِيَةُ الْاِيْمَانْ

بسم الله الرحمن الرحيم ط

In the name of Allah, Most Gracious, Most Merciful

Praised be to You O' Allah that You conferred on me right guidance by Your blessings; raised me from the *Ummah* of the Holy Prophet (peace and blessings of Allah be upon him); set me to the path of pure unity; saved me from the path of innovation and appointed an *Ummi* (unlettered one) Your Messenger for my guidance by giving him the Qur'an. O' Allah send your blessings to your Apostle who checked people from ploytheism and innovation, guided to your path, described in detail the virtues of unity and vices of polytheism, and to his family members and his companions who set his *sunnah* in action and rejected *bid'at.*

It should be kept in view that a learned and pious person described in detail the evils of *shirk* and *bid'at* and the treatise was entitled as "Taqwiatul Iman." Here the writer collected verses and *ahadith* and divided the collection in two parts. In the first part, he described the virtues of 'Tauheed' and vices of *shirk*. In the second part, he described the virtues of the following of *sunnah* and vices of *bid'at*.

It must be known that what the Holy Prophet (peace and blessings of Allah be upon him) refrained from doing, did not ask anybody to do nor saw anybody doing anything and did not disapprove, nor was circulated by his companions, nor any authentic companion accepted by his companions, nor any authentic companion accepted it as true, nor found currency in times of *tabi'in* (successors of the Companions of the Holy Prophet) and their followers, nor its example was found in any of the four periods, nor the religious directors proved it anyhow; but the Companions of the Prophet, his successors and their followers invented such a faith on their own with the hope of some reward therein; all these are *bid'at* and act of perversion. Moreover, it is also *bid'at* that something new is added to what has been in currency during the four periods. Similarly, what was done by the Holy Prophet (peace and blessings of Allah be upon him) or approved when it was done by anyone or it was done by most of the Companions of the Apostle, is an act of *sunnah*, or what was practised by the successors of the Companions and their followers and what was put into circulation by the religious directors, is also adopted as *sunah*.

It is abundantly clear from the above discussion that any division of *bid'at* as *bid'at-e-hasnah* and *bid'at-e-sayiah* is totally wrong and baseless. It is just a battle of words and nothing else.

Chapter - One

About Practising 'Sunnah' and Saving Oneself from Bid'at

فِي الْاِعْتِصَامِ بِالسُّنَّةِ
وَالْاِجْتِنَابِ عَنِ الْبِدْعَةِ

Allah, the Almighty says in Surah A le Imran of the Holy Qur'an

وَاعْتَصِمُوا بِحَبْلِ اللّٰهِ جَمِيعًا وَّلَا تَفَرَّقُوا وَاذْكُرُوا نِعْمَةَ اللّٰهِ عَلَيْكُم اِذْ كُنْتُم اَعْدَآءً فَاَلَّفَ بَيْنَ قُلُوبِكُم فَاَصْبَحْتُم بِنِعْمَتِهٖ اِخْوَانًا ـ

> "Cling one and all to the faith of Allah and let nothing divide you. Remember the favours He has bestowed upon you: how He united your hearts when you were enemies, so that you are now brothers through His grace......."
>
> (Q. 3:103)

That is, it is a great blessing of Allah, the Almighty that He raised you as an *Ummah* of His Prophet and gave a Book to act according to it unitedly and not to create disruption and dissension. One should not invent a new religion and someone else invent another to combat the former and thus come into conflict with one another. Hence it was said that all of them should remain clung to the Book of Allah. As one lying in a ditch comes out by holding a string so you also do it because unless one in a ditch catches the string he will remain lying there and falls down if he catches it carelessly. Hence all of you should hold the Holy Qur'an fastly and refrain from inventing new things; do not create dissension and do not keep aloof from those who follow the *Sunnah* of the Messenger of Islam

It is clear from the above-mentioned verse that the root cause of all perversions and deviations is to keep aside the Holy Qur'an and invent new things instead.

Allah, the Almighty says in Surah A'le Imran of the Holy Qur'an

وَلَاتَكُونُوا كَالَّذِينَ تَفَرَّقُوا وَاخْتَلَفُوا مِنْ بَعْدِ مَاجَآءَهُمُ
الْبَيِّنَاتُ وَأُولٰئِكَ لَهُم عَذَابٌ عَظِيمٌ ط يَومَ تَبيَضُّ وَجُوهٌ وَ
تَسوَدُّ وَجُوه فَأَمَّا الَّذِينَ اسوَدَّت وَجُوهَهُم أَكَفرتُم بَعدَ
إِيمَانِكُم فَذُوقُوا العَذَابَ بِمَا كُنتُم تَكفُرُونَ -

"Do not follow the example of those who became divided and opposed to one another after clear proofs had been given them. These shall be sternly punished on the day when some faces will be bright (with joy) and others blackened (with grief). To the blackfaced sinners it will be said: "Did you disbelieve after embracing the true faith? Taste then our scourage, for you were unbelievers:"
(Q. 3:105-106).

That is, clear instructions were given to the former *Ummahs* but, later on, they got themselves divided. Thus the Jews and the Christians were divided in seventy two sects and were liable to be sternly punished. Hence you do not become like them and do not create dissension. You have got clear injunctions in the Holy Qur'an and hence do not invent new rites and customs, new faiths and creeds and new ways. Some of them become Mu'atazali, Kharji, Rafizi while others have turned Nasibi, Jabari, Qadri, Marji etc. Some of them get clean-shaved, keep long hairs and declare themselves Fakirs and from among them come out Quadri, Suhrawardy, Naqshbandi etc. It is the injunction from Allah, the Almighty that the Qur'an and *hadith* should be followed and be a Muslim according to *Sunnah*, do not get yourself divided like the Jews and the Christians and by inventing new things and by creating dissension and disruption. On the Day of Resurrection, there will be some bright-faced and some black-faced. The black-faced persons will be told that, at first, you became Muslims and confessed to follow the Book of Allah but, later on, they invented new rites and customs and gave currency to *bid'at*. Thus they ceased to practise according to the Book of Allah. Gradually, they started loving new rites and failed to abandon them. Their hearts, therefore, refused to accept the injunctions of Allah given in the Holy Qur'an. Now they have to taste the result of their misdeeds.

It is clear from the above verse that one who invents new things and practise them, he is, in fact, a person not believing the Holy Qur'an and hence will be raised on the Day of Judgment as black-faced. Thereafter, he will be severely punished.

Allah, the Almighty says in Surah Al-An'am of the Holy Qur'an:

إِنَّ الَّذِينَ فَرَّقُوا دِينَهُمْ وَكَانُوا شِيَعًا لَسْتَ مِنْهُمْ فِي شَيْءٍ
إِنَّمَا أَمْرُهُمْ إِلَى اللَّهِ ثُمَّ يُنَبِّئُهُمْ بِمَا كَانُوا يَفْعَلُونَ ـ

> "Have nothing to do with those who have split up their religion into sects. Allah will call them to account and declare to them what they have done."
>
> (Q. 6:159).

That is, those who built up several avenues in Faith and split themselves up into different sects and do not pay heed to the call of right guidance and follow not the path shown by Allah and His Prophet (peace and blessings of Allah be upon him), are those who have been set aside to be sternly punished by Allah, the Almighty. Only then they will come to know how filthy were the acts of *bid'at*.

It is clear from the above verse that when people refrain from practising according to the injunctions of Allah and His Apostle, create new avenues and do not pay heed to the warnings Allah will lift His grace and mercy from them, and they are left in the deviated state. At last, they will be administered severe punishment on the Day of Judgment.

Allah, the Almighty says in Surah Al-Rum of the Holy Qur'an

وَلَاتَكُونُوا كَالَّذِينَ فَرَّقُوا دِينَهُمْ وَكَانُوا شِيَعًا كُلُّ حِزْبٍ بِمَا لَدَيْهِمْ فَرِحُونَ -

> ".... be not of those who associate others with Allah, those who split up their religion into sects, each exculting in its own beliefs."
>
> (Q. 30:32).

That is, what is an evil and a vice according to *Shari'ah* is known by one and all. But what one invents from his reason or what learns from anybody else he does not find it mentioned either in the Holy Qur'an or in *Sunnah* and feels happy and satisfied. Moreover, every sect has its own innovations which make people differ and dissent. This attitude splits up the *Ummah* into small groups. For example, a particular sect considers Hadrat Ali Murtaza (may Allah be pleased with him) better than all other Companions of the Holy Prophet (peace and blessings of Allah be upon him) and named themselves *"Tafziliah"*, another sect rose to adore Hadrat Ali Murtaza (may Allah be pleased with him) more than what *'Tafziliah'* did, and looked down upon the Companions of the Messenger of Allah, invented congregations of 'Muharram', observance of mourning in Muharram, reciting of elegy, putting on of black clothes, celebrating of *'Eid-e-Ghadir'* (the festival of the succession of Hadrat Ali, as the Prophet's successor) and that of Baba Shuja'a, celebrating of 'nawroz' etc. and called themselves *Shi'a* and brought about amendments in prayers, wudu (ablution) etc. In opposition to this sect, another one came up condemning and denigrating Hadrat Ali Murtaza (may Allah be pleased with him) and called themselves *'Kharji'*. One more sect came to the fore, developed enmity with Hadrat Ali Murtaza (may Allah be pleased with him) and called themselves *Nasbi*; another one refused to accept intercession and sight of Allah, the Almighty and considered the major sin the cause of breaking off from Islam and called themselves *Muatazib.* There were still a number of sects which started a life of seclusion; abandoned lawful and unlawful and ceased to practise many tenets of Islam and invented a number of chantings and recitations, soothsayings, amulets and *'ganda'* (knotted string tied round the neck as a charm) *urs* (anniversary of a saint), falling into meditation on a grave, hearing of music and songs, and getting in *haal* (state of ecstacy) and were called 'peer' (religious guide) and *'masha'ikh'* (holy persons). Later on, they were called *Chishti*, *Quadri*, *Naqshbandi*, *Suhrawardi*, *Rifa'i* etc. Some people get clean-shaved, put on large-sized cap or crown growing long hair, coffin etc. and get the name of *Madaria* or *Jalalia.* A few of them got by heart some of the jargons of logic, arithematic and digits etc. and tried to make themselves known as Molvi and Alim (religious scholar). In short, they created thousands of avenues and each of them was happy and satisfied and took pride in his righteousness. Hence, Allah, the Almighty commanded not to get split up into sects and follow the path shown by Allah as the Jews and the Christians did and divided themselves in groups. They must follow the Qur'an and *hadith* and obey the Holy Prophet (peace and blessings of Allah be upon him) and avoid dissension.

It is clear from the above verse that one must not remain static to his own faith, way, rites, attitude and habit and be satisfied with what he has; he should rather keep on trying to know the truth. He must be constantly comparing his faith and action with those ordained by the Holy Qur'an and *hadith* and follow what is right while reject the wrong and baseless. A large number of people have deviated from the right path only by neglecting the path shown by Allah and His Messenger. They follow only the way of their forefathers in lieu of the one mentioned in the Holy Qur'an and *hadith*.

Allah, the Almighty says in Surah Al-Anam of the Holy Qur'an:

وَاَنَّ هٰذَا صِرَاطِى مُسْتَقِيمًا فَاتَّبِعُوهُ وَلَا تَتَّبِعُوا السُّبُلَ
فَتَفَرَّقَ بِكُم عَن سَبِيلِهِ ذَٰلِكُم وَصّٰكُم بِهِ لَعَلَّكُم تَتَّقُونَ ـ

> "Verily, this is My Way leading straight: follow it: Follow not (other) paths: They will scatter you about from this path: Thus doth He command you, that ye may righteous".
> (Q. 6:153)

That is, Allah, the Almighty has said that He has revealed the Qur'an to them to adopt the right course and this is the only way to reach Him. Hence they should avoid the ways shown by the ancestors, teachers, guides, rites and rituals, and the paths dictated by the kings, Their ways will cause you deviate from the path of Allah , it has been made clear so that no body is left without being warned.

The example of what has been said above is that anyone is being called by a king who has to pass a long way in order to reach the court. A messenger is being sent to guide him through the way. Moreover, the right way is being shown to follow, wrote down all the signs. He has already been informed that a number of ways and sub-ways come out of the main road, but they have to follow it leaving aside others, otherwise they will go astray and get deprived of the opportunity to reach the destination. Now, if the person referred to here, goes alongwith the messenger to some distance but leaves the main road thereafter and takes to other avenues and keeps aside the right advice and even warning of the messenger, he is bound to reach his doom instead of reaching the king. One cannot get access to the king by following others. It is the same that the people of all ages has been doing. It only led to the process of division and sub-division. The Jews and the Christians have adopted this course and even the Muslim followed suit and got split up into thousands of sects. Similarly, Allah the Exalted sent the Holy Prophet (peace and blessings of Allah be upon him) as His Messenger with His Message for the people to be guided to the right path. He commanded them to follow the Qur'an as it shows the right path and it is the only path which leads directly to Allah, the Almighty. Now if they follow the course set by the Jews and Christians, Zoroastrians or the Hindus or invent their own, they will be certainly misguided and bound to go astray.

From the above verse it is apparent that the right and straight way is to follow the Holy Qur'an in letter and spirit. It leads to Allah without any risk, and one who takes to any other course goes astray, away from the path of Allah, whether it be the path of the pagans of the bygone days or of the present age or of the 'ignorants', innovators etc. At present a large number of persons have adopted the path of various sects leaving aside the way shown by the Qur'an and *hadith*.... that is, not to give *Zakat*, not to perform *hajj* etc. and to avoid all kinds of prayers, to adopt the path of heretics and transgressors and to do whatever is akin to attitude and likeness. Similarly, to adopt the path of the hypocrites, to build shrines and mosques over the graves, to think that the dead saints have become one with Allah or Allah has absorbed in them, to beg the dead persons for fulfilling their needs, to vow for something, to adopt the course of the ancestors and the pagans in opposition to the way of Allah and His Messenger, to take pride in lineage, to cry and beat the breast on someone's death and lament loudly, to consider the second marriage of a widow as a vice, to fasten *'sehra'* at the time of marriage, to shave the beard, to embrace others on the Eid day, to kindle lights on the occasion of *shubrat*, to consider mounting of an ass, a donkey and a camel to be improper, to practise augury, to consider some dates, days and moments unfortunate and others fortunate, to adore the pictures and photographs of the ancestors, to celebrate death anniversaries, *teja*, *daswan*, *chaliswan* etc. to adore the footprints of the Holy Prophet (peace and blessings of Allah be upon him) these are all rites of the Hindus or those invented by the religious teachers and guides. They adopted many ways of deviations and perversions, discarding the only way of Allah and His Messenger. And in spite of these transgressions they claim to be following the way of Allah, the Almighty.

Allah, the Exalted says in Surah A'le-Imran of the Holy Qur'an:

قُلْ إِن كُنتُمْ تُحِبُّونَ اللهَ فَاتَّبِعُونِي يُحْبِبْكُمُ اللهُ وَيَغْفِرْ لَكُمْ
ذُنُوبَكُمْ وَاللهُ غَفُورٌ رَّحِيمٌ ۔

> "Say : "If ye do love Allah, Follow me : Allah will love you and forgive you your sins; For Allah is Oft-Forgiving, Most Merciful."
>
> (Q. 3 : 31)

That is, people of every religion claim that they love Allah; they are His servants; whatever task they perform it is for the sake of his love so that He is happy and love them too and forgive them inspite of shortcomings. Almighty Allah has said: "Tell them O' Prophet that if you are true in your love for Allah, it is He who has sent me to you and hence you obey me accordingly; do whatever work I entrust with you; follow my way so that it is known that your love for Allah is true and He forgives you in return for He is forgiver and Merciful for such men." Now if a person doesn't follow the way of the Prophet of Allah (peace and blessings of Allah be upon him) and claim his love for Allah even after innovating new courses, he is a liar. Almighty Allah is annoyed with him and the Prophet of Allah (peace and blessings of Allah be upon him) inflicts and sends his curses on such a person. It is because of this the person claims his love for Allah while in fact he claims prophethood for himself and intends to eshtablish his own *Shariat*. Hence he is in no way faithful to the Prophet of Allah (peace and blessings of Allah be upon him); he is rather against him out and out.

It becomes clear from the above *ayah* that one who refrains from obeyaing the Prophet (peace and blessings of Allah be upon him) and claims his love for Allah at the same time, is a liar. One is true in love for Allah only when he follows the *Sunnah* of the Prophet. Only such a person is beloved of Allah; Allah loves him and He will forgive his sins and confer his forgiveness and mercy on him.

Allah the Exalted says in Surah Nisa of the Holy Quran

فَلَا وَرَبِّكَ لَا يُؤمِنُونَ حَتّٰى يَحكَمُوكَ فِيمَا شَجَرَ بَينَهُم ثُمَّ
لَا يَجِدُوا فِيٓ اَنفُسِهِم حَرَجاً مِمَّا قَضَيتَ وَيُسَلِّمُوا تَسلِيماً

"But no by thy Lord, they can have no (real) faith. Untill they make thee judge in all disputes between them. And find in their souls no resistance against thy decisions, but accept them with the fullest conviction."

(Q. 4:65)

That is, when any dispute arise regarding religious matters or worldly affairs or concerning rites, rituals and customs ..... each having his own claim of right and wrong—— one should accept the judgement of the Holy Prophet (peace and blessings of Allah be upon him) whether it is to one's likeness or not. It is only then the claim of being a believer may be accepted as true. And one who does not consider the Holy Prophet (peace and blessings of Allah be upon him) as the real judge and arbiter and differs from his judgment and evades his rulings, he is bound to go astray and lose his faith. Such a person is, in fact, a transgressor, hypocrite and an unbeliever. He calls himself to be a Muslim only in name; he is in no way liable to be included among the believers of the

Messenger of Islam and his *Ummah*. In the same way thousands of rites and customs find circulation among Muslims of India; like slaughtering of a goat at the birth of a child and firing; keeping of an arrow and the Holy Qur'an on the bed of a woman who has recently given birth tò a child, performing of ceremony on the sixth day after child birth, naming the child as certain 'Baksh' and 'Ghulam' of so and so, considering a woman dirty and unclean for forty days even if her bleeding is stopped much before it, fixing up four years and four months for the first lesson of a baby and celebrate the occasion with pomp and show, holding festivities on the occasion of circumcission, taking the circumcised to graves for saluting, wearing red or yellow clothes, applying myrtle, typing comb, serving food to the community, causing women to abstain from sexual intercourse and beautifying themselves and sleeping on the cot, making *ta'ziyah* (a model of the tombs of Imam Hasan and Husain carried in procession during Muharram), holding congregations of Muharram, considering thirteen days of 'Safar' to be inauspicious, going for recreation on every Wednesday and holding assemblies for celebrating birthday of the Holy Prophet (peace and blessings of Allah be upon him) during the month of 'Rabi-ul-aw'wal (third month of Hijri year) and getting up and keep standing while the birth of the Messenger of Allah is mentioned keeping in mind that the soul of the Apostle visits such a gathering, observing "the Eleventh" of Rabi'us-sani (the fourth month of the Hijri year), cracking of fireworks and cooking 'halwa' in the month of Sha'ban (the eighth month of the Hijri year) and observing the last Friday of the Ramdhan the day of 'farewell address', preparing 'siwayyan' (paste turned into slender threads) on the Eid day, shaking hands and embracing after Eid prayer, avoiding marriage during the month of Ziqa'd (the eleventh month of the Hijri year) etc. and considering the cot of the dead as inauspicious, thinking the name of Hadrat Izra'il and Surah Ya'sin as something bad, writing Kalimah (Word of Allah) on the Coffin, putting genealogy in the grave, observing the tenth, the fortieth, six-monthly and anniversary of the deceased, causing *hafiz* (one who knows the Holy Qur'an by heart) to sit at the graves, putting sheets on the graves, building tombs, writing dates and life-sketch on the graves, kindling lights there, condemning the mention of the death, mourning the dead after three days, visiting graves after making a long journey, depriving the daughters from the estate of a deceased person, performing 'totka' (a superstitious remedy) for the sick, holding Tuesday, Wednesday and a Saturday as inauspicious and some dates as impure and unclean, reciting an invented supplication while lighting a lamp; observing Holi, Diwali and other religious rites and rituals of the Unbelievers, thinking mounting of camel, ass and donkey as an evil, and thinking the same about the exchange of 'salam' (salutation) between man and female and between elders and youngers, refusing to accept the existence of fortune, preferring Hadrat Ali (may Allah be pleased with him) to Hadrat Abu Bakr and Hadrat Umar (may Allah be pleased with them), considering the Caliphates of Hadrat Abu Bakr and Hadrat Umar (may Allah be pleased with them) to be based on untruth, have low opinions about 'ahle-bait' and Companions of the Apostle and condemning them, spending lavishly on marriages, lamenting laudly and beating breast on one's death.

In short, thousands of such impure and invented rites and rituals, manners and customs are observed and practised without taking care of do's and don'ts. But the most safe and righteous way is to follow the sayings and practices of the Holy Prophet (peace and blessings of Allah be upon him). Even during the life-time of the Messenger of Allah, children were born, male children were circumcised, first lesson was taught to them, people of that period also got married, fell ill and expired and were buried, they also passed the months of Muharram and Safar. Now the question arises as to what the Messenger of Allah would do on such occasions and what did his Companions do. Every Muslim is bound by the *Sunnah* of the Holy Prophet (peace and blessings of Allah be upon him). But one who opposes or disagrees with the *Sunnah* of the Apostle must bear in mind that he has gone astray: And if it is accepted beyond any doubt that these rites and practices have been invented later after the days of the

Companions of the Apostle, their successors and after the followers of their successors, then the verdict of the Holy Prophet (peace and blessings of Allah be upon him) is mentioned here under:

Bukhari and Muslim reports from Hadrat Ayesha (may Allah be pleased with her) that the Holy Prophet (peace and blessings of Allah be upon him) :

من احدث فی امرنا هذا مالیس منه فهو رَدٌّ -

> "One who invents a new thing in my religion which is not found in it, is certainly wrong and rejected."

That is, one who invents such a thing in the religion which in not based on truth stands wrong and rejected. New things are of two kinds: One, something that was not needed during the days of the Holy Prophet (peace and blessings of Allah be upon him), his holy Companions, his successors and the followers of the successors; Secondly, those things that were needed later on. For example, books of grammar, diacritical points of the Qur'an and *fiqh* (Islamic jurisprudence) were not written in those days, because the earlier Muslims were Arabs; they could understand the Holy Qur'an without grammar and diacritical points. They could read it correctly and since most of them wre scholars of Islamic laws and had least differences among them. Hence they were not in need of a book on *fiqh* etc. But, later on, when Islam went out of Arab and came to India etc. the Believers needed all these things. When these things were written or compiled or edited or researches carried on are not *bid'at* (innovation). *Bid'at* is one that was disapproved also during the days of the Holy Prophet (peace and blessings of Allah be upon him) and his Companions and their successors and followers of the successors. Such innovations are wrong and stand rejected. For example, people would die and get buried even in those days but the *tenth* or *fortieth* was not observed nor *Fatiha* (prayer for the dead) was recited; these rites were not even considered. For example, marriages were celebrated those days but without 'sachaq' and fireworks and 'mushaf-arsi'; all such rites are wrong and stand rejected. Religious act is one which has virtues and rewards in doing them and losing rewards in case of undoing. Hence, religious acts are of two kinds: One, which belongs to heart, like faith, creed, reason, attention, love, enmity etc.; secondly, those which have behavioural features like prayers, financial matters, rites and habits. Now it was the rights of the Holy Prophet (peace and blessings of Allah be upon him) alone to put any thing right or wrong and for this purpose alone, he was sent as the Messenger of Allah. And the Messenger of Allah has said that one who invents a new faith, prayer, rite without having any example in the religion, it stands as *bid'at* and hence wrong and rejected. An analogy is to be found out by a religious director alone.

Muslim reports from Jabir that the Holy Prophet (peace and blessings of Allah be upon him) said:

فان خير الحديث كتاب الله وخير الهدى هدى محمد صلى
الله عليه وسلم وشر الامـور محدثاتها وكل بدعةٍ ضلالة -

> "The best among the words is the Word of Allah; the best among the ways is the way of Messenger of Allah; the worst among the affairs is the affair which is new and every new thing (attached to religion) is deviation "

That is, Allah, the Almighty is more merciful to man than his father that He sent the Holy Qur'an for the guidance of man by abrogating the former ones and described all things good for this world and the Hereafter. Hence all should follow them. The Messenger of Allah was sent to explain and elucidate the meaning of Qur'anic verses in clear words and put all into practice. Nothing was left to be invented and added later. Hence, if, in spite of all this, anything new is added to the religion it is sheer evil and to corrupt the pure and clean code of Allah. It is to assert that what was sent earlier was imcomplete and hence was to be completed by the coming generations. And since an innovator acts keeping in view that he is righteous in all his performances, hence he has almost no chance to revert to the right path. Thus he keeps on going along the deviated path.

Bukhari reports from Ibn Abbas that the Holy Prophet (peace and blessings of Allah be upon him) said:

ابغـض النـاس الى الله ثـلاث ملحد بالحرم ومتبغ فى الاسلام سنة الجاهلية ومطلب دم امرء مسلم بغير حق ليهريق دمه -

> "Three men of all incur wrath of Allah: one who commits sin inside *haram*; another one who adopts the rites and practices of the former pagans and; the third one who sheds blood of a Muslim only for blood sake."

That is, one who commits a sin he incurs displeasure of Allah and wrath of Allah turns towards him. But, of all, the wrath of Allah befalls on one who commits sin inside the *haram* of the holy Ka'bah; on one who tries to restore the rites of the pagans and on one who sheds blood of a Muslim without rhyme or reason. It is because he, in fact, opposes the Will of Allah. Allah, the Almighty proclaimed the holy Ka'bah His House and commanded to observe esteem of it and say prayer in it. Hence one who fails to observe the esteem of Ka'bah and shows utter disrespect to it, is a transgressor. Allah, the Almighty created man and gave him eyes, nose, ears etc. and put all organs right and let them grow, gave him a place on this earth and conferred Faith on him and hence, if one, tries to kill him means that he wants to oppose Allah. He wants to kill and remove from the face of the earth whom Allah wants to keep living. People of the past invented something new considering it to be right, clean and virtuous. But since those rites and practices were based on deviations from the right path. Allah, the Almighty, sent His Messenger with thè Holy Qur'an to obliterate all the rites and practices of the bygone days. Here also the Unbelievers are in constant conflict with Allah, the Almighty, since they try to popularise their beliefs and practices among the masses as against the Will and Pleasure of Allah. They want to maintain what Allah wants to obliterate. Thus, they are enemies of Allah. Pagans of the past considered the sayings and practices of their religious guides as true and virtuous and superior to those dictated by Allah. Thus, to refrain from speaking the truth in matters of what is right or because of some greed and worldly gain, to bring about alterations and distortions in the Qur'an and *hadith,* to give a different interpretation of an obvious meaning of a word, to fabricate religious tenets according to one's own desire, to adopt an attitude of peace with all, to think highly of one's ancestory, to beat and cry for the dead, to wear black clothes, to build high graves and tombs over them, to write dates and life-sketches on the graves and tombs, to build mosques over the graves, to offer food to the shrines, to consider music and songs as a part of prayer, to consider thirteen days of the month of Safar to be inauspicious, to take stars as auspicious and inauspicious, to believe in jinns and fairies, to practise augury, to make offerings to elders and saints, to adore pictures, to refuse to consider anyone Prophet or Friend of Allah if he does not perform any miracle etc. Thousands of such rites and practices come from the Jews, Christians, Zoroastrians, hypocrites and pagans of Makkah. Many more rites and rituals were adopted from the Hindus. The Holy Prophet (peace and blessings of Allah be upon him) came to wipe out such rites and rituals and for the same purpose the Holy Qur'an was revealed. Thus, one who adopts and practises such pervasive rites and customs and tries to give currency to them among Muslims, in general, is accursed and rejected by Allah, the Almighty, as per the above-mentioned *hadith.*

It should be borne in mind that to restore and keep going the rites and customs of the pagan past is also a form of innovation. It is also wrong to think that what is not proclaimed to be evil in the Holy Qur'an and *hadith* should not be taken as evil. It is wrong because what is not permitted by Allah and His Apostle is certainly forbidden.

Muslim reports from Ibn Mas'ud that the Holy Prophet (peace and blessings of Allah be upon him) said:

ما مـن نبـى بعثـه فـى قبلـى الا كان له فى امته حواريون واصحاب يـاخذون بسـنته ويقتدون بامره ثـم انهـا تخلـف مـن بعدهـم خلـوف يقولون مـا لايفعلـون ويفعلـون مـا لا يومـرون فمـن جاهد هم بيده فهو مؤمن ومن جاهد هم بلسانه فهومؤمن ومن جاهد هم بقلبه فهو مؤمـن وليـس ورآء ذلك من الايمان حبة خردل -

> "Any Prophet who was sent to his *Ummah* before me was opposed by some and supported by others; they were followed by bad-natured persons who did not do what they were asked and did what they were not asked for; thus, one who makes supreme efforts against them with hands, he is a perfect Muslim; one who makes supreme efforts from his tongue is also a Muslim and; one who makes supreme efforts with his heart is a Muslim too; but there is not an iota of Faith thereafter."

The Holy Prophet (peace and blessings of Allah be upon him) has narrated the affairs of the *Ummah* of the past Prophets. The people of his own *Ummah* were virtuous and good-natured; they helped the Apostle in carrying out the commands of Allah and they themselves practised as they were preached. Hence, Allah, the Almighty said that those who make supreme efforts in killing the innovators and wipe out their machinery of innovation, is a perfect Muslim and achieves the first rank in Islam; one who makes use of his tongue for forbidding acts of *'bid'at'* and counsels the innovators against the evils of *bid'at*, is also a Muslim but of the second rank and; one who looks down upon the acts of *bid'at*, finds out ways and means of its removal and does not go hands in hands with the innovators; is also a Muslim, but belongs to the third grade and is, therefore, weak in Faith, But after this there is not an iota of Faith left in him.

It is obvious from the above discussion that everyone should try his best to eliminate *'bid'at'*. He must make all-out efforts to bring to light the evils of *bid'at*, look it down and condemn it from the bottom of his heart, refrain from keeping any friendship and intimacy with the innovators. If he does so his Faith is bound to get spotted. Hence he should save himself acts of *bid'at* as far as possible and practicable. It is also a *bid'at* to practise something which has not been forbidden. For instance, it is obligatory to wash hands up to elbow during Wudu (ablution) and it is, however, not forbidden to wash up to armpit. Thus, if one washes up to armpit thinking it to be right because it is not forbidden he is a transgressor because he does a thing he is not asked for; or, for example, one should call *Allah-o-Akbar* four times at the outset during *Adhan* but if he calls it five times on the plea that calling *Adhan* five times is not forbidden. But this plea is rejected outright because it is not commanded to call *Adhan* more than four times. Two *rak'ats* (a part of the prayer which includes standing, bending and prostration) of *Sunnah* prayer are fixed in the *Fajr* prayer. But if one says three or four *rak'ats*, he will be forbidden to do so on the same basis that one has not been asked to do so.

Tirmidhi reports from Abdullah bin Umar (may Allah be pleased with him) that the Holy Prophet (peace and blessings of Allah be upon him) said:

ليأتين زمان على امتى كما اتى على بنى اسرآئيل حذوا
النعل بالنعل حتى ان كان منهم اتى امه علانية لكان فى

امتـى مـن يصنـع ذلك وان بنى اسرآئيل تفرقوا على
ثنتين وسبعين ملـة وتفترق امتى على ثلاث وسبعين
ملة كلهم فى النـار الا ملة واحدة قالوا من هى
يا رسول الله قال مـا انـا عليه واصحابى وانه سيخرج
فى امتى اقوام تتجـارى بهم تلك الاهوآء كما يتجارى
الكلب لصاحبه لايبق منه عرق ولامفصل الا دخله ـ

"A time will come in the life of my *Ummah* as it came in the life of Bani Isra'il, and there will not be an iota of difference so that anyone will perfrom dirty act openly with his mother, if anyone from Bani Isra'il would have done so; Bani Isra'il were split up into seventy two sects; my *Ummah* will get split up into seventy three sects, and all of them will be hellish except one."

"Which one sect, O' Messenger of Allah?" the Companions asked.

"They will follow my way and that of my companions," said the Apostle, and added:

"My *Ummah* will include such people who will circulate *bid'ats* among people so that they turn into ones who have been bitten by a mad dog resulting in the loss of all veins and joints."

That is, my *Ummah* will pass through a period when people will adopt acts of *bid'ats*. They will find themselves involved in such faiths, prayers, chantings, recitations, fastings, charities etc. Which are quite new to Islam. They will face disunity and dissension more than what the Jews and the Christians faced because they got split up into seventy-two sects, while the Believers will get split up into seventy-three. So it happened according to the prophecy. Hence, the Holy Prophet (peace and blessings of Allah be upon him) had prophesied that the sect following his way and that of his Companions will enter Heaven, while all others will go to Hell.

It is clear from the above-mentioned *hadith* that one who acts according to the sayings and practices of the Messenger of Allah and his Companions is the man of Heaven, while one who goes against the way of the Apostle and his Companions will go straight to Hell.

Tirmidhi reports from Anas (may Allah be pleased with him) that the Holy Prophet (peace and blessings of Allah be upon him) said:

يا بنـي ان قـدرت ان تصبـح وتمسـى
وليس فى قلبك غـش لاحـد فـافعل ثـم قـال يـا بنـى
وذلك من سنتى ومن احـب مـن سـنتى فقـد احبنـى
ومن احبنى كان معى فى الجنة ـ

"O child! pass your days and nights in a way that you keep no malice and enmity" and added, 'my child, it is my *Sunnah* and; one who befriends my *Sunnah*, befriends me, and one who keeps my friendship will accompany me to the Heaven."

It comes to know from the above *hadith* that keeping friendship with the Holy Prophet (peace and blessings of Allah be upon him) means following his way and only such a person will enter the Heaven.

Baihaqi reports from Abu Hurairah (may Allah be pleased with him) that the Holy Prophet (peace and blessings of Allah be upon him) said:

من تمسك بسنتی عند فساد امتی فله اجرمأئة شهيد -

> "One who follows my *Sunnah* at the time of crisis and disruption will get reward equal to those of a hundred martyrs."

That is, when thousands of *bid'ats* will go in circulation and each one will claim to be righteous and virtuous, anyone who follows my way and keeps aloof from *bid'at* will get reward equal to those of one hundred martyrs. It is because thousands of innovators will condemn him and will be thirsty of his life and esteem and he will keep patience in all opposition and trouble. Now the time has come for all to think over the matter and act accordingly.

Ahmad and Baihaqi report from Jabir that once Umar (may Allah be pleased with him) appeared before the Holy Prophet (peace and blessings of Allah be upon him) and said:

انا نسمع احاديث من

يهود فتعجبنا فتراه ان نكتب بعضها فقال امتهوكون

انتم كما تهوكت اليهود والنصرى لقد جئتكم بها

بيضآء نقيةً لوكان موسى حيا ما وسعه الا اتباعی -

> "We hear something from the Jews and like them; will you please allow us to get them preserved in writing?"

Thereupon the Messenger of Allah said:

> "Are you amazed as did the Jews and the Christians?
>
> Certainly, I have brought for you an enlightenedCode and had Musa been alive he would have no alternative but to

follow me."

That is, in a religion where commands and injunctions are not very clear and in detail, both the religious scholars and the masses are at a loss what to do and how to solve the problem and unfasten the knot. In such a state of embarrassment, they learnt some tenets and codes of other religions and made a mess of everything. But Islam deals each and everything in great detail beyond any doubt and suspicion and abrogated all other religions and their codes and laws. Had their Prophet Musa been alive in the present age, he must have followed the Codes of Islam.

It is clear from the above *hadith* that learning and adopting rites and affairs of other religions is not allowed except those that could help preach Islam among others and restore Unbelievers to the path of guidance. But for this a Believer must be well-versed in the tenets of Islam. Since the Jews and Christians know very little about their religions, they adopted many things from the Hindus and others and mixed them up with their own. Similarly most of the ignorant persons saw many prohibited things in others and adopted them for their own. And when they are said that the things are alien to Islam they come into conflict with the righteous persons.

Imam Ahmad and Tirmidhi report from Abu Umama (may Allah be pleased with him) that the Holy Prophet (peace and blessings of Allah be upon him) said:

اضل قوم بعد هده كا نوا عليه الا اوتوا الجدل ثم
قرا رسول الله صلى الله عليه وسلم هذه الاية ما
ضربوه لك الاجدلا بل هم قوم خصمون -

"No nation deviated from the path of guidance after receiving guidance but for dispute." Thereafter, reciting a verse he further said:

"The infidels do not argue thee (the Apostle) but with dispute since the infidels are totally a disputer by nature."

Here dispute means to falsify one who is righteous. When the people of the past remained stuck to the truth, they had been on the right path. But as soon as they objected to the right course of life, they went astray. Hence a Muslim should not raise any dispute in matter of *bid'at* and follow the truth as written in the Qur'an and *hadith*. And one who fights for *bid'at* tries to keep in going, he is truly misguided. During the times of the Holy Prophet (peace and blessings of Allah be upon him) most of the pagans knew the truth very well but they fought still. Hence, Allah, the Almighty declared them sheer disputer; they do not enter into an argument to arrive at the truth but just to deviate from it knowingly.

Allah be praised ! A Muslim proves an act as *bid'at* and asks anyone to refrain from it, but the later argues that he will do it because his ancestors, religious guides or people of his city do so Such a person abandons the path of truth shown by Allah, the Almighty and His Messenger (peace and blessings of Allah be upon him).

Abu Dawud reports from Hadrat Anas (may Allah be pleased with him) that the Holy Prophet (peace and blessings of Allah be upon him) would say :

لا تشددوا على انفسكم فيشدد الله عليكم فان قوما شددوا على انفسهم فشدد الله عليهم فتلك بقايا هم فى الصوامع والديار رهبانية ابتدعوها ما كتبنها عليهم -

> "Do not put any hardship on yourselves otherwise Allah will put hardship on you. Any nation which followed the path of hardship was put to hardship by Allah. And Allah, the Almighty said:
>
> "The monkery they have invented was certainly not made obligatory on them by Me."

That is, some of the Jews and Christians took to monkery and left for forests. They wore sack clothes and put a chain round their neck and became eunuch for fear of committing adultery. And by doing all this, they considered them to be righteous. Hence, Allah, the Almighty, says that the monkery and *faqiri* (vocation of a fakir) adopted by them is not by the Command of Allah. Hence, our Prophet (peace and blessings of Allah be upon him) said to his *Ummah* that when a person gets himself indulged in hardship is left by Allah, the Almighty in the same hardship, and he does not understand it at all. You should, therefore, keep away from such acts of deviation. Allah, the Almighty, has made His *Shari'ah* very easy and hence one should not impose hardships upon himself. Thus to consider utensils, water and clothes of a Muslim dirty and unclean; using too much water for performing *wudu*, forming intention vocally for *salat* again and again, to take bath like Hindus for each task, keeping away from the company of others, chanting *Durud* , etc., against the mode of *Sunnah*.

Moreover, to abandon eating meat once in a day, to refrain from wearing good clothes and good and lawful food, vegetables, to abandon the use of any particular thing once a month or on a particular day, to perform any rite of death or marriage and carry it on and to consider the marriage and death inauspicious without performing those rites, to make delay in performing circumcision or marriage unless those rites are performed at the proper time and in proper manner, are all acts of *bid'at*. And to celebrate *urs* of a saint once in a year or to visit the shrine of a particular religious guide etc. also form part of *bid'at*. People of the past got in trouble only by indulging in such acts.

It is obvious from the above-mentioned facts that one should not invent anything of his own; he should, rather, follow only the path shown by Allah and His Apostle. However, an even lawful act may be temporarily abandoned for some particular gain or for fulfilling the demand of the situation; for example, a patient may desist from eating meat and bread on the advice of a physician. But he should resume eating it as soon as he is cured. Nobody is permitted to eat one thing and desist from eating another on his own and only by way of caution

Imam Malik reports from Hadrat Malik bin Anas (may Allah be pleased with him) that the Holy Prophet (peace and blessings of Allah be upon him) said:

تركت فيكم امرين لن تضلوا
ما تمسكتم بهما كتاب الله وسنة رسوله

> "I am leaving two things for you so that you will never go astray till you keep holding these two——one is the Book of Allah and the second is the *Sunnah* of His Messenger."

Every individual is living in a state of constant stress and strain. The world, the Satan, parents, the ruler, teacher, religious guide, friends, acquaintances, wife and children pull him towards own way. A man gets his needs fulfilled by almost each of them. Hence, Allah, the Almighty, has put in His Book and His Messenger (peace and blessings of Allah be upon him) in his *Sunnah* the ways and means of solving all such problems. The Holy Qur'an and *Sunnah* provide guidline in all affairs of life. Hence, if one follows the way of those other than Allah, the Almighty, he is bound to go astray. Very unfortunate he is who is led by Satan keeping aside the way of Allah and His Messenger (peace and bessings of Allah be upon him).

Razin reports from Hadrat Abdullah ibn Mas'ud (may Allah be pleased with him) to have said:

من كان مستناً
فليستن بمن قدمات فان الحى لاتومن عليه الفتنة
اولئك اصحاب محمدٍ صلى الله عليه وسلم كانوا
افضل هذه الامة وابرها قلوبًا واعمقها علما واقلها
تكلفا اختارهم الله لصحبة نبيه ولاقامة دينه فاعرفو

هـم فضلهـم واتبعوهـم على اثـارهم وتمسكو بما استطعتم من اخلاقهم وسيرهم فانهم على الهدى

"One who wants to follow the right path should follow those who are no more, for the persons alive are in the grip of evils and mischiefs. Those during the life-time of Muhammad (peace and blessings of Allah be upon him) were better and more virtuous, deep in knowledge and devoid of formalities. They were raised by Allah for the company of His Apostle and for establishing His religion on firm ground. Hence you should follow them step by step and hold their habits and manners firmly for they were certainly on the right path."

That is, one should refrain from inventing new methods and form new attitudes but go along the way of the Holy Prophet (peace and blessings of Allah be upon him) and his companions and adopt their rites and customs; for they were good-natured and simple-hearted. They had deep knowledge, understanding and wisdom. They were above all formalities. It is because of this they were made courtiers of the Messenger of Allah so that the religion of Allah, the Almighty was established by them. Hence, try to know and discover their high traits and characters. They were certainly on the right path. But more the distance from their period, more Satan made inroads on the Faith and actions of the Believers. They became victim of pomp and luxuries and differences among them widened day by day. Now at a time when the Muslims are victim of dissensions and disruptions, the Believers should stick to the way of the Holy Prophet (peace and blessings of Allah be upon him) and his Companions without inventing new ideas and attitude. Otherwise the Day of Judgment is quite at hand and one will have to taste the result of his thoughts and actions.

Bukhari reports the Holy Prophet (peace and blessings of Allah be upon him) saying:

انی فرطکم علی الحـوض مـن

مر علی شرب ومن شرب لم یظما ابدًا لیردن علی اقـوام

اعرفهم ویعرفوننی ثم یحال بینی وبینهم فاقول انهم منـی

فیقا ل انـك لا تـدری مـآ احدثـوا بعـدك فـاقول سـحقا

سحقا لمن غیر بعدی

> "First of all I shall arrive at the `Fountain of Kausar" (the name of a fountain in paradise) and put the matter right. Whoever will come to me will get his thirst quenched and from that day on he will never feel thirsty. Thereafter, some groups of people will appear who will know me and I shall know them, but a screen will be drawn between them and myself. I shall say that they belong to me but I shall be given to know that these people invented new things after I am gone. Thereupon, I shall say: keep them off ! Keep them off, those who changed my religion after me."

That is, on the Day of Resurrection when the sun will come very near and the Hell will be visible, the heat will touch its height and the people will feel thirsty, a fountain will be seen there whose water will be whiter than milk, sweeter than honey, and colder than ice. The Holy Prophet (peace and blessings of Allah be upon him) will arrive there ahead of all, and will give water to every one passing that way. But when innovators will go to that fountain, the Messenger of Allah will recognise them to be the people of his *Ummah* because of their chanting Word of Allah and saying Salat and thus having particular signs; they will also recognise the Messenger of Allah as their Apostle. But a group of angels will stand between them and the Apostle, stopping them to advance further. When the merciful Prophet will tell the angels that these people belong to his *Ummah*, the angels will say in reply that these people had invented new things in his religion after his departure which is unknown to him, he will, in spite of the hard times and their thirst will ask the angels to keep them off from him. It was because they had added new things to his religion and changed its feature beyond recognition. The Holy Prophet (peace and blessings of Allah be upon him) was sent to uproot innovations but they added to them instead. This is to be borne in mind that Allah, the Almighty sent His Apostle with His Book for spreading His Message and for demonstrating His codes and laws through actions. When the Holy Qur'an was completed and the time of the final departure of the Apostle came near, Allah, the Almighty said:

اَلْيَوْمَ اَكْمَلْتُ لَكُمْ دِيْنَكُمْ وَاَتْمَمْتُ عَلَيْكُمْ نِعْمَتِي وَرَضِيْتُ لَكُمُ الْاِسْلَامَ دِيْنًا

> ."Today I have perfected your religion for you, and I have completed My Favour upon you and I have approved for you al-Islam as the (Divine) Code of life."
>
> (Q.5:4).

That is, when the religion of Allah was perfected and His Favour was completed, then, if one adds something new to the religion, it is out of the realm of the Qur'an. In the same manner, if anyone curtails anything from the injunctions of the Qur'an, he certainly reduces the importance and virtues of the Message of Allah.

In short, when the Prophet of Allah (peace and blessings of Allah be upon him), his Companions, successors of the Companions and their followers departed and the knowledge of the Holy Qur'an lessened, new sections of people rose to add new things in religion and their followers took these new things as part of true religion. Thus the pure religion was tainted. Many new and ridiculous rites and rituals were added to circumcision and marriage. May Allah save all of us from such *bid'ats*.

Chapter -Two

Mention of Facts About Faith

فِي ذِكْرِ حَقِيْقَةِ الْإِيْمَانِ

This chapter consists of mention of such verses of the Holy Qur'an and *ahadith* which brings to light facts concerning Iman (faith) so that every wise person may come to know that actions against the verses and *ahadith* are actions of Faithlessness.

One should bear in mind that all acts of *Iman* (Faithfulness) are performed according to the dictates of Allah and His Messenger and not guided by one's wisdom and logic. Had it been so, great philosophers and wise men like Aristotle etc. would have been perfect men. But this is not the fact. Reason must be subordinate to Shari'ah; Shari'ah must not obey reason. Allah, the Almighty says in Surah Muminun of the Holy Qur'an:

قَدْ اَفْلَحَ الْمُؤمِنُونَ الَّذِينَ هُمْ فِي صَلَاتِهِمْ خٰشِعُونَ وَالَّذِينَ
هُمْ عَنِ اللَّغْوِ مُعْرِضُونَ وَالَّذِينَ هُمْ لِلزَّكٰوةِ فَاعِلُونَ
وَالَّذِينَ هُمْ لِفُرُوجِهِمْ حٰفِظُونَ اِلَّا عَلٰى اَزْوَاجِهِمْ

اَوْمَامَلَكَتْ اَيْمَانُهُمْ فَاِنَّهُمْ غَيْرُ مَلُوْمِيْنَ فَمَنِ ابْتَغٰى وَرَآءَ
ذٰلِكَ فَاُولٰٓئِكَ هُمُ الْعٰدُوْنَ وَالَّذِيْنَ هُمْ لِاَمٰنٰتِهِمْ وَعَهْدِهِمْ
رٰعُوْنَ وَالَّذِيْنَ هُمْ عَلٰى صَلَوٰتِهِمْ يُحَافِظُوْنَ اُولٰٓئِكَ هُمُ
الْوٰرِثُوْنَ الَّذِيْنَ يَرِثُوْنَ الْفِرْدَوْسَ هُمْ فِيْهَا خٰلِدُوْنَ –

"Successful indeed are the Believers,—— those who humble themselves in their prayers; who avoid vain talk; who are active in giving *Zakat*; who guard their modesty, except with those joined to them in the marriage bond, or (the captives) whom their right hands possess, — for (in their case) they are free from blame, but those whose desires exceed those limits are transgressors;——— those who faithfully observe their trusts and their covenants; and who (strictly) guard their prayers;—these will be the heirs, who will inherit paradise; they will dwell therein (forever).

(Q.23:1-11)

That is, those Muslims who look to Allah in *salat*, keep pressed with fear of Allah, the Almighty, concentrate on their prayer and keep aloof from futile, worthless and meaningless activities are righteous. Same is the case with those who do not indulge in music and fun and evasion of *Zakat*, commit sexual intercourse only with their wives or slave-girls and not with any other woman and do not commit sexual acts elsewhere like arranging of *muta'h* (a temporary marriage) or to indulge in adultery with a hired woman or do it by way of friendship or by force or do masturbation. All such persons are righteous. And needs and desires of all those are fulfilled who keep promise, say prayers in time and do not neglect it at any cost. Only these people are true successors of Hadrat

Adam (peace be upon him); they will inherit the Heaven and will remain there forever.

It is clear from the above-quoted verses that if the Believers say prayers with all humility and from the bottom of heart; pay *Zakat* if wealth is available, keep promise and trust and keep from indulging in sexual intercourse with women other than their wives and slave-girls, they will attain Favours of Allah, the Almighty and get Heaven as a reward. Allah, the Almighty says in Surah al-Anfal of the Holy Qur'an:

إِنَّمَا الْمُؤْمِنُونَ الَّذِينَ إِذَا ذُكِرَ اللّٰهُ وَجِلَتْ قُلُوبُهُمْ وَإِذَا تُلِيَتْ عَلَيْهِمْ آيَاتُهُ زَادَتْهُمْ إِيمَانًا وَعَلٰى رَبِّهِمْ يَتَوَكَّلُونَ ط الَّذِينَ يُقِيمُونَ الصَّلٰوةَ وَمِمَّا رَزَقْنٰهُمْ يُنفِقُونَ ط أُولٰئِكَ هُمُ الْمُؤْمِنُونَ حَقًّا لَهُمْ دَرَجٰتٌ عِندَ رَبِّهِمْ وَمَغْفِرَةٌ وَرِزْقٌ كَرِيمٌ -

"For, Believers are those who, when Allah is mentioned, feel a tremor in their hearts, and when they hear His revelations rehearsed, find their faith strengthened, and put (all) their trust in their Lord; who establish regular prayers and spend (freely) out of the gifts we have given them for sustenance: such in truth are the Believers: they have grades of dignity with their Lord, and forgiveness, and generous sustenance."

(Q.8:2-4)

It is the sign of Faith that one fears and shudders with terror when the name of Allah, the Almighty is mentioned before him; hears with fondness when the Book of Allah is recited; obey every order; consider everything to be right and believe it; rely on his Lord alone; say *salat* properly; and spend from what Allah has bestowed on him only he is the true Muslim. He becomes closer to Allah with every virtue of his

It is clear from the above discussion that the person lacking in the virtues must not make any claim regarding his Muslimhood.

Allah, the Almighty says in Surah Al-Anfal of the Holy Qur'an:

وَالَّذِينَ آمَنُوا وَهَاجَرُوا وَجَاهَدُوا فِي سَبِيلِ اللَّهِ وَالَّذِينَ آوَوا وَّنَصَرُوا أُولَٰئِكَ هُمُ الْمُؤْمِنُونَ حَقًّا لَّهُم مَّغْفِرَةٌ وَرِزْقٌ كَرِيمٌ -

> "Those who believe, and emigrate, and fight for the faith, in the Cause of Allah as well as those who give (them) asylum and aid, these are (all) in very truth the Believers: for them is the forgiveness of sins and a provision most generous."
>
> (Q.8:74)

That is, those who embraced Islam and left their house in the territories of the Unbelievers in accordance with the Command of Allah; fought in the way of Allah and those who gave asylum and helped them are true Muslims. They will get a place of respect in the Heaven.

Allah, the Almighty said in Surah Al-Hujurat of the Holy Qur'an:

إِنَّمَا الْمُؤْمِنُونَ الَّذِينَ آمَنُوا بِاللَّهِ وَرَسُولِهِ ثُمَّ لَمْ يَرْتَابُوا وَجَاهَدُوا بِأَمْوَالِهِمْ وَأَنفُسِهِمْ فِي سَبِيلِ اللَّهِ أُولَٰئِكَ هُمُ الصَّادِقُونَ -

"Only those are Believers who have believed in Allah and His Messenger, and have never since doubted, but have striven with their belongings and their persons in the Cause of Allah: Such are the sincere ones."

(Q.49:15)

To believe in Allah means to consider Allah one's Creator, Master, Nourisher, Reliever of needs and Remover of difficulties; to accept these commands from the bottom of heart, to be thankful to Him in comforts and discomforts, and to obey His Will at all costs. To believe in the Messenger of Allah means to consider him better than every creature of Allah, to carry out what he says thinking it to be according to the Will of Allah, without putting his own reason into it, is indeed a true Believer.

Allah, the Almighty says in Surah An-Nisa'a of the Holy Qur'an:

فَلَا وَرَبِّكَ لَا يُؤْمِنُونَ حَتَّى يُحَكِّمُوكَ فِيمَا شَجَرَ بَيْنَهُمْ ثُمَّ
لَا يَجِدُوا فِي أَنفُسِهِمْ حَرَجاً مِمَّا قَضَيْتَ وَيُسَلِّمُوا تَسْلِيماً

"But no by thy Lord, they can have no (real) Faith. Until they make thee judge in all disputes between them. And find in their souls no resistance against thy decisions, but accept them with the fullest conviction."

(Q.4:65)

It is amply clear by the verse quoted above that it is the symbol of Faith that any dispute arising in matters of this world or the Hereafter, should be settled according to the sayings and practices of the Holy Prophet (peace and blessings of Allah be upon him) without any ifs and buts. If one follows the path of Allah and His Messenger, he is a Believer, otherwise not.

Bukhari and Muslim report from Hadrat Abdullah ibn Umar (may Allah be pleased with him) that the Holy Prophet (peace and blessings of Allah be upon him) said:

بنى الاملام على خمس شهادة ان لا الــه الا اللــه وان محمداً وعبده ورسـولـه واقـام الصلـوة وايتـاء الزكـوة والحج وصـوم رمضـان -

> "Islam is based on five things: to bear witness that none is liable to be worshipped except Allah; Muhammad (peace and blessings of Allah be upon him) is His Servant and Messenger; to establish Salat; to give Zakat; and to observe fast during the month of Ramadan."

That is, everything has its base and root, and if the base and root are absent, the thing is also no more. In the same way, Islam is based on five things mentioned above. These are the basic principles of Islam. First of all, one has to bear witness that there is none liable to be worshipped other than Allah, the Almighty and Muhammad (peace and blessings of Allah be upon him) is the Servant and Messenger of Allah; this belongs to heart and tongue. The second base of Islam is to establish *Salat*; this belongs to body and soul. The third base of Islam is to give *Zakat*; this belongs to wealth of a person. The fourth base of Islam is to observe fast in the whole month of Ramadan. The fifth and the last one is to perform Hajj of the holy Ka'bah; this is the prayer of body and wealth.

To believe means to be certain about anything. If one makes confession of anything but acts against it, he is a liar and hypocrite. The hypocrites did the same during the life-time of the Holy Prophet (peace and blessings of Allah be upon him).

Allah, the Almighty has said in the Holy Qur'an that those people were liars and hypocrites, because they confessed one thing from their tongue and negate it by their action. When a person claims to believe in the Oneness of Allah, the Almighty, by his tongue and actions, it means he kept himself away from all other relgions like those of idol-worshipping, star-worshipping,

worshipping of religious guides etc. And when one claims that there is none liable to be worshipped other than Allah, it means he has to worship Allah alone in letter and spirit, like bowing, prostrating, going round Ka'bah, spending in His name, observing fast for Him, vowing in His name, asking help from Him, calling His name in time of difficulties, chanting and reciting His Words, fighting those who oppose Him etc. One should worship One Who is independent of needs and care-free and all others be dependents on him. Hence all others are themselves needy and destitues, how can a needy person fulfils needs of others? One who is totally and completely independent must have come into being of his own and has not been created by any other agency, one who is eternal, free from all defects and shortcomings, omnipotent and omnipresent, deciding everything out of his own will, knows the unseen. Thus, when one says "La ilaha illallah", he accepts in letter and spirit all powers centred in Him. And whatever there is in the form of a saint, reason, body, spirit, dead or alive, jinn, ghost, fairy, tree, stone, standard, sign and symbol, house, shrine, grave, picture, paw, image etc., are all to be rejected and discarded outright. None is there for whom one should bow down in prayer or spend in his name or do any prayer whether physical, spiritual and financial. It is because none is eternal and care-free save Allah, the Almighty. All creatures are needy to Him. All of them have been created by Him; all are mortal; all are to be perished.

Further, one has to believe in Muhammad (peace and blessings of Allah be upon him) as the Messenger of Allah and that he has been sent by Allah with His Message. But the basic thing is that he is a servant of Allah. Had he not been so, he would not have brought message from anybody else. And when he was himself the servant of Allah, he had to worship and obey Him. But Since he was picked up for prophethood, he must have been above all creatures in regard to wisdom, mercy, sobriety, forsightedness, morality, humility, obedience, content, piety, generosity, valour, fear of Allah etc.

For the Messenger of Allah, three things are but necessary:

1) He must be truthful and not a liar.

2) He must be innocent, committing no sin.

3) He must convey the Message of Allah to His servants.

Hence, if the Apostle is a liar, nobody will believe, and instead of receiving guidance, they will go astray. He must be innocent because a sinner cannot ask others to keep from sins. Similarly, if he fails to carry out his responsibility as conveyer of the Messenger of Allah and hides it instead, he is, in fact, not the true messenger of Allah at all. It would be futile to appoint such a person as messenger, and Allah, the Almighty, is not supposed to do anything futile.

Thus, anyone who says "*Ash'hado anna Muhammadan abduhu wa rasulohu*," he confesses that Muhammad (peace and blessings of Allah be upon him) was the servant of Allah and it was a must for him also to worship and obey Allah. Moreover, he was above all creatures of Allah in human traits. Whatever he said was the Command of Allah, the Almighty. All his performances were according to the Will and Pleasure of Allah. None is innocent except the Holy Prophet (peace and blessings of Allah be upon him) and one who is not innocent may commit sins and crimes, and such a person cannot guide anyone along the path of Allah.

The second pillar of Islam is *Salat* (prayer). These are seventeen *reka'hs* ('*raka't*' means a part of the *salat* which includes standing, bending and prostration). It is performed five times a day including night. None has the power to bring about any change in the rule. Nobody is permitted to add or substract from the fixed number of *raka'hs*. It can be likened to a sovereign who chooses a very suitable person from among his subjects to attend his court times a day and declares terrible punishment for being absent. Now if the chosen fellow is at fault in carrying out the order of the king, he is liable to be condemned and punished. But, if he carries out the order of the king according to his will and pleasure and attends the court in the prescribed manner, praises him in a befitting way, describes his obligations and extends his thanks for what Allah, the Almighty, has bestowed upon him, places his needs before the king with due respect and obeys all the wills, orders of the king with pride and sincerity, and leaves the place only after the permission of the king, he is certainly to get the greatest favour of the king.

Similarly, Allah, the Almighty, chooses some persons from among His creatures to attend His Court five times a day. But if he fails to perform his duty adequately, he is to be condemned by all the creatures and the result is wrath and punishment from Allah, the Almighty. However, if the person prepares himself for attending the Court of Allah by cleansing himself from all dust, dirt and pollution, and the filth of polytheism and innovation, stands on the carpet for saying prayer having his face in the direction of Ka'abah, the sacred House of Allah and performs his prayer as he has been directed, praising Him in the most suitable words possible, professing that none is liable to be worshipped but He, seeking salvation from the Fire of Hell, he is a pure, sincere and true slave of Allah, the Exalted, liable to be favoured by his Creator, Sustainer and Master.

The third pillar of Islam is *Zakat* (two and half per cent of annual profits to be given in charity by Muslims to the class of people specified in the Qur'an). This can be likened to the tax or revenue or duty or excise or customs collected from the cultivators, traders, industrialists etc., for their protection and safety. If he claims that all wealth and property belong to Allah, he should testify it by giving from it to Allah, as prescribed by Him. He has raised the poor and needy from among them to receive the amount on His behalf. Thus one who evades *Zakat* is liable to incur punishment.

The fourth pillar of Islam is *Hajj*. It is likened to those who are ordained to make representation before the king in his seat of power, since the person has been appointed on an important post. He may appear before the king in order to get his honour and status redeemed. In the same way, one has to call at the appointed place.

to make special representation before Allah, in the House of Allah. Thus, all his big and small sins are pardoned and he comes back home so pure and clean as if he is born from the womb of his mother.

The fifth pillar is observing fasts during the whole month of Ramadan. It is likened to sending expedition for the conquest of a country so that the army is kept alert through movements and exercises. Similarly, the Behievers are to move and fight against the evil forces of Satan during this month as an annual exercise. During this month, the Behievers have to wage a war against their personal and internal enemies also. They have not only to keep from eating, drinking and sexual intercourse in the state of fasting but also to make more exercises in prayers and try to achieve more reward and virtues during this sacred month. This is, in fact, the month of training which if received properly, leads to change for the best. Such a training not only prepares the Believers to fight against evils but also do exercises in hard work, endurance, patience and forbearance. They keep aloof from un-Islamic acts as they refrain from eating, drinking and carnal desires during this period.

Bukhari and Muslim report from Hadrat Abu Hurairah (may Allah be pleased with him) that the Holy Prophet (peace and blessings of Allah be upon him) said:

الايمان بضع وسبعون شعبةً فافضلها قول لا اله الا الله وادنها اماطة الاذى عن الطريق والحياء شعبة من الايمان -

> "Faith has more than seventy branches. The most excellent of all the branches is to say 'La ilaha illallah; the smallest branch is to remove hurdle from the way and to keep modesty."

Faith is like a tree which has green leaves and of varied colours and fruits of different tastes. Similarly, there are more than seventy branches; the biggest among them is the Word (Kalimah) of Allah. In fact, this branch is like the root of the tree and the tiny branches are removing bricks, stones, thorns from thoroughfare so that nobody is troubled. One branch of faith is modesty and shame. In short, to recite Word of Allah, to observe modesty and to save creatures from trouble are the demand of Faith.

Bukhari and Muslim report from Hadrat Anas bin Malik (may Allah be pleased with him) that the Holy Prophet (peace and blessings of Allah be upon him) said:

لايؤمن احدكم حتى اكون احب اليه من والديه وولده
والناس اجمعين -

> "Nobody can become a Muslim unless I am dearer to him than his father, son, and all others."

That is, one cannot become a Muslim unless he keeps the Messenger of Allah (peace and blessings of Allah be upon him) dearer than his parents and all the creatures; loves him more than all others, follows his *'sunnah'* in letter and spirit and translates them into action. This is what is called true love. Confessing love only from tongue without feeling it at heart and not following it is not love at all.

It is clear from the above statement that one who follows the sayings of his religious guides, parents, kings etc. rejecting those of the Messenger of Allah (peace and blessings of Allah be upon him), he is not a Muslim in the real term of the word.

Bukhari and Muslim report from Hadrat Anas bin Malik (may Allah be pleased with him) that the Holy Prophet (peace and blessings of Allah be upon him) said:

ثلاث من كن فيه وجدبهن حلاوة الايمان من كان الله
ورسوله احب اليه مما سواهما ومن احب عبداً لايحبه

الا الله ومن يكره ان يعود فى الكفر بعد ان انقذه اللـه
منه كما يكره ان يلقى فى النار -

"One who retains three things has the taste of Faith; one who befriends Allah and His Messenger most; one who keeps friendship with a slave of Allah for the sake of Allah; and one who abhors going back to unbelief after being purified by Allah, as he desists falling into Fire."

That is, anyone who has three traits i.e., he loves Allah and His Messenger more than others; befriends a slave of Allah for Allah's sake; and abhors going back to unbelief after being saved from unbelief by Allah and considers this as falling into Fire, has the real taste of Islam i.e., the true character of Islam appears to him without an iota of doubt.

Muslim reports from Hadrat Abbas (may Allah be pleased with him), the son of Abdul Muttalib that the Holy Prophet (peace and blessings of Allah be upon him) said:

ذاق طعم الايمان من رضى بالله رباً وبالاسلام دينا
ومحمدٍ رسولاً -

"One has the real taste of Islam, who is happy with having Allah, the Almighty as his Lord; having Islam as his religion; and have Muhammad (peace and blessings of Allah be upon him) as his Prophet."

That is, one who is happy and satisfied that Allah is his Lord; Islam is his religion; and Muhammad (peace and blessings of Allah be upon him) is his Prophet —— has the real taste of Faith. And for real taste, Faith in these things should take firm root in one's heart, and one who has these things inculcated in heart gets the real satisfaction. One who believes that none but Allah is his Lord, he will never turn towards anybody other than Allah; one who believes firmly that only Islam is his religion, he will never follow any religion except Islam; and one who is satisfied that Muhammad (peace and blessings of Allah be upon him) is his Prophet, he will never follow the ways of others against the will of the Messenger of Allah.

Bukhari reports Hadrat Anas bin Malik (may Allah be pleased with him) that the Holy Prophet (peace and blessings of Allah be upon him) said:

من صلى صلوتنا واستقبل قبلتنا واكل ذبيحتنا فذلك المسلم الذى له ذمة الله وذمة رسوله فلا تحفرْوا الله فى ذمته ـ

> "Anyone who says *salat* like me; turns his face towards Ka'abah like me; and eats from the animal sacrificed as I do —— he is a Muslim; he is under the protection of Allah and His Messenger —— hence, do not break covenant under the security of Allah."

Salat is the mark of Islam. It is like the uniform of Islam without which nobody can become a Muslim. The Jews had no *ruku* (bending) in *salat* while the Christians had no *Sajda* (prostration). Both the Jews and the Christians would say their prayers facing *Baitul Maqdis*. Hence it has been said that anyone who performs *salat* like him with *ruku* and *sajda* and faces Ka'abah during *salat*, belongs to him; when he eats from the animal sacrificed by Muslims, he becomes their brothers and should be accepted as a Muslim because he has come under the protection of Allah and His Messenger. Thus it is *haram* (prohibited) to kill him without reason. So give him protection and don't kill him nor snatch away his property from him. It is sheer interference with the protection given to him by Allah and breach of promise. It is now clear that to spare a Muslim from the sufferings of life and property is the sign of Islam. Hence anyone practising these tenets of Islam is a Muslim beyond doubt and he should be treated accordingly. However, Allah alone knows the feelings of heart.

Abu Dawud reports from Umama (may Allah be pleased with him) that the Holy Prophet (peace and blessings of Allah be upon him) said:

من احب لله وابغض لله واعطى لله ومنع لله فقد استكمل الايمان -

> "Anyone who befriends someone for the sake of Allah and shows enmity against Him alone, gives something to anyone for Allah and refuses to give for His sake, he perfects his Islam."

That is, one who loves anyone with a purpose in view; for examples, he loves his parents because they nursed him; he shows respect to his religious guide and teacher because they taught him and guided him along the right path; he pays regards to an officer or a king because he seeks his protection he loves someone because he is generous; and he is attracted to someone because he has charming appearance. Moreover, one loves someone because he is friend of his friend. Apart from these persons, there are some others who deserve our love and respect because Allah, the Almighty, has commanded to do so, like Prophets, friends of Allah, martyrs, religious scholars, derveshes, all the Muslims and the angels etc. On the other hand, there are some who are to be shown disrespect, spite and enmity by the Order of Allah, the Almighty, because they are accursed by Him, like Satan, unbelievers, unbelieving jinns. Hence a Muslim is required to love anyone for Allah's sake and to show enmity to anyone for Allah. Similarly, a Believer is asked to donate something with the permission of Allah and refuse to contribute anything to anyone for fear of the displeasure of Allah. Such a person is perfect in Faith.

It is clear from the above discussion that one's love and enmity, generosity and misery should be under the Will and Pleasure of Allah, the Exalted. This is the Faith at its height.

Tirmidhi, Nasai and Baihaqi report from Abu Hurairah (may Allah be pleased with him) that the Messenger of Islam (peace and blessings of Allah be upon him) said:

المسلم من سلم المسلمون من لسانه ويده والمؤمن من امنه الناس على دمآئهم واموالهم -

"The perfect Muslim is one from whose tongue and hand other Muslims remain safe; and the perfect Believer is one who is regarded as trustworthy with respect to their lives and properties."

That is, a Muslim who is safe from another Muslim, for example, one who keeps away from inflicting any trouble to his fellow Muslims by hand, by refraining from backbiting, ridiculing, cursing, abusing, taunting, quarrelling, disclosing secrets, using harsh words, bearing false witness; and spares a Muslim by hand, by not killing, beating and wounding without any reason, snatching away his property, setting his housing on fire — — he is surely a perfect Muslim. A perfect Believer is one that instead of fearing, people make him trustee of their lives and properties.

Baihaqi reports from Anas (may Allah be pleased with him) in its chapter on Iman (Faith) that very rarely the Messenger of Islam (peace and blessings of Allah be upon him) addressed us without mentioning that :

لا ايمان لمن لا امانة له ولادين لمن لاعهد له -

'one who has no trustworthiness has no Faith, and one who has no promise to keep, has no religion'

It is now clear that one who fails to practise trustworthiness and keep promise and agreement is not a Muslim in its perfectness.

Muslim reports from Jabir that the Messenger of Allah (peace and blessings of Allah be upon him) said:

ثنتان موجبتان قال رجل يا رسول الله ماالمؤجبتان قال من مات يشرك بالله شيئاً دخل النار ومن مات لايشرك بالله شيئاً دخل الجنة ۔

"There are two deciding factors."

"Are there only two deciding factors", O' Messenger of Allah,' asked a person.

"Yes, one who died establishing partners to Allah, would go to Hell; and one who died never associating anyone else to Allah, would go to Heaven."

Ahmad reports from Abu Umama that someone asked the Messenger of Allah (peace and blessings of Allah be upon him):

ماالايمان قال اذا

سرتك حسنتك وسآءتك سيئتك فانت مؤمن ۔

"What is Faith ?'

"You are a Believer if your virtue keeps you happy and vice sad."

It means if there is left no distinction between virtue and vice, Islam is no more.

Imam Ahmad reports from Umar, the son of Anbasah that a person came to the Messenger of Allah (peace and blessings of Allah be upon him) and submitted:

يا رسول الله من معك على هذا الامر قال حر وعبد
قلت ماالاسلام قال طيب الكلام واطعام الصائم قلت
ماالايمان قال الصبر والسمآحة ۔

"For whom you are the Prophet?"

"I am Messenger of Allah for the free and the slaves," he said.

"What is Islam?" I asked.

"To speak the truth and to feed others," replied the Apostle.

"What is Faith?' I submitted again.

"To keep patience and to show valour," he said.

That is, the visitor put three questions to the Messenger of Allah (peace and blessings of Allah be upon him): the first question was, whom for you are sent as a Prophet and who are to obey you?" The Apostle replied that he is Prophet for all whether they are free or slave. The second question was, "What is Islam?" To which he replied, `to speak the truth, to be polite and sociable, to salute and feed others. The third question was, 'What is Faith?' The Apostle replied, 'to keep patience, to show valour and manliness."

The above statement emcompasses scores of things like: evading not the saying of prayers, not getting embarrassed at any suffering, nor keeping away from adultery and sodomy, nor abstaining from the detestables, nor running away from fighting against the infidels, nor disclosing anybody's secret, to prove oneself trustworthy ——are all acts of patience and valour.

Imam Ahmad and Abu Dawud report Irbaz, the son of Sa'ria:

صلى بنا رسول الله صلى ا لله عليه وسلم ذات يومٍ فاقبل علينا بوجهه فوعظنا موعظةٍ بليغةٍ ذرفت منها العيون ووجلت منها القلوب فقال رجل يا رسول الله كان هذه موعظة مودع فاوصينا فقال اوصيكم بتقوى الله والسمع والطاعة وان كان عبداً حبشياً فانه من يعش منكم بعدى فسيرى اختلافاً كثيراً فعليكم بسنتى وسنة الخلفاء الراشدين المهديين تمسكوا بها وعضوا عليها بالنواجذ واياكم ومحدثات الامور فان كل محدث بدعة وكل بدعة ضلالة ۔

"Once the Messenger of Allah (peace and blessings of Allah be upon him) led the prayer and then turning towards us he admonished intensively so that we burst into tears and submitted:

"If this admonition is of one who seems to depart, then admonish us perfectly."

Thereupon he said:

"Fear Allah, obey your superiors, even if they had once been slaves; you will face much differences after me and then you should hold my *Sunnah* and those of my successors firmly because they are the guided and the righteous. Hence hold our ways with your teeth, keep away from innovations, because everything new (added to the religion) is innovation, and every innovation is deviation "

That is, one should fear Allah to keep safe from evils and if an evil is committed, he reports out of fear and he is pardoned. Fear of Allah leads one to perform virtuous deeds. A Believer has been ordered to obey the ruler even if he is an Abyssinian slave, save that he is not ordering to do anything against the Command of Allah, the Almighty. Moreover, differences, dissensions and disruptions will emerge in the last days of this world, hence one should then obey the Apostle and his Companions in all matters. One should hold firmly the way of Allah, His Messenger and his Companions and reject all innovations because innovations lead to deviation from the right path. Details about innovations have already passed. In short, fear of Allah is the symbol of Islam.

Imam Ahmad, Nasai and Darimi report from Abdullah bin Mas'ood (may Allah be pleased with him):

خط لنا رسول الله صلى الله عليه وسلم خطاً ثم قال
هذا سبيل الله ثم خط خطوطاً عن يمينه وشماله وقال
هذا سبلٌ على كل سبيلٍ منها شيطانٌ يدعوا اليه وقراء
وان هذا صراطى مستقيماً فاتبعواه الاية

> "The Messenger of Allah drew a line and said, 'This is the way of Allah; thereafter, he drew a few other lines right and left of the former one and said: 'There is one Satan on every way calling towards him and thereafter recited the verse *'Inna haza serati mustaqima'* up to the end.

That is, Allah, the Almighty says that His *Shari'ah* is simple and straightforward, hence one should follow it and not others which will lead astray. The Messenger of Allah (peace and blessings of Allah be upon him), therefore, drew lines to show the straight line leading to Allah, the Exalted while others leading astray. It is because Satans are sitting on each way calling men towards it. Hence, one should refrain from treading on the ways of Satan. One should keep in mind that the straight way is one which is shown by Allah and His Messenger and none others. This is the demand of true Faith.

Tirmidhi reports from Bilal bin Harith Muzanni that the Messenger of Allah (peace and blessings of Allah be upon him) said:

من احيى سنةً من سنتى قد اميتت بعدى فان له من الاجر مثل اجور من عمل بها من غير ان ينقص من اجورهم شيئاً ومن ابتدع بدعة ضلالةٍ لا يرضاه الله ورسوله كان عليه من الاثمم مثل مثل آثام من عمل بها لا ينقص ذلك من اوزارهم شيئاً ـ

> "Anyone who revives any *Sunnah* from among my *Sunnahs* which has been wiped out after me, he will get the reward equal to all those who will follow it without lessening from the reward of the reviver; similarly, one who innovates something new which is not approved by Allah and His Messenger, he will incur sin equal to the sins of all those who will follow his innovated idea without deducting from his sins."

That is, when the followers of *Sunnah* increase in number, innovations are eradicated; when innovators exceed in number, *Sunnah* get obliterated. In such a situation anyone riviving the dead *Sunnah* will get reward equal to all those who will practise it.

In the same way, anyone who revives an abandoned innovation so that others start following it, the innovator will incur punishment equal to all those who will practise it till the end of this world.

Tirmidhi reports from Amr bin Auf (may Allah be pleased with him) that the Messenger of Allah (peace and blessings of Allah be upon him) said:

ان الديـن كيـارزُ الـى الحجـاز كمـا تـارزُ الحيـة الـــى جحرها وليعقلن الذين من الحجاز معقل العرويـةِ مـن رأس الجبـل ان الـد يـن بـدأ غريبـاً وسيعود كمـا بـدأ فطوبى للغرباء هم الذين يصلحون ما افسد الناس من م بعدى من سنتى -

"The religion will come back to Mak'kah as a serpent recoils to its hole, and the religion will find refuge in Mak'kah as the herd seeks refuge from the peak of a mountain. Truly speaking, the religion will look like a traveller, but these travellers (unknown persons) will put the matter right after being polluted by some people after me."

That is during last days the original Islam will be like a traveller who is unknown to one and all, as it was at the earlier stage, some people will come out to eradicate innovations and set everything right. It has also become clear that in the last days Islam will come back to stay in Arabia leaving all other parts of the world. In such a situation those who will revive the dead *Sunnahs* and eradicate innovations will find their status elevated.

Imam Ahmad reports from Hadrat Muadh bin Jabal (may Allah be pleased with him) to have asked the Messenger of Allah (peace and blessings of Allah be upon him):

عـن افضـل الايمـان قـال ان تحـب للـه وتبغـض للـه وتعمل لسانك فى ذكر الله قال ومـاذا يـا رسـول اللـه

قال ان تحب للناس ما تحب لنفسك وتكره لهم مــاتكره لنفسك -

"What is the best Faith?"

"To keep friendship and enmity for the sake of Allah and keep one's tongue engaged in praising Allah."

"Anything more?" he asked.

"To consider good for others what is good for oneself, and to consider bad for others what is bad for oneself."

That is, one should keep friendship and enmity for the sake of Allah.

The above mentioned verses and *ahadith* make it clear that the acts of a Muslim is to consider Allah as one in all His traits, to consider Muhammad (peace and blessings of Allah be upon him) as His Messenger, to say prayer with perfect attention, to give *Zakat*, to observe fasts during the month of Ramadan, to refrain from doing nonsense work, to keep away from adultery, to act as trustworthy, to keep promise, to fear at the mention of Allah's name, to hear the Book of Allah with rapt attention and believe in it, feed the people, to give charity, to leave the country of the infidels, to fight in the way of Allah, to entertain the migraters, to spend on holy war, to act according to the *Sunnah* of the Messenger of Allah (peace and blessings of Allah be uopn him), to maintain shame and modesty, to keep the Apostle dearer than one's parents and children etc., to love the beloveds of Allah, to show disgust at the acts of unbelief, to rely on Allah, the Almighty, to raise no doubt about Islam, to keep one's love, enmity, generosity and misery obedient to the Will of Allah, not to inflict trouble on any Muslim, to show happiness at virtuous deeds and annoyance at misdeeds, to obey the Muslim rulers, to hold firmly the way to Apostle and his Companions, to keep from *bid'at* (innovations), to revive the dead *Sunnah* and to eradicate *bid'at* etc. These are all religious acts, and to oppose them is irreligious. May Allah, the Almighty save from all these.

Chapter - Three

Concerning Faith in Divine Decree

فِي ذِكْرِ الْإِيمَانِ بِالْقَدَرِ

This chapter consists of verses and *ahadith* which signify the occasions where Divine decree should be taken into account and where not.

One should bear in mind that Divine Command and valuation put togehter are called destiny. Allah, the Almighty decided the destiny of all creatures before their creation. Everything was predistined to act in a particular manner. Its do's and don'ts, beginning and end were predetermined. Every living being was created by Allah, the Almighty and it is He Who puts every thought in heart. To profess and be sure about it is called Faith in Divine Decree. Thus one who believes that a person acts of his own and acts without the Will of Allah and His Knowledge, is called *Qadria* i.e., one who denies the role of destiny. On the other hand, one who believes that man has no power over his will and action and whatever good or bad occurs, it is from Allah, the Almighty, and men and animals are so powerless that it is Allah Who make them indulge in sin and infidelity is called *Jabria* i.e., such a person believes in compulsion from Allah. Hence this creed is also wrong.

Man has, no doubt, some power and autonomy, and hence he has power of discretion, power to act and not to act, power to differentiate between good and bad. There is clear difference between a man and a stone; man can move at will but a stone cannot. A palsied hand moves of its own while a healthy hand is to be moved. And because of this much of autonomy a man acts in good faith and gets reward while he acts in bad faith and gets punishment. It is Allah who created both the right and the wrong ways, no doubt, but it does not mean that Allah likes the wrong way and He wants His slave to follow the wrong way. This example can be likened to an astrologer who, writing the horoscope of a boy, foretells that the boy will be caught in theft and put to jail. If it heppens according to what was said, there is no fault of the astrologer, because he had foretold according to his knowledge. Similarly, Allah, the Almighty wrote beforehand what was to happen and what was not, denoted the good and evil in clear terms, commanded to do good and forbade to do wrong. For example, He permitted to eat the meat of a goat and prohibited to eat the flesh of swine. Thus, if one eats pork instead of meat, how Allah, the Almighty is to be blamed for his senseless act. Allah had given him power to eat either of the two. But due to having perfect knowledge of the future lives and actions of each of His Creatures, He had destined for him to eat the pork. But He never permitted it; He had, rather, prohibited it.

Allah, the Almighty says in Surah Qamar of the Holy Qur'an:

إِنَّا كُلَّ شَيْءٍ خَلَقْنَاهُ بِقَدَرٍ -

"Verily, all things have We created in proportion and measure."

(Q.54:49).

That is, Allah's Creation is not haphazard. Everything goes by law, proportion, and measure. Everything has its appointed time, place, and occasion, as also its definite limitation. Everything open and concealed, the Throne and Authority, *lauh-o-qalam* (the tablet and the pen with which the decrees of Allah are written), angels, Heaven and Hell, firmament, stars, movement of the skies, earth and what lies between them, trees, fire and whatever are made of these, are all created by Allah, the Almighty. He is All-Wise and He perfectly knows what is going to happen and what will happen in future. Similarly, He knows who will do what at an appointed time. It is true that a wise and learned person knows his mission well and acts according to his scheme and plan with a certain result in view. Hence, Allah, Who is Wisest of all, performs nothing without a Planning Will. Thus whatever occurs remains in His Knowledge and nothing comes out without His Will. So one should thank Allah for the good happened to him and think for the harm or loss that it happened as was destined for him with the perfect Knowledge of Allah.

Allah, the Almighty says in Surah As-Saffat of the Holy Qur'an:

وَاللّٰهُ خَلَقَكُمْ وَمَاتَعْمَلُونَ ـ

"But Allah has created you and your handiwork,"

(Q.37:96)

That is, it is Allah Who created you. You can't do anything if He stops you from doing anything. Thus, a man wants to do something but he cannot do; and he does not want to do something but it is done of its own. Hence man is the doer of everything and he should do whatever is good and virtuous, and thank Allah if he is treated nicely. If man is not free to do anything according to his choice, to declare anything lawful and unlawful is useless. Similarly, to establish Heaven and Hell, to send Messengers to this world, to install kings or officers are all fruitless. However, the man is not perfectly independent and autonomous. If it happens so, Allah's sovereignty will be of no use.

Allah, the Almighty says in Surah Anfal of the Holy Qur'an:

وَاعْلَمُوا اَنَّ اللّٰهَ يَحُولُ بَيْنَ الْمَرْأ وَقَلْبِه ـ

> "And know that Allah cometh in between a man and his heart......"
>
> (Q.8:24).

First of all an idea enters the heart of a man and thereafter, it is translated into action. Thus, whatever Allah decides not to let happen, He stops it from being done. It is a fact that a man wants to perform thousands of works, but all these cannot be possibly done.

It is, therefore, clear that there is someone who stands in the way of carrying out any business of life. It is likened to the example of an animal who is free to graze but it is fastened with a string and it is allowed to graze from one field and not to do so from another field lying nearby. Now it is up to the animal to graze from the permitted or prohibited field.

Allah, the Almighty says in Surah Kuwirat (At-Takwir) of the Holy Qur'an:

وَمَا تَشَاءُونَ إِلاَّ أَن يَّشَاءَ اللهُ رَبُّ الْعَالَمِينَ ـ

> "But ye shall not will except, as Allah Wills,—— the Cherisher of the Worlds."
>
> (Q.81:29).

If it is an undeniable fact that it is Allah who instils in the heart of a man to do something or not to do something. Hence one should rely on Allah in all his affairs. None is there to make or mar his business of life. Thus, it is quite useless to turn towards others for help; it is an act that brings about disgrace and nothing else. It is He alone Who manages and regulates all activities of human life. One should, therefore, refrain from meddling in the matter with one's incomplete power of reasoning, otherwise Faith will be at stake.

Tirmidhi reports from Ali (may Allah be pleased with him) that the Holy Prophet (peace and blessings of Allah be upon him) said:

لا يؤمن عبدٌ حتى يؤمن باربعٍ يشهدُ ان لا اله الا اللـه انى رسولٌ بعثنى بالحق ويُؤمن بـالموت و البعـث بعـد الموت ويؤمن بالقدر -

> "None can become a Muslim unless he believes in four things: to bear witness that none is liable to be worshipped but Allah; that, I am the Messenger of Allah with truth; to believe in death and to trust that one is to come back to life after death; and to believe in destiny."

That is, as one should believe that Allah, the Almighty, is One, the Messenger of Allah stands on truth, the death is sure; in the same way, one should believe that destiny is definite. One who disbelieves the above-mentioned items is not a Believer at all.

Tirmidhi reports from Abdullah ibn Abbas (may Allah be pleased with him) that the Holy Prophet (peace and blessings of Allah be upon him) said:

صنفـان مـن امتـــى ليـس لهـا فـى الاسـلام نصيـبٌ المرجيئة و القدرية

> "Two types of people are there in my *Ummah* who have nothing from Islam; they are Murjea and Qadria."

That is, one who thinks that he is quite powerless and passive and he does what Allah wants him to do and hence he will not be accountable on the Day of Resurrection for his deeds and actions, and the inevitable result will be his salvation —— such a person is called *Jabri* or *Merji*. Such a person claims that Allah, the Almighty, makes him to do anything by force and He, at the same time, requires one to keep from sins. Such a notion is tantamount to the refusal of Divine Code. On the other hand, there is one who believes that he does everything of his own and he is free to act as he likes without the Will of Allah; such a person is known as Qadria. He is a person who denies the power of destiny and gives himself an air of divinity. Both of them are not Believers and they have to play no part in Islam.

Abu Dawud and Tirmidhi report from Abdullah ibn Umar (may Allah be pleased with him) that the Holy Prophet (peace and blessings of Allah be upon him) said:

فى امتى خسفٌ ومسخ وذلك فى المكذبين بالقدر -

> "From my *Ummah*, those who deny the power of destiny will be sunken into the earth and will find their faces changed like animals."

From this and other *ahadith* it becomes clear that the people of the *Ummah* of the Holy Prophet (peace and blessings of Allah be upon him) will not sink into the earth as it had happened to men like Qarun nor their faces will get changed like the past *Ummah* like the Jews and Christians whose faces were changed into those of monkeys and swines. This *hadith* shows that those who will deny the existence of destiny despite believing in *Kalimah* (Word) of Allah, they will find their faces changed or will be sunk into the earth at the end.

Imam Ahmad and Abu Dawud report from Abdullah bin Umar (may Allah be pleased with him) that the Holy Prophet (peace and blessings of Allah be upon him) said:

القدرية مجوسٌ من هذ ه الامة ان مرضوا فلا
تعودوهم وان ماتوا فلا تشهدوهم -

> "Qadri Magies belong to such an *Ummah* that their health must not be enquired about in case they fall ill, and prayer should not be said for them if they are dead."

'Majus' (Magi) is one who worships the sun and fire and believes in the effect of stars. When a person does not rely on

destiny and Allah, the Almighty, his heart is divided and he starts adoring countless objects. Sometimes he begins to adore the graves and the lamp of a shrine; at times he considers a certain day or night as auspicious and inauspicious, although there is nothing like it. A man believing in these things cannot retain his belief. Hence, the Holy Prophet (peace and blessings of Allah be upon him) says that a person who does not believe in the force of destiny is like the *Majus* of his *Ummah*, and if he falls ill, his health should not be enquired into, and his burial should not be attended if he passes away. It is because such a treatment is meted out to Believers only.

Ahmad and Abu Dawud report from Hadrat Umar bin Khattab (may Allah be pleased with him) that the Holy Prophet (peace and blessings of Allah be upon him) said:

لاتجالسوا اهل القدر ولاتفاتحوهم -

> "Do not let the person (disbelieving destiny) sit beside you nor start talking with him."

That is, do not develop love and sympathy with such a person; do not, rather, let him sit beside him nor you yourself sit beside him; do not start talking with him, but, however, there is no harm if you make a reply to his question: such a person is out of the circles of humanity. A disbeliever is known to one and all and nobody follows him, but a *Qadri* claims to be a Muslim and will mislead the ignorants by distorting some verse, *ahadith* and peotic verses on his own behalf. Thus, it is better to keep aloof from such a person so that he may not try to mislead the people or abandon his creed thinking it wrong and baseless.

Baihaqi and Razeen report from Hadrat Aisha (may Allah be pleased with her) that the Messenger of Allah (peace and blessings of Allah be upon him) said:

ستةٌ لعنتهم ولعنهم الله وكل نبى يجابُ الزائد فى

كتاب اللــه والمكـذب بقـدر اللـه والمتسـلط بـالجبروت
ليعز من اذله الله ويذل من عزه الله والمستحل لحرام
الله والمســتهل مـن عشـرتى ممـا حـرم اللـه والتـارك
السنتى -

"Six persons have been cursed by Allah and me; one who adds something to the Book of Allah; one who denies the destiny of Allah; one who becomes a ruler by force, so that he put to grace whom Allah disgraced, and put to disgrace whom Allah graced; one who declars *haram* what Allah declared as *halal*; those among my relatives who declare *halal* what Allah prohibited, and one who abandons my *Sunnah*."

That is, one who desists from the *Sunnah* of the Messenger of Allah (peace and blessings of Allah be upon him) without any religious reason and abandons it permanently, he has no faith in the Apostle; if he belongs to the lineage of the Apostle, he commits greater sin. For instance, if the son of a minister (vazir) steals something of a king or the king who shows no respect to his own laws so that his subject follow him in misdeeds, they deserve greater punishment. In short, one who denies the existence of destiny deserves curse from Allah and His Messenger.

Imam Ahmad, Abu Dawud and Ibn Majah report from Zayd bin Thabit (may Allah be pleased with him) that the Messenger of Allah (peace and blessings of Allah be upon him) said:

لو ان الله عـذب اهـل سـماواته واهـل ارضـه عذبهـم
وهو غير ظالمٍ لهم ولـو رحمهـم كـانت رحمتـه خـيراً
لهم من اعمالهم ولو انفقت مثـل احدٍ ذهبـاً فـى سبيل

الله ماقبله الله تعالى منك حتى تؤمن بالقدر وتعلـم ان
ما اصابك لم يكن ليخطئك و ان ما اخطـأ ك لـم يكـن
ليصيبك وان مت على غير هذا لدخلت النار۔

> "If Allah, the Almighty punishes the animates of the heavens and earth He cannot be labelled as cruel; and if He shows mercy to them, He is All-Merciful; if you spend gold equal in quantity to Mount Uhad, all this may go unaccepted unless you are a true believer in destiny and think that what happened to you was destined to happen, and if you pass away believing against this creed, you are bound to enter the Hell."

That is, what Allah has destined will happen at any cost. His decree cannot go unheeded. Hence, all griefs, miseries, sickness, comfort, happiness, health, victory, defeat, poverty and richness etc. come to him as written in destiny. And these cannot be avoided and discarded even if all the creatures oppose it unitedly. If it hapens that one wants to recover from an illness and he failed; one wants to become rich and he was not able to achieve it; a snake passes through one's hand without biting him; and he wants to achieve victory and fails in his mission—— all these happened according to what was destined to be. Hence a person who thinks against it is certainly a hellish person because he refuses the verdict of Allah, the Almighty. He is the Creator, Lord and Sustainer, and has every authority over His creatures, so if, he desires to send all to the Fire, He will not be accused to be cruel. Similarly, if He wants to show mercy to His creatures, nobody can stop Him from doing so.

Tirmidhi reports from Abu Huraírah (may Allah be pleased with him):

خرج علينا رسول الله صلى الله عليه وسلم ونحن نتنازعُ فى القدر فغضب حتى احمر وجهه كانها فقى فى وجهه حب الرمان فقال ابهذا امرتم ام بهذا ارسلت اليكم انما هلك من كان قبلكم حين تنازعوا فى هذا الامر عزمت عليكم عزمت عليكم ان لاتنازعوا فيه -

> "Once the Holy Prophet (peace and blessings of Allah be upon him) came out and found us in hot dispute regarding destiny. He grew so angry that his face turned red as if seeds of pomigranate were squeezed on his face and he then remarked:
>
> "Have I been towards you for this? People of the past were ruined because of their dispute over this topic. Hence I ask you not to enter into any conflict over this."

Allah, the Almighty has denoted what was beneficial to mankind. He delineated in clear and open words how to worship Him and how to carry out the business of life. However, He refrained from giving full detail about those things which were useless and worthless from the wordly point of view as well as from the standpoint of the Hereafter. All these He left to the wisdom and discretion of man. Thus, Allah, the Almighty did not disclose how the sun and moon came into being and what were the matters and their composition that led to the formation of the sun and moon, water, land, fire, etc. because the revealation of all these facts were futile and useless. Allah deliberately avoided to make people know what were above their power of reasoning and understanding. The same is the case with the problem of destiny. One should avoid any discussion on the topic of destiny because such discussions and disputes are likely to lead one astray. It is because of this the messenger of Allah (peace and blessings of Allah be upon him) showed his utmost anger upon discussion over destiny going on among his Companions including Abu Hurairah (may Allah be pleased with him).

Ibn Majah reports from Hadrat Aisha (may Allah be pleased with her) that the Holy Prophet (peace and blessings of Allah be upon him) said:

من تكلم فی شیء من القدر سئل عنه یوم القیامة ومن لم یتکلم فیه لم یسئل عنه ۔

> "Whoever discusses the problem of destiny will be punished on the Day of Judgment and one who does not do so will be saved."

It is clear from this that a Muslim should avoid such a discussion. Everyone should keep in mind that it is bound to happen what Allah, the Almighty has already decreed. A man has to act and act and the result should be left to One Who instils everything in the heart. He should believe what is written in the Book of Allah and the book of *hadith*.

Tirmidhi reports from Ubadah bin Samit that the Holy Prophet (peace and blessings of Allah be upon him) said:

ان اول ما خلق الله القلم فقال له اكتب فقال ما اكتب قال القدر فكتب ماكان وما هو كائنٌ الى الابد ۔

> "Allah, the Almighty ordered the Pen to write. It requested to know 'What to write?'
>
> "Write Destiny !" He said

'Thus it happened for everyone what was written."

Muslim reports from Abdullah bin Umar (may Allah be pleased with him) to have heard from the Holy Prophet (peace and blessings of Allah be upon him) said:

كتب الله مقادير الخلائق قبل ان يخلق السموات والارض بخمسين الف سنةٍ وكان عرشه على الماء -

> "Allah, the Almighty wrote the destiny of His creatures fifty thousand years before their creation, although His Throne was put on water."

Imam Ahmad and Abu Dawud report from Musa that he heard the Holy Prophet (peace and blessings of Allah be upon him) say:

ان الله خلق آدم من قبضةٍ قبضها من جميع الارض فجآء بنوم دم على قدر الارض منهم الاحمر والابيض والاسود وبين ذلك والسهل والحزن والخبيث والطيبُ -

> "Allah, the Almighty created Adam (peace be upon him) with a handful of dust taken from the earth —— red, white, black, soft, hard, unclean and clean."

That is, the standing differences in the complexion of men i.e., some are red and white while others are black; some are mild and polite, others are hard and rash; some are good-natured, others are wicked are due to the fact that Allah, the Almighty made Adam by taking dust from different kinds of earth. And Adam's progeny has the same complexion and nature.

Imam Ahmad and Tirmidhi report from Abdullah bin Umar (may Allah be pleased with him) that he heard the Messenger of Allah (peace and blessings of Allah be upon him) say:

ان اللہ تعالی خلق خلقه فی ظلمةٍ فالقی علیهم من نوره فمن اصابه من ذلك النور اهتدی ومن اخطآءه ضل فلذلك اقول جف القلم علی علم الله تعالی-

> "Allah, the Almighty created His creatures in darkness and then cast His Light over them. Now those who got it were guided while those who did not, went astray. Hence the pen wrote what Allah, the Almighty Commanded it to do."

That is, the pen wrote according to the Order of Allah, the Almighty and thereafter it got dried and hence does not write anymore.

Moreover, Islam is due to the Light of Allah, the Almighty. One who received the Light in Eternity was guided along the right path and one who failed to get it remained unguided and therefore deviated.

Imam Ahmad reports form Abi Darda'a (may Allah be pleased with him) that the Holy Prophet (peace and blessings of Allah be upon him) said:

ان الله عزوجل فرغ الی عبدٍ من خلقه من خمس من اجله وعمله ومضجعه واثره ورزقه -

> "Allah, the Almighty accomplished five things about His creatures: about its death, its acts abode, attitude and livelihood."

That is, He knows where one will die; what acts he will perform, what attitude he will adopt, what manners he will show, wherefrom he will get his livelihood. Everything will occur as ordained without the least change.

Thus a man should rely on the decrees of Allah, the Almighty, and he should not keep on striving very hard in worldly affairs because nothing will occur against the decrees of Allah, the Almighty.

Imam Ahmad reports from Abu Darda'a (may Allah be pleased with him) that the Holy Prophet (peace and blessings of Allah be upon him) said:

خلق الله آدم حين خلقه فضرب كتفه اليمنى فاخرج ذريةً بيضاء كانهم الذر فضرب كتفه اليسرى فاخرج ذريةً سوداء كانهم الحسم فقال للذى فى يمينه الى الجنةِ ولا ابالى وقال للذى فى كتفه اليسرى الى النار ولاابالى -

> "Allah, the Almighty created Adam on the appointed time. Thereafter, ant-like white progeny was taken out by striking at his right shoulder, and coal-like black progeny by striking at his left shoulder and said: These who are on the right hand side belong to Heaven and those on the left belong to Hell and He has least care for the result of both of them."

That is, Allah, the Almighty, declared some people Heavenly while others Hellish before the creation of Adam without having least care for their consequences because He has unchallenged authority and power over everything.

Muslim reports from Hadrat Aisha (may Allah be pleased with her) that the Messenger of Allah (peace and blessings of Allah be upon him) said:

ان الله خلق للجنة اهلاً خلقهم لها وهم فى اصلابِ آبائهم وخلق للنار اهلاً خلقهم لها وهم فى اصلاب آبائهم -

"Allah, the Almighty created people liable to be sent to Heaven even when they were in the back of their fathers; and the Hellish people when they were in the back of their fathers."

That is, Allah, the Almighty confirmed the hellishness and heavenliness before their birth in this world and they acted accordingly.

Bukhari and Muslim report from Ibn Mas'ood (may Allah be pleased with him) that the Holy Prophet (peace and blessings of Allah be upon him) said, he was truthful and was called truthful by Allah, the Almighty:

ان خلق احدكم يجمع فى بطن امه اربعين يوماً نطفة ثم يكون علقةً مثل ذلك ثم يبعث الله اليه ملكاً باربعِ كلماتٍ فيكتب عمله واجله ورزقه وشقىٌ او سعيدٌ ثم ينفخُ فيه الروح فوالذى لا اله غيره ان احدكم ليعملُ بعمل اهل الجنة حتى ما يكون بينه وبينها الا زراعٌ فيسبق عليه الكتاب فيعمل بعمل اهل النار فيدخلها وان احدكم ليعمل بعمل اهل النار حتى مايكون بينه وبينها الا زراعٌ فيسبقُ عليه الكتاب فيعمل بعمل اهل الجنة فيدخلها ـ

"The process of creation is the same for one and all. Every person remains in the womb of his mother in the form of sperm for forty days; thereafter, he takes to the form of blood for another forty days, followed by forty days in the form of a lump of flesh. Thereafter, Allah, the Almighty, sends toward it for performing four things: he writes his (man's) deeds, death, livelihood, and good or bad nature. After that he breaths the spirit in it concerning that none is liable to be worshipped but Allah. Afterwards, he goes on performing Heavenly acts so that there is a distance of a cubit between him and the Heaven and then he starts doing like Hellish men and enters the Hell. And some of you go on performing Hellish acts and there remains a distance of a cubit between him and the Hell that he starts doing like Heavenly persons and enters the Heaven."

That is, the Messenger of Allah was truthful and Allah, the Almighty, has also called him truthful. He has denoted that every human being takes the human form in the womb of his mother in one hundred twenty days. Thereafter Allah, the Almighty sends an angel to him who writes for him that he will do such and such things, will die in such and such year, in such and such place, how much he will eat and whether he will be of good nature or bad. Only after writing all these things, the angel will breathe spirit in the form. After birth he goes to Heaven and Hell according to what has already been written for him.

In short, none should be proud of his wisdom and should not rely on it but on the blessings and benedictions of Allah alone. One should keep fearing his end, for if his end is good, it is good for him otherwise it is terrible for him.

Muslim reports from Abu Musa (may Allah be pleased with him) that the Messenger of Allah (peace and blessings of Allah be upon him) got up and addressed signifying five things:

ان اللـه لاينـام ولاينبغـى لـه ان ينـام يخفـضُ القسـط
ويرفعه يرفع اليه عمل اليل قبل عمل النهـار و عمـل
النهار قبل عمل الليل حجابه النور لو كشفه لاحرفت
سبحان وجهه ما انتهى اليه بصره من خلقه -

"Lo! Allah does not sleep because sleeping causes neglect and negligence is harmful, and Allah, the Almighty is away from harm and loss; He raises the scale for whom He wants and lowers it for whoever He wants; He knows before the night what His servants do in the day and He comes to know before the day what His servants do in the night; He is so great and magnificent that if He unveil Himself His Light get everything burnt till the reach of an eye."

This *hadith* makes it clear that although nobody can change the decrees of Allah, He can Himself effect any change according to His Will. He has in His Hand the scale of destiny. He raises the scales and lowers it down at His Will. He is aware of everything.

Tirmidhi and Ibn Majah report from Anas (may Allah be pleased with him) that the Messenger of Allah (peace and blessings of Allah be upon him) would so often say:

يَا مُقَلِّبُ القُلُوب ثَبِّت قلبى على دينك فقلت يا نبى اللـه
آمنا بك وبما جئت به فهل تخافُ علينا قال نعم ان
القلوب بين اصبعين من اصابع الله يقلبها كيف يشآء

"O turner of heart, keep my heart stuck to my Faith !"

"O Messenger of Allah ! Do you fear that we will turn away from our Faith ?" I submitted.

"Yes ! the heart lies between two fingers of Allah and He turns it as He likes."

It is an undeniable fact that all the Prophets are Heavenly and all the Prophets leave the world on Faith. Hence the Apostle have no fear of losing Faith. Anas (may Allah be pleased with him), therefore, rightly thought that the supplication (cited above) belonged to them.

It means it lies in the hand of Allah to let one keep going along the right or the wrong path. Hence, everybody should keep looking towards Him for true Guidance.

Muslim reports from Abdullah bin Umar (may Allah be pleased with him) that the Holy Prophet (peace and blessings of Allah be upon him) once came out with two books and asked:

اتدرون ما هذان الكتابان قلنا لايا رسول الله الا ان تخبرنا فقال للذى فى يده اليمنى هذا كتابٌ من رب العالمين فيه اسمآء اهل الجنة واسمآء آبآئهم وقبآئلهم ثم اجمل على آخرهم فلا يزادُ فيهم ولا ينقص منهم ابداً ثم قال للذى فى شماله هذا كتابٌ من رب العالمين فيه اسمآء اهل النار واسمآء آبآئهم وقبآئلهم ثم اجمل على آخرهم فلا يزادُ فيهم ولاينقص منهم ابداً

"Do you know what these books are about?"

"We don't know O'Messenger of Allah, please tell us" we submitted.

"The book in my right hand has been sent from Allah, the Lord of the worlds, and herein are written the names of the Heavenly people with the names of their fathers and relatives; and about the book in his left hand he said that this book has also been sent from the Lord of the worlds; and herein are written the names of the Hellish people with the names of their fathers and relatives."

Thereupon the Companions (may Allah be pleased with them) said:

اصحابه ففيمَ العمل يا رسول الله إن كان امرٌ قد فرغ
منه فقال سددوا وقاربوا فان صاحب الجنة يختم له
بعمل اهل الجنة وان عمل اى عملٍ وان صاحب النار
يختم له بعمل اهل النار وان عمل اى عملٍ ثم قال
رسول الله صلى الله عليه وسلم بيديه فنبذهما ثم قال
قد فرغ ربكم من العباد فريقٌ فى النار -

"What is the use of doing anything when everything is decided beforehand?"

"Keep the right line and serve Him because the Heavenly people have their end on good and Hellish have their end on bad deeds," he said.

The Apostle, thereafter, threw away the books behind him and said:

"Your Lord has already made a decision regarding the Heavenly and the Hellish people."

That is, when the Messenger of Islam (peace and blessings of Allah be upon him) denoted that Allah, the Almighty has put down names of the Heavenly and Hellish people with their parenthood and with the remark that there will be no change at all. Allah the Almighty has already decided about their Heavenliness and Hellishness. Thereupon the Companions of the Messenger of Allah (peace and blessings of Allah be upon them) said as to what was the use of doing good deed when Heaven or Hell was destined beforehand. Thereupon, the Apostle denoted that those who are Heavenly start doing good deeds and vice versa. Hence one should keep doing good and leave the result to Allah, the Almighty.

Ahmad, Tirmidhi and Ibn Majah report from Abi Khuzamah

that he heard his parents say that they submitted:

يا رسول اللـــه ارأيـت رُقـىً رقيهـا ودواءً فتـداوى بـه وتقاةً فتقيها هل ترد من قـدر اللـه شـيئاً قـال هـى مـن قدر الله ـ

> "O' Messenger of Allah! We repeat incantation over a patient and try to save him with medical treatment, but can these devices recover a patient if written destiny had decided otherwise? 'All these (devices) are also a part of his destiny written by Allah, the Almighty."

That is, the Companion of the Holy Prophet (peace and blessings of Allah be upon him) thought that repeating incantation over the patient, medical treatment, supplication, charity etc. and other such devices are futile if the decision about patient has already been taken. Thereupon, the Messenger of Allah (peace and blessings of Allah be upon him) said that adopting such devices also belong to destiny. Hence, one should not apply his power of reasoning on such occasions and do as ordained by Allah and His Messenger.

Bukhari and Muslim report from Ali (may Allah be pleased with him) that the Holy Prophet (peace and blessings of Allah be upon him) said:

ما منكم من احدٍ الا وقد كتب مقعدهُ من النار ومقعـدهُ من الجنة قالوا يا رســول اللـه افـلا نتكلُ علـى كتابنـا وندعُ العمل قال اعملوا فكلٌ ميسرٌ لما خلق له اما من كان من اهل السعادة فسيسره لعمل السعادة وامـا مـن كان من اهل الشقاوة فسيسر لعمل اشقيآء ثم قرأ فَاَمَّـا مَن اعطى وَاتَّقى وَصَدَّقَ بِالحُسنى الاية ـ

> "For everyone of you a place has already been fixed either in the Heaven or Hell."

Thereupon, the Companions submitted:

> "O' Messenger of Allah! should we not rely on what is written and abandon doing anything?"

> "Go on doing deeds for he will get for which he has been created; good-natured persons are assigned good tasks and bad-natured persons bad tasks."

Thereafter, the Messenger of Allah (peace and blessings of Allah be upon him) recited a verse meaning:

> "One who maintains piety and believed the Qur'an as true, he will find his path easy to tread on; one who practised misery and chose to pass a careless life and sought to falsify the Qur'an will find his path difficult."

That is, for a virtuous person, virtuous resources are collected so that his path becomes smooth and easy; for wicked person foul resources are accumulated and his path becomes difficult and arduous. Hence, if anyone finds virtues around him he should pay his thanks for this mercy and try to follow the path of virtue. Similarly, if one feels that vices have surrounded him, he should desist from them and abandon them as soon as possible.

Bukhari and Muslim report from Sahl, the son of Sa'd that the Holy Prophet (peace and blessings of Allah be upon him) said:

ان العبد يعمل عمل اهل النار وانه من اهل الجنة
ويعمل عمل اهل الجنة وانه من اهل النار وانما
الاعمال بالخواتم -

> "One is destined to get Heaven although he acts like Hellish people; similarly, one is Hellish but he acts like

Heavenly people —— hence it is the end which is decisive."

This and other *ahadith* mentioned in this chapter occur in the 'Chapter On Faith' in Mish'kat. The obvious meaning of these *ahadith* is that a person is Heavenly but in the beginning he acts like Hellish people but goes to Heaven by doing virtuous acts at the later years of his life. Similarly, one is destined to be Hellish, but in the beginning he acts like Heavenly people, but goes to Hell by doing evil acts at the latter part of his life. In short, to believe the destiny is obligatory. Virtue and vice are indicated by Allah, the Almighty.

Chaptre - Four

About Companions and Ahl-e-Bait of the Messenger of Allah

فِي ذِكْرِ
الصَّحَابَةِ وَاَهْلِ الْبَيْتِ رَضِيَ اللهُ عَنْهُمْ

This chapter consists of the verses and *ahadith* which establish the virtues and excellences of the Companions and *ahle-e-bait* (members of the family of the Holy Prophet, consisting of Hadrat Ali, Hadrat Fatima and their children). A Companion is one who kept the company of the Messenger of Allah (peace and blessings of Allah be upon him) as a Believer. *Ahl-e-bait* means family members like wives, children, son-in-law, grand children etc. Slaves, slave-girls, adopted children also belong to this category. Hence Abu Bakr Siddiq, Umar Farooq, Uthman, Ali, Talha, Zubair, Abdur Rahman, Sa'd, Sa'id, Abu Ubaidah, Abu Hurairah, Anas, Belal, Mua'wiyya together with those the Muhajir, the Ansar, crusaders in the way of Allah, participaters of the battles of Badr Uhad, Khayber and Treaty of Hudaibiya etc. (may Allah be pleased with all of them) were all Companions of the Apostle. Their traits and virtues have been described in the Holy Qur'an and *ahadith*. To keep loving to follow their path is the sign of Faith. Hence, one who shows disrespect to them is one who rejects the Qur'an and *hadith* and obviously his abode is Hell. Similarly, Hadrat Khadija, Hafsa, Aisha, Zainab, Umm Salma, Umm

Habiba, Javiriah, Maimuna, Maria Qibtiya (all wives of the Apostle): Fatima, Umm Kulthum (daughter of the Apostle), Ali Murtaza, Uthman (sons-in-law) etc. (may Allah be pleased with all of them) ——all these include the house of the Messenger of Allah. So, to love them and follow their courses is the symbol of Islam and Iman. Hence, one who loves them not or reproaches them is a man of defective Faith, for their praise and eulogy is testified by the Qur'an and hadith. Thus a person who looks down upon them commits renouncement of the Qur'an and hadith. Naturally, such a person will find his abode in the Hell. These Companions of the Messenger of Allah (peace and blessings of Allah be upon him) followed him and helped him in spreading the message of Allah, were true ideals for the Believers to follow.

Allah, the Almighty says in Surah A'raf of the Holy Qur'an:

وَرَحْمَتِى وَسِعَتْ كُلَّ شَىْءٍ فَسَأَكْتُبُهَا لِلَّذِينَ يَتَّقُونَ
وَيُؤْتُونَ الزَّكوٰةَ وَالَّذِينَ هُم بِآيَاتِنَا يُؤْمِنُونَ الَّذِينَ يَتَّبِعُونَ
الرَّسُولَ النَّبِى الأُمِىَّ الَّذِينَ يَجِدُونَهُ مَكْتُوباً عِندَهُمْ فِى
التَّوراةِ وَالإِنجِيلَ يَأْمُرُهُم بِالْمَعْرُوفِ وَيَنهَاهُمْ عَنِ الْمُنكَرِ
وَيُحِلُّ لَهُمُ الطَّيِّبَاتِ وَيُحَرِّمُ عَلَيهِمُ الْخَبَآئِثَ وَيَضَعُ عَنهُم
إِصرَهُم وَالأَغلاَلَ الَّذِى كَانَتْ عَلَيهِمْ فَالَّذِينَ آمَنُوا بِهِ
وَعَزَّرُوهُ وَنَصَرُوهُ وَاتَّبَعُوا النُّورَ الَّذِى أُنزِلَ مَعَهُ أُولَٰئِكَ هُمُ
الْمُفلِحُونَ ـ

"My Mercy extendeth to all things. That (Mercy) I shall ordain for those who do right, and pay *Zakat* and those who believe in Our Signs; those who follow the Messenger, the unlettered Prophet, whom they find mentioned in their own (Scriptures), in the Taurat and the Gospel; for he commands them what is just and forbids them what is evil; he allows them as lawful what is good (and pure) and prohibits them from what is bad (and impure): He releases them from their heavy burdens and from the yokes that are upon them. So it is those who believe in him, honour him, help him, and follow the Light which is sent down with him, it is they who will prosper."

(Q.7:156-157).

That is, Allah, the Almighty says that although His Mercy encompasses all, but it will be noted down for those who put their faith in the unlettered Prophet i.e., the Messenger of Allah (peace and blessings of Allah be upon him), migrated with him to Madinah leaving their households in Mak'kah; those who accommodated the Apostle in Madinah and extended all kinds of help, followed the Holy Qur'an in letter and spirit; those who fear Allah, pay *Zakat*, believe in the commands of Allah, such persons acheive success and get the Heaven as reward. The Companions, particularly four of them, were the true comrades of the Messenger of Allah (peace and blessings of Allah be upon him); they helped a lot in spreading Islam; they feared Allah, the Almighty most; they were pious; paid *Zakat* and followed the Commands of Allah in all the departments of life. Hence, the Almighty wrote for them a Heavenly life and denigrating them means renouncing the Mercy of Allah.

Allah, the Almighty says in Surah Al-Anbiya' of the Holy Qur'an:

وَلَقَدْ كَتَبْنَا فِى الزَّبُورِ مِن م بَعدِ الذِّكْرِ اَنَّ الاَرضَ يَرِثُهَا عِبَادِىَ الصَّالِحُونَ ـ

"Before this We wrote in the Psalms, after the Message (given to Moses): My servants the righteous, shall inherit the earth."

This verse also goes in favour of the Companions of the Messenger of Allah (peace and blessings of Allah be upon him). Here, Allah, the Almighty says that He revealed Taurat (Torah) to Hadrat Musa (peace be on him), then sent down Psalms to Hadrat Dawud (peace be upon him). Hence, first in Taurat and then in Psalms, I have already written that from now on only My righteous slaves will inherit the earth. Accordingly, Hadrat Abu Bakr, Umar, Uthman and Ali (may Allah be pleased with them) became the ruler of a large territory and Hadrat Imam Mehdi is to appear.

It is clear from this that the Caliphs were the righteous servants of Allah and one who renounces them as hypocrites and transgressors is the rejector of this verse.

Allah, the Almighty says in Surah Al-Hajj of the Holy Qur'an:

اَلَّذِينَ إِنْ مَّكَّنّٰهُمْ فِى الْاَرْضِ اَقَامُوا الصَّلٰوةَ وَاٰتَوُا الزَّكٰوةَ

وَاَمَرُوْا بِالْمَعْرُوْفِ وَنَهَوْا عَنِ الْمُنْكَرِ وَلِلّٰهِ عَاقِبَةُ الْاُمُوْرِ:

"(They are) those who, if We establish them in the land, establish regular prayer and give *Zakat*, enjoin the right and forbid wrong: with Allah rests the end (and decision) of (all) affairs."

(Q.22:41).

Prior to this verse, Allah, the Almighty has mentioned about the Holy Companions of the Messenger of Allah (peace and blessings of Allah be upon him), how they were driven out due to be of Faith. Hence Allah, the Almighty helped them and praising them said that if they were installed as ruler on earth they will establish *Salat*, pay *Zakat*, enjoin the right and forbid wrong: Allah keeps control over all affairs.

It is also clear from this verse that the Muhajirin (migrants), particularly four Caliphs of Islam, enjoined upon people tasks which were accepted to Allah, the Almighty. Hence, Allah fulfilled His promise and conferred on them power on earth.

Allah, the Almighty says in Surah Al-Fat'h of the Holy Qur'an:

مُحَمَّدٌ رَّسُولُ اللَّهِ وَالَّذِينَ مَعَهُ أَشِدَّاءُ عَلَى الْكُفَّارِ رُحَمَاءُ
بَيْنَهُمْ تَرَاهُمْ رُكَّعًا سُجَّدًا يَبْتَغُونَ فَضْلًا مِّنَ اللَّهِ وَرِضْوَانًا
سِيمَاهُمْ فِي وُجُوهِهِم مِّنْ أَثَرِ السُّجُودِ ذَٰلِكَ مَثَلُهُمْ فِي
التَّوْرَاةِ وَمَثَلُهُمْ فِي الْإِنجِيلِ كَزَرْعٍ أَخْرَجَ شَطْأَهُ فَآزَرَهُ
فَسْتَغْلَظَ فَاسْتَوَىٰ عَلَىٰ سُوقِهِ يُعْجِبُ الزُّرَّاعَ لِيَغِيظَ بِهِمُ
الْكُفَّارَ وَعَدَ اللَّهُ الَّذِينَ آمَنُوا وَعَمِلُوا الصَّالِحَاتِ مِنْهُم
مَّغْفِرَةً وَأَجْرًا عَظِيمًا :

> "Muhammad is the Messenger of Allah; and those who are with him are strong against Unbelievers, (but) compassionate amongst each other. Thou wilt see them bow and prostrate themselves (in prayer), seeking Grace from Allah and (His) Good Pleasure. On their faces are their marks, (being) the traces of their prostration. This is their similitude in the Taurat, and their similitude in the Gospel is: Like a seed which sends forth its blade, then makes it strong; it then becomes thick, and it stands on its own stem, (filling) the sowers with wonder and delight. As a result, it fills the Unbelievers with rage at them. Allah has promised those among them who believe and do righteous deeds forgiveness, and a great Reward."
>
> (Q.48:29).

This verse eulogizes Muhammad (peace and blessings of Allah be upon him) and his Companions (may Allah be pleased with them) so that their traits and chracters come to light for those who seek guidance and right path.

It has also been clear that the company of the Messenger of Allah (peace and blessings of Allah be upon him) brings about radical change among his Companions. One of their traits is that they are strong against Unbelievers but compassionate among themselves, keep themselves engaged in prayer, have Light of Allah on their faces and are recognized among thousands due to their prostrations. Their internal trait is that they keep dear the Pleasure of Allah and exert for His Favour. They neither want wealth nor power. They harbour no hypocracy. When the Believers achieved power on earth, Allah and His Messenger (peace and blessings of Allah be upon him) were happy and satisfied while the Unbelievers got angry and annoyed. The holy Companions of the Apostle will be rewarded while the Unbelievers will be severely punished.

Hadrat Abu Bakr Siddiq (may Allah be pleased with him) loved the Holy Prophet (peace and blessings of Allah be upon him) beyond all descriptions; he accompanied the Apostle in the Cave of *Thaur*, and was buried with the Messenger of Allah. Thus, he set the example of being one with the Prophet of Islam.

The day Hadrat Umar ibn Khattab (may Allah be pleased with him) embraced Islam, the Muslims came out in the open to say their prayer. Before this, they used to say their prayers in hiding. With his embracing of Islam, the Muslims got stronger and stronger and the Unbelievers got frightened. During his Caliphate the Muslim got hold in thousands of cities. Thus he exemplified how the Muslims can become strong against the Unbelievers.

Hadrat Uthman (may Allah be pleased with him), the third Caliph of Islam showed with his glittering example how one can become compassionate to the Muslims. When he was surrounded by the rebels, about two thousand armed slaves were on guard for him. But he freed them all saying that he did not want bloodshed even if he was killed. With the result, the freed slaves left and the insurgents killed the Caliph.

Hadrat Ali (may Allah be pleased with him) showed with

personal example how to get lost in prayer. He was slain in the state of prostration. Hence *tarahum ruk'ka'an sujjadan* is fully applied to them. Moreover, if you ponder over you would find that each of them retained all these four qualities and all of them were obliged to Allah alone. In short, this *ayah* makes it clear that the inward and the outward of these Companions was one and the same and they had towards them the Mercy of Almighty for ever. The torah and the Gospel had reference about them. Moreover, Allah made these Companions praiseworthy and of highest qualities to arouse jealousy annoyance and irritations among the unbelievers. It means one who is displeased at the praise and virtues of the Companions is an Unbeliever and rejected by Almighty Allah. It is also clear from the *ayah* that if any Companion commits any sin he stands as forgiven for Almighty Allah has made a promise to forgive them.

Allah, the Almighty says in Surah Al-Hashr of the Holy Qur'an:

لِلْفُقَرَاءِ الْمُهَاجِرِينَ الَّذِينَ أُخْرِجُوا مِن دِيَارِهِمْ وَأَمْوَالِهِمْ
يَبْتَغُونَ فَضْلًا مِّنَ اللَّهِ وَرِضْوَانًا وَيَنصُرُونَ اللَّهَ وَرَسُولَهُ
أُولَٰئِكَ هُمُ الصَّادِقُونَ وَالَّذِينَ تَبَوَّءُوا الدَّارَ وَالْإِيمَانَ مِن قَبْلِهِمْ
يُحِبُّونَ مَنْ هَاجَرَ إِلَيْهِمْ وَلَا يَجِدُونَ فِي صُدُورِهِمْ حَاجَةً
مِّمَّا أُوتُوا وَيُؤْثِرُونَ عَلَىٰ أَنفُسِهِمْ وَلَوْ كَانَ بِهِمْ خَصَاصَةٌ
وَمَن يُوقَ شُحَّ نَفْسِهِ فَأُولَٰئِكَ هُمُ الْمُفْلِحُونَ :

"(Some part is due) to the indigent Muhajirs, those who were expelled from their homes and their property, while seeking Grace from Allah and (His) Good Pleasure, and aiding Allah and His Messenger: such are indeed the truthful; — and those who before them, had homes (in Madinah) and had adopted the Faith, show their affection to such as came to them for refuge, and entertain no desire in their hearts for things given to the (latter), but give them preference over themselves, even though poverty was their (own lot). And those saved from the covetousness of their own souls, they are the ones that achieve prosperity."

(Q.59: 8-9).

Among the Companions of the Messenger of Allah (peace and blessings of Allah be upon him) were those who left their homes and properties for the sake of Allah and came to Madinah to fight with the Apostle in the way of Allah. Allah, the Almighty declared them righteous.

Another section of people lived in Madinah and they were called Ansar. They accommodated the Muhajirs and provided them food and clothes and preferred them to their own lives. They starved to feed their Muhajir brethren. Both these groups lived and died in the Cause of Allah without any wordly greed. Allah, the Almighty has praised both the Muhajirs and Ansar in the Holy Qur'an. The Muhajirs left their all for the Pleasure of Allah and the Ansar spent lavishly in the cause of Allah. They rose above all selfishness, greed and avarice, and became successful.

Allah, the Almighty says in Surah Al-Hadid of the Holy Qur'an:

لَايَستَوِى مِنكُم مَن اَنفَقَ مِن قَبلِ الفَتحِ وَقَاتَلَ اُولٰئِكَ
اَعظَمُ دَرَجَةً مِّنَ الَّذِينَ اَنفَقُوا مِن بَعدُ وَ قَاتَلُوا وَكُلًّا
وَّعَدَاللّٰهُ الحُسنٰى وَاللّٰهُ بِمَا تَعمَلُونَ خَبِيرٌ:

"Not equal among you are those who spent (freely) and fought, before the victory, (with those are higher in rank than those who spent (freely) and fought afterwards. But to all has Allah promised a goodly (reward). And Allah is well acquainted with all ye do."

(Q.57:10).

Before the conquest of Mak'kah, most of the Muslims were economically weak and needy. *Jihad* (holy war) made them stronger and established their superiority on them. Moreover, they have great status in the eyes of Allah, the Almighty. Some of the Companions have greater status in regard to fighting and spending in the cause of Allah.

Allah, the Almighty says in Surah At-Tauba of the Holy Qur'an:

وَالسّٰبِقُونَ الاَوَّلُونَ مِنَ الْمُهٰجِرِينَ وَالاَنصَارِ وَالَّذِينَ اتَّبَعُوهُم بِاِحسَانٍ رَضِيَ اللّٰهُ عَنهُم وَرَضُوا عَنهُ وَاَعَدَّ لَهُم جَنّٰتٍ تَجرِي مِن تَحتِهَا الاَنهَارُ خٰلِدِينَ فِيهَا اَبَدًا ذَالِكَ الفَوزُ العَظِيمُ :

"The vanguard (of Islam) the first of those who forsook (their homes) and of those who gave them aid, and (also) those who follow them in (all) good deeds, well-pleased is Allah with them, as are they with Him: For them hath He prepared Gardens under which rivers flow, to dwell therein for ever: that is the supreme Triumph."

(Q.9:100)

Those who embraced Islam till the Battle of Badr are supposed to be old and senior and those who confessed Islam after the Battle were junior to them. *'Muhajirs'* were those who migrated from Mak'kah with the Holy Prophet (peace and blessings of Allah be upon him); Ansar were those who were the inhabitants of Madinah and accommodated the Muhajirs with fooding and lodging. Allah, the Almighty declared that He became pleased with all those people and they with Him. And Allah, the Almighty has created Heaven for them under the gardens of which will be flowing canals and will remain there for ever. This is the greatest reward for the Heavenly people. How unfortunate and wicked is that section who keep malice and enmity against these pious and virtuous people.

Allah, the Almighty says in Surah Al-Fat'h of the Holy Qur'an:

لَقَدْ رَضِيَ اللّٰهُ عَنِ الْمُؤْمِنِيْنَ اِذْ يُبَايِعُوْنَكَ تَحْتَ الشَّجَرَةِ فَعَلِمَ مَافِيْ قُلُوْبِهِمْ فَانْزَلَ السَّكِيْنَةَ عَلَيْهِمْ وَاَثَابَهُمْ فَتْحًا قَرِيْبًا :

> "Allah's Good Pleasure was on the Believers when they swore Fealty to thee under the Tree: He knew what was in their hearts, and He sent down Tranquillity to them; and He rewarded them with speedy victory."
>
> (Q.48:18).

The Messenger of Allah (peace and blessings of Allah be upon him) once reached Mak'kah with the sole intention of performing *Umrah* (pilgrimage to Mak'kah on days other than the Hajj days). After making a halt at Hudaibiyah near Mak'kah, the Apostle sent Uthman (may Allah be pleased with him), a Companion of his to tell the pagans of Mak'kah that they had come only to perform *Umrah* and not to fight against them. Circumstances at Mak'kah led him to overstay there giving birth to rumour that Uthman (may Allah be pleased with him) was martyred. Thereupon, the Messenger of Allah (peace and blessings of Allah be upon him) asked his Companions to assemble under a tree to take the bai'at (oath of allegiance) to wage *Jihad* against the Unbelievers of Mak'kah. Thus one thousand five hundred Companions took *bai'at* to fight against the Mak'kans. Thereupon, Allah, the Almighty revealed this ayah (verse) so that their sincerity and obedience came to light.

This *ayah* reveals that Allah became pleased with them and for others nothing can be said.

Allah, the Almighty says in Surah An-Nur of the Holy Qur'an:

وَعَدَاللّٰهُ الَّذِينَ اٰمَنُو مِنكُم وَعَمِلوُالصّٰلِحٰتِ لَيَستَخلِفَنَّهُم
فِى الاَرضِ كَمَا استَخلَفَ الَّذِينَ مِن قَبلِهِم وَلَيُمَكِّنَنَّ لَهُم
دِينَهُمُ الَّذِى ارتَضٰى لَهُم وَلَيُبَدِّلَنَّهُم مِنْ بَعدِ خَوفِهِم اَمنًا
يَّعبُدُونَنِى لاَيُشرِكُونَ بِى شَيًاً وَمَن كَفَرَ بَعدَ ذَالِكَ
فَاُولٰئِكَ هُمُ الفَاسِقُونَ :

> "Allah has promised, to those among you who believe and work righteous deeds, that He will, of a surety, grant them in the land, inheritance (of power), as He granted it to those before them; that He will establish in authority their religion the one which He has chosen for them; and that He will change (their state), after the fear in which they (lived), to one of security and peace: 'They will worship Me (alone) and not associate aught with Me,' If any do reject Faith after this, they are rebellious and wicked."
> (Q.24:55)

That is, those who had confessed Islam by the time this *ayah* was revealed, were promised to be installed as ruler on earth. Thus a few of them became caliphs as Hadrat Dawud (peace be upon him) and several others had been appointed caliphs and rulers in the past.

It is also clear that their Faith and attitude were loved by Allah, the Almighty. Thus, those who refuse to accept and pay regards to them as Caliphs of Allah are the transgressers. They reject what Allah has graced.

Allah, the Almighty says in Surah Al-Lail of the Holy Qur'an:

وَسَيُجَنَّبُهَا الاَتقَى الَّذِى يُوتِى مَالَهٗ يَتَزَكّٰى وَمَالِاَحَدٍ عِنْدَهٗ
مِن نِعمَةٍ تُجزٰى اِلَّا ابتِغَاءَ وَجهِ رَبِّهِ الاَعلٰى وَلَسَوفَ يَرضٰى

> "But those most devoted to Allah shall be removed far from it, those who spend their wealth for increase in self-purification, and have in their minds no favour from anyone for which a reward is expected in return, but only the desire to seek for the Countenance of their Lord Most High; and soon will they attain (complete) satisfaction."
> (Q.92: 17-21)

This *ayah* is being revealed in favour of Hadrat Abu Bakr Siddiq (may Allah be pleased with him), because he had spent his all in the way of Allah on needy and destitues, for purchasing land for building a mosque and for freeing slaves and slave-girls from the tortures of the pagans. He bought sixty Muslims slaves and slave-girls and freed them in the way of Allah. One of them was Hadrat Bilal (may Allah be pleased with him), who was a slave of an Unbeliever. When he embraced Islam, his accursed master kept him lying in the scorching heat surrounded by blazing fire and kept on beating him the whole night but he (Bilal) would cry and say: 'Allah is One.' When Hadrat Abu Bakr Siddiq (may Allah be pleased with him) came to know about this unfortunate event, he went to that infidel and asked him to desist from doing so. But he did not refrain from his cruelties. However, one day the pagan master of Bilal told Hadrat Abu Bakr (may Allah be pleased with him) in plain words that if he (Abu Bakr) would give him his Roman slave together with two thousand guineas, he (Bilal) would be handed over to him. Hadrat Abu Bakr (may Allah be pleased with him) purchased Hadrat Bilal (may Allah be pleased with him) in return for the Roman slave and two thousand guineas, adding forty 'Oqiah' more. He then brought Hadrat Bilal (may Allah be pleased with him) before the Messenger of Allah (peace and blessings of Allah be upon him) and set him free. Thereafter, this *ayah* was revealed in his favour. Here Allah, the Almighty Himself says that this person (Abu Bakr) is very pious, virtuous and God-fearing; he spends his wealth in the way of Allah, with the sole purpose of achieving His Favour and Pleasure. Hence I shall save him from the Fire.

It is clear from this *ayah* that Hadrat Abu Bakr Siddiq (may Allah be pleased with him) has a great status in the sight of Allah, the Almighty. And none is greater than him after the Apostle.

Allah, the Almighty says in Surah Al-Ahzab of the Holy Qur'an:

وَمَن يَقْنُتْ مِنكُنَّ لِلَّهِ وَرَسُولِهِ وَتَعْمَلْ صَالِحًا نُّؤْتِهَا
أَجْرَهَا مَرَّتَيْنِ وَأَعْتَدْنَا لَهَا رِزْقًا كَرِيمًا يَٰنِسَاءَ النَّبِيِّ لَسْتُنَّ
كَأَحَدٍ مِّنَ النِّسَاءِ إِنِ اتَّقَيْتُنَّ فَلَا تَخْضَعْنَ بِالْقَوْلِ فَيَطْمَعَ
الَّذِي فِي قَلْبِهِ مَرَضٌ وَقُلْنَ قَوْلًا مَّعْرُوفًا وَقَرْنَ فِي بُيُوتِكُنَّ
وَلَا تَبَرَّجْنَ تَبَرُّجَ الْجَاهِلِيَّةِ الْأُولَىٰ وَأَقِمْنَ الصَّلَوٰةَ وَآتِينَ
الزَّكَوٰةَ وَأَطِعْنَ اللَّهَ وَرَسُولَهُ ط إِنَّمَا يُرِيدُ اللَّهُ لِيُذْهِبَ
عَنكُمُ الرِّجْسَ أَهْلَ الْبَيْتِ وَيُطَهِّرَكُمْ تَطْهِيرًا ه وَاذْكُرْنَ مَا
يُتْلَىٰ فِي بُيُوتِكُنَّ مِنْ آيَاتِ اللَّهِ وَالْحِكْمَةِ ط إِنَّ اللَّهَ كَانَ
لَطِيفًا خَبِيرًا ه

"But any of you that is devout in the service of Allah and His Messenger, and works righteousness, to her shall we grant Her reward twice: and We have prepared for her a generous Sustenance. O Consorts of the Prophet ! Ye are

> not like any of the (other) women: If ye do fear (Allah), be not too complaisant of speech, lest one in whose heart is a disease should be moved with desire: but speak ye a speech (that is) just. And stay quietly in your houses, and make not a dazzling display, like that of the former. Times of Ignorance; and establish regular prayer, and give *Zakat* and obey Allah and His Messenger. And Allah only wishes to remove all abomination from you, ye Members of the Family, and to make you pure and spotless. And recite what is rehearsed to you in your homes, of the Signs of Allah and His Wisdom: for Allah is All-Subtle, All-Aware."
>
> (Q.33: 31-34).

Allah, the Almighty asks the wives of the Messenger of Allah (peace and blessings of Allah be upon him) to obey Allah and His Messenger so that they be doubly rewarded. They have a place of respect in this world and the Hereafter. They have also been ordained to talk and address other men like their mother. Don't behave with them in a polite manner so that the hypocrites and transgressors make it an issue to propagate against them; keep yourselves inside your homes with honour and dignity and refrain from showing yourselves like the women of the Age of Ignorance; say prayer; give *Zakat* ; obey the Commands of Allah and His Messenger. Allah wants you to be above all evils. Keep in mind that Allah, the Almighty knows everything hidden.

This *ayah* makes it known that the consorts of the Messenger of Allah (peace and blessings of Allah be upon him) are doubly rewarded for their virtuous acts. Hence the consorts of the Apostle and other women cannot be equal in status. Allah, the Almighty Himself wanted that their inside and outside be the same.

Allah, the Almighty says in Surah Al-Ahzab of the Holy Qur'an:

النَّبِىُّ اَوْلٰى بِالْمُؤْمِنِيْنَ مِنْ اَنْفُسِهِمْ وَاَزْوَاجُهٗٓ اُمَّهٰتُهُمْ :

> "The Prophet is closer to the Believers than their own selves, and his wives are their mothers."
>
> (Q.33:6)

That is, the Believers keep the Messenger of Allah (peace and blessings of Allah be upon him) dearer to even their own selves, because the Messenger is the vicegerent of Allah, the Almighty. None has power over his life and property as much as the Apostle has over theirs. And since the consorts of the Messenger of Allah (peace and blessings of Allah be upon him) are the mothers of the *Ummah*, they cannot be married to any of them.

Bukhari and Muslim report from Sa'yeed al-Khudri (may Allah be pleased with him) that the Messenger of Allah (peace and blessings of Allah be upon him) said:

ان من امن الناس على فى صحبته وماله ابى بكر :

> "Abu Bakr is above all others in keeping company with me, in spending money (in the way of Allah) and in obliging me in all respects."

That is, Abu Bakr Siddiq (may Allah be pleased with him) obliged the Messenger of Allah (peace and blessings of Allah be upon him) in all respects. He kept constant company with the Apostle through thick and thin; spent money lavishly with his (Prephet's) will and pleasure. Now, when the chief of all the Muslims is obliged to Abu Bakr Siddiq (may Allah be pleased with him) what to speak of his status. The entire Muslim world, till the Day of Resurrection, will remain obliged to him.

Tirmidhi reports from Abu Hurairah (may Allah be pleased with him) that the Holy Prophet (peace and blessings of Allah be upon him) said:

مالاحد عندنا يد الا كافيناه ما خلا ابا بكر يكا ن الله

يوم القيمة ما نفعنى ما ل احد قط ما نفعنى مال ابى

بكر ولوكنت متخذا خليلا غير ربـى لا تخـذت ابـابكر خليلا الاوان صاحبكم خليل الله :

"None is there whose obligation I have not paid back but Abu Bakr, who will be paid by Allah, the Almighty on the Day of Judgment; none is there whose wealth has helped me in the cause of Allah more than that of Abu Bakr; had I made friendship with anybody else other than Allah, it is Abu Bakr; let it be known to you that your Companion is the bosom Friend of Allah."

By habit and nature, the Messenger of Allah (peace and blessings of Allah be upon him) paid back more than what others did for him. But he confessed that he could not return the obligations of Abu Bakr in this material and transitory world, and hence only Allah, the Almighty will pay him back on the Day of Judgment because only He has the Power and Capacity to do so. Moreover, objects and items of the Paradise are of permanent nature. Abu Bakr Siddiq (may Allah be pleased with him) spent his all in the way of Allah and turned a pauper.

It is now clear beyond doubt that Allah and His Messenger loved Abu Bakr (may Allah be pleased with him) too much and he will be amply rewarded on the Day of Judgment, we should all pay our regard to him because it will carry Reward and Favour of Allah, the Almighty.

Tirmidhi reports from Umar (may Allah be pleased with him) to have said:

ابوبكر سيدوخيرنا واحبنا الى رسول الله صلى الله عليه وسلم :

"Abu Bakr is our chief; best of all us; and the best friend

> of the Messenger of Allah (peace and blessings of Allah be upon him)."

In order to make others pay regards to Abu Bakr, he (Umar) used to lay stress on his high status by declaring him the chief of the Muslims and the best of all in the *Ummah* of the Apostle.

Razin reports from Aisha (may Allah be pleased with him) that once the Messenger of Allah (peace and blessings of Allah be upon him) was lying with his head in my lap in a moonlit night that I asked him:

هل يكون لا حد من الحسنات عدد نجوم السماء قال نعم عمر قلت فاين حسنات ابى بكر قال انما جميع حسنات عمر كحسنة واحدة من حسنات ابى بكر :

> "Could there be virtues of anyone equal to the number of stars in the sky?"
>
> "Yes, those of Umar," he replied.
>
> "Where gone the virtues of Abu Bakr?" I asked.
>
> "All the virtues of Umar equalize one virtue of Abu Bakr," he said in reply.

Bukhari and Muslim report from Abu Hurairah (may Allah be pleased with him) that the Messenger of Allah (peace and blessings of Allah be upon him) said:

لقد كان فيما قبلكم من الامم محدثون فان يك فى امتى احد فانه عمر :

> "Certainly some persons of the past *Ummahs* had inspiration and had virtuous thoughts inculcated in their hearts; if anyone of my *Ummah* will be so, it is Umar."

That, it is the status of Hadrat Umar (may Allah be pleased with him) that virtuous thoughts would come to him on the part of Allah, the Almighty.

Tirmidhi reports from Uqbah bin Amir (may Allah be pleased with him) that the Messenger of Allah (peace and blessings of Allah be upon him) said:

لوكان بعدى نبى لكان عمربن الخطاب :

"Had anyone been a Prophet after me, it would have been Umar, the son of Khattab."

Tirmidhi reports from Jabir that Umar (may Allah be pleased with him) once said to Abu Bakr (may Allah be pleased with him):

يا خيرالناس بعد رسول الله صلىالله عليه وسلم فقال ابوبكر اما انك ان قلت ملقد سمعت رسول الله صلىالله عليه وسلم يقول

"O' the best of all, after the Messenger of Allah (peace and blessings of Allah be upon him) !"

Thereupon Abu Bakr (may Allah be pleased with him) said:

"Listen! what the Messenger of Allah (peace and blessings of Allah be upon him) said:

ما طلعت الشمس على رجل خير من عمر

"The sun never shone over anyone better than Umar."

That is, Hadrat Umar ibn Khattab (may Allah be pleased with him) once said to Abu Bakr (may Allah be pleased with him):

"You are the best of all after the Messenger of Allah (peace and blessings of Allah be upon him)."

Thereupon, Hadrat Abu Bakr Siddiq (may Allah be pleased with him) said in reply:

'You say I am the best, although I have heard the Holy Prophet (peace and blessings of Allah be upon him) say that none over whom the sun shines is better than Umar."

That is, none of the men born on this earth was better than Umar. It means none is better than Umar after the Messenger of Allah (peace and blessings of Allah be upon him).

Bukhari and Muslim report from Hadrat Abdullah bin Umar (may Allah be pleased with him) that he heard the Messenger of Allah (peace and blessings of Allah be upon him) say:

بین انا نائم اوتیت بقدح لبن فشربت حتی انـی لا ری
الری یخرج فی اظفاری ثم اعطیت فضلی عمر ابـن
الخطاب قالو افما اولته یارسول الله قال العلم :

"I was asleep that I was given a cup of milk and I drank to the fill; Thereafter, I gave the cup to Umar, the son of Khattab."

Thereupon, the Companions (may Allah be pleased with them) submitted:

"What is the interpretation of this dream, O' Messenger of Allah?"

"Knowledge!" the Apostle replied.

That is, the cup of milk given to the Messenger of Allah (peace and blessings of Allah be upon him) was the cup of Knowledge which he gave Umar after drinking to the fill.

This *hadith* makes it clear that none had so much knowledge of religion as Hadrat Umar (may Allah be pleased with him) had after the Messenger of Allah.

Tirmidhi reports from Abdullah ibn Umar (may Allah be pleased with him) that the Holy Prophet (peace and blessings of Allah be upon him) said:

ان الله جعل الحق على لسان عمرو قلبه

> "Allah, the Almighty has affixed truth on the heart and tongue of Umar."

That is, what comes out of the tongue of Umar (may Allah be pleased with him) is nothing but Truth; and what enters his heart is also truth. Nothing comes out or goes in his heart but from Allah and His Messenger.

Abu Dawud, Tirmidhi and Ibn Majah report from Abu Sayeed al-Khudri (may Allah be pleased with him) that the Holy Prophet (peace and blessings of Allah be upon him) said:

ان اهل الجنة ليترون اهله عليين كما ترون الكوكب

الدرى فى افق السماء وان ابابكر وعمر منهم وانعما

> "Certainly, the Heavenly people will see Hadrat Abu Bakr and Umar (may Allah be pleased with them) as you see bright stars in the sky."

That is, Hadrat Abu Bakr and Umar (may Allah be pleased with him) will have such an elevated position in the Heaven that Heavenly beings will see them like the bright stars.

Ibn Majah reports from Ali and Tirmidhi from Anas (may Allah be pleased with them) that the Holy Prophet (peace and blessings of Allah be upon him) said:

ابوبکر وعمر سید اکهول اهل الجنة من الاولین والاخرین الاالنبین والمرسلین:

"Both Abu Bakr and Umar will be chiefs of the aged men of the Heaven save Prophets and Messengers."

That is, one who dies after being aged and goes to Heaven, will find Hadrat Abu Bakr and Umar (may Allah be pleased with them) as his chiefs. And if they will be the chiefs of aged persons, they will naturally be chiefs of the youths as well. It means they will be the chiefs of all the Heavenly people except the Prophets. None can be equivalent to Hadrat Abu Bakr Siddiq and Umar ibn Khattab (may Allah be pleased with them); neither in this world, nor in the Hereafter.

Tirmidhi reports from Hudhaifa (may Allah be pleased with him) that the Holy Prophet (peace and blessings of Allah be upon him) said:

انی لا ادری ما بقائی فیکم فاقتدوابالذین من بعدی ابی بکر وعمر :

"I don't know how long I shall live; you should follow those following me like Abu Bakr and Umar."

From the injunction to follow the course of Abu Bakr and Umar after him, it becomes clear beyond doubt that in religious activities and administration, welfare and reformation of the *Ummah*, these two persons had no equal.

Tirmidhi reports from Talha, the son of Obaidullah (may Allah be pleased with him) that the Messenger of Allah (peace and blessings of Allah be upon him) said:

لکل نبی رفیق ورفیقی فی الجنة عثمان :

> "Every Prophet has a Companion, and my Companion in the Heaven is Uthman."

That is, every Prophet has Companions who keep company with him, in this world and the Hereafter; hence, according to the Apostle, Uthman will be his Companion in the Heaven.

Imam Ahmad reports from Abdur Rahman bin Samurah:

جاء عثمان الى النبى صلى الله عليه واله وسلم بالف دينار فى كمه حين جهزجيش العسرة فنشرها فى حجره فرايت النبى صلى الله عليه وسلم يقلبها يقول ما ضر عثمان ماعمل بعداليوم مرتين :

> "Uthman brought one thousand guineas under his sleeve to the Messenger of Allah (peace and blessings of Allah be upon him) and put them into the lap of the Apostle for the preparation of an army. The Holy Prophet (peace and blessings of Allah be upon him) would scatter the amount in his lap and say: Let Uthman do whatever he likes from this day on and he will have no harm." The Apostle repeated these words twice.

That is, Uthman rendered such an exclusive service to the cause of Allah, the Almighty and it was accepted and honoured in such a manner that if any sin would have been committed by Uthman it was pardoned leaving no trace of harm behind it. This *hadith* makes it amply clear that even if any sin of Uthman is proved, it must have been pardoned forthwith. Hence none has the right to reproach him for any sin. It is as if a person regains health after sickness.

Tirmidhi and Ibn Majah report from Murrah bin Ka'b (may Allah be pleased with him) to have heard from the Messenger of

Allah (peace and blessings of Allah be upon him):

وذكر الفتن فقربها فمر رجل مقنع فى ثـوب فقـال هـذا يومئذ على الهدى فقمت اليه فاذاهو عثمـان بـن عفـان قال فاقبلت عليه فقلت هذاقال نعم :

"Disruptions will raise head in the near future."

In the meantime a man passed that way with his head covered with a piece of cloth. The Apostle, pointing him out said:

"During that period that man will be on the right track."

The man was Uthman bin Affan (may Allah be pleased with him).

That is, the Holy Prophet (peace and blessings of Allah be upon him) was once narrating the occurrences in future and disruptions taking place after he was no more. In the meantime, Hadrat Uthman (may Allah be pleased with him) passed that way. Then, pointing him out, the Messenger of Allah remarked that that person will remain on truth and righteousness.

This remark of the Apostle came true when disruption was caused after his demise, during the Caliphate of Hadrat Uthman. Thus during the uprisings against Hadrat Uthman, he was on truth till he was martyred by the insurgents.

Bukhari reports from Hadrat Anas (may Allah be pleased with him) that the Messenger of Allah (peace and blessings of Allah be upon him) once climbed on Uhad accompained by Abu Bakr, Umar and Uthman (may Allah be pleased with him). Meanwhile, Mountain Uhad moved a little. Thereupon, the Messenger of Allah (peace and blessings of Allah be upon him) said, striking the mountain with his feet:

اثبت احد فانما عليك نبى وصديق وشهيدان

> "Keep motionless, for, here on you are one Prophet, one Siddiq (truthful) and two martyrs."

Martyr (Shaheed) is one who is in deep love with Allah, the Almighty and lays down his life for seeking His Pleasure. So, the Messenger of Allah (peace and blessings of Allah be upon him) pointed out Hadrat Umar and Uthman (may Allah be pleased with them) to be martyrs; and Hadrat Abu Bakr Siddiq (may Allah be pleased with him) was called 'Siddiq' (truthful) and after Prophets, none is higher than him in status.

Abu Dawud reports from Jabir (may Allah be pleased with him) that the Holy Prophet (peace and blessings of Allah be upon him) said:

ارى الليلة رجل صالح كان ابى بكر نيط برسول الله
صلعم ونيط عمر بابى بكر ونيط عثمان بعمر قال
جابر فلما قمنا من عند رسول الله صلى الله عليه
وسلم قلت اما الرجل الصالح فرسول الله صلى الله
عليه وسلم وامانوط بعضهم ببعض فهم ولاة الامر
الذى بعث الله به نبيه صلى الله عليه وسلم :

> "I have dreamt tonight that a virtuous man is getting embraced with me; and he is Abu Bakr; Umar is getting embraced with Abu Bakr; and Uthman with Umar."
>
> When we left the place, we remarked that these three persons are the managers of the affairs for which the Messenger of Islam was sent.

This *hadith* makes it clear that Hadrat Abu Bakr, Umar and Uthman (may Allah be pleased with them) were the managers and care-takers of Islam.

Bukhari and Muslim report from Sa'd bin Abi Waqqas (may Allah be pleased with him) that the Messenger of Allah (peace and blessings of Allah be upon him) said:

لعلی انت منی بمنزلة هرون من موسی الاانه لانبی بعدی :

> "Ali to me is like Harun to Musa, but there is no Prophet after me."

That is, Hadrat Musa (peace be on him) was very close to Hadrat Harun (peace be on him) and they were brothers and managers of the affairs of the world. In the same way, the Apostle indicated that Ali to him is like Harun, with the difference that there would be no Prophet after him. However, there is no affinity between Harun and Ali in respect of Caliphate. Hadrat Harun (peace be upon him) was not appointed Caliph after Hadrat Musa (peace be on him); Hadrat Harun (peace be on him); had passed away forty years before the death of Hadrat Musa (peace be on him).

Muslim reports from Zarin Hubaish that Ali (may Allah be pleased with him) said:

والذی فلق الحبة وبرء النسمة انه لعهد النبی الامی صلی الله علیه وسلم الی ان لا یجبنی الا مومن ولا یبغضنی الا منافق –

> "By One who takes out grains from seeds and created all creatures that the Messenger of Allah (peace and blessings of Allah be upon him) said to me:
>
> 'One who is a Muslim will keep friendship with me; and one who shows enmity to me will be a hypocrite."

This *hadith* makes it clear that love of Ali (may Allah be pleased with him) is the sign of Iman (Faith); and keeping enmity and malice towards him is hypocricy.

Tirmidhi reports from Zaid bin Arqam (may Allah be pleased with him) that the Messenger of Islam (peace and blessings of Allah be upon him) said:

من كنت مو لا ه فعلى مو لاه –

"Ali is friend of one whose friend I am."

That is, one who keeps friendship with me should love Ali too with the only difference that Muhammad (peace and blessings of Allah be upon him) was a Prophet but Ali was not.

Tirmidhi reports from Anas bin Malik (may Allah be pleased with him):

كان عند رسول الله صلى الله عليه وسلم طير فقال اللهم اتنى بـاحب خلقك اليك يـاكل معى هذا الطير فجاء ه على فاكل معه

"The Messenger of Allah (peace and blessings of Allah be upon him) had a cooked bird to eat. He supplicated:

"O Allah! Send to me one who is the dearest among your friends so that he may share this bird." Meanwhile, Hadrat Ali (may Allah be pleased with him) appeared on the scene and the Messenger of Allah (peace and blessings of Allah be upon him) ate the bird with him."

Tirmidhi reports from Ali (may Allah be pleased with him) that the Holy Prophet (peace and blessings of Allah be upon him) said:

انا دار الحكمة وعلى بابها –

"I am the house of wisdom and Ali is its gate."

Tirmidhi reports from Umm Atiya (may Allah be pleased with her): that the Messenger of Allah (peace and blessings of Allah be upon him) once sent an expedition which consisted of Ali too. I heard the Apostle saying with his hands raised:

اللهم لا تمتنى حتى ترينى عليا –

"O Allah! Keep me alive till I see Ali again."

That is, the Apostle supplicated Allah, the Almighty to send back Hadrat Ali (may Allah be pleased with him) safe and sound. It showed his depth of love for Ali who was beloved of Allah, the Almighty.

Imam Ahmad reports from Umm Salma (may Allah be pleased with her) that the Messenger of Allah (peace and blessings of Allah be upon him) said:

من سب عليا فقد سبنى

"One who reproaches Ali, reproaches me."

Imam Ahmad reports from Ali (may Allah be pleased with him) that the Messenger of Allah (peace and blessings of Allah be upon him) said:

فيك مثل من عيسى ابغضته اليهود حتىبهتوامه واخبة
النصارى حتى انزلوه بالمنزلة التى ليست لـه ثم قال
يهلك فى رجلان محب مفرط كفرطنى بما ليس فى
ويبغض يجعله شبانى على ان ينهتنى–

"You somewhat resemble to Isa (peace be on him) for the Jews degraded him by putting blame on his mother; the Christians raised his status so much so that he did not deserve it. And he will meet his doom who eulogises Ali beyond all limits; and also one who degrades him to the level that he puts blame on me."

That is, the true position of Hadrat Isa (peace be on him) was that he was a Prophet and was born without a father only with the Spirit of Allah. The Christians raised him so high in status that he was called son of Allah. They also used to pray to him for fulfilling his needs and desires. The Jews, on the other hand, showed enmity to him and accused his mother Maryam (Mary), labelled him as a liar and refused to accept his Prophethood.

Hence the Messenger of Allah (peace and blessings of Allah be upon him) told Hadrat Ali (may Allah be pleased with him) that he resembles to Isa (peace be on him) because both of them face the same situation. Some people will show so much love towards him that they will describe him what he is not. It happened exactly so: Some people accused him that he was not a Muslim; he loved the world and disgraced Hadrat Aisha (may Allah be pleased with her), the consort of the Apostle; caused the martyrdom of Hadrat Uthman (may Allah be pleased with him); remained against Hadrat Abu Bakr (may Allah be pleased with him) for several months; fought against Muslims without valid reasons; refrained from the decision of the jury; kept on concealing his creed etc. Another section of people raised him in status so high and described something which he did not have; for instance, they say that Prophethood was sent to Ali but Jibril handed it over to Muhammad (peace and blessings of Allah be upon him); Allah had disguised Himself in the form of Ali; he is higher than Abu Bakr and Umar in status; on the Day of Judgment he will send people to Heaven and Hell at his discretion; he is trouble-shooter; the one loving Ali will go to Heaven in spite of evil-doings.

But Ali (may Allah be pleased with him) declared both the sections to have been ruined with their Faith. From this statement, it came to be known that both the *Kharjis* and *Rafezis* had lost their Faith.

Imam Ahmad reports from Bra'a bin A'zib and Zaid bin Arqam qmay Allah be pleased with them):

ان رسول الله صلى الله عليه واله وسلم لما نزل بغد-
يرخم اخذبيد على فقال الستم تعلمون انى اولى
بالمومنين من انفسهم قالوا بلى فقال الستم تعلمون انى
اولى بكل مومن من نفسه قالوا بلى فقال اَللّٰهُمَّ مَن
كُنتُ مَولَاه اَللّٰهُمَّ وَالِ مَن وَالَاهُ وَعَادِمَن عَادَاهُ فلقيه
عمر بعد ذالك فقال له هنيا يا بن ابى طالب اصبحت
وامسيت مولا كل مومن ومومنة

"When the Messenger of Allah (peace and blessings of Allah be upon him) arrived at Ghodair-e-Khum, he caught the hand of Ali and said to the people present there:

"Don't you know I love the Muslims more than their lives?

'Yes,' they replied.

The Apostle said again:

"O Allah! Ali loves whom I love; O Allah! love those who love Ali and hate those who hate Ali.

Thereafter, Umar (may Allah be pleased with him) met Ali (may Allah be pleased with him) and greeted him by saying:

"O Son of Abu Talib! You pass your morning ana evening in a state that every Muslim male and female loves you."

Ghodair-e-Khum is a house where the Messenger of Allah

(peace and blessings of Allah be upon him) stayed with his Companions. It was a time when some hypocrites had cast aspersion on Ali. Hence the Apostle assembled people there and addressed them holding the hand of Ali: 'Do I not love the Muslims more than their lives?" The Muslims replied in the affirmative. After their confession, the Apostle invoked Allah: Saying 'O Allah! as you have enjoined upon Muslims to love me so make others to love Ali and love those who love Ali; and be at enmity with those who is enemy of Ali."

After this address of the Apostle, when Umar met Ali, he said:

> "How glorious you are! It has been enjoined upon all the Muslim males and females to love you."

It is clear from this *hadith* that as every Muslim male and female has been enjoined to love the Apostle more than their lives, so they are to love Ali. Moreover, one should praise Ali in suitable words and balanced terms.

Imam Ahmad reports from Ali (may Allah be pleased with him) that the people once asked:

يا رسول الله صلى الله عليه وسلم من نومر بعدك

> "O Messenger of Allah, Whom should we appoint our ruler after you?"

قال ان تومروا ابابكر تجدوه امينا زاهدا فى الدنيا
راغبا فى الاخرة وان وان تومرواعمر تجدوه قويا
امينا لايخاف فى الله لومة لائم وان تومروا عليا ولا
اركم فاعلين تجدوه هاديا مهديا يا خذبكم الطريق
المستقيم

"If you appoint Abu Bakr as your ruler, you will find him trustworthy, unattached to the world, and attracted to the Hereafter; if you appoint Umar as ruler, you will find him trustworthy of the highest order, undaunted by those who oppose him in the management of the affairs of Allah; and if you appoint Ali as your ruler, and you may not do so, you will find him a guide to the right path."

The Holy Companions (may Allah be pleased with them) were anxious to know as to who will deputize for the Prophet of Allah (peace and blessings of Allah be upon him) to manage the affairs of the Muslims. Hence they wanted to know from the Apostle as to who should be appointed as deputy to him. Replying the question, the Messenger of Allah (peace and blessings of Allah be upon him) named three persons with their personal traits.

Naming Abu Bakr Siddiq (may Allah be pleased with him) he said that if he be appointed *Amir* (ruler) after me, he will keep trustworthiness, pay the rights of the people, keep eye on religiosity, will remain indifferent to the world, will not seek anything other than the Pleasure of Allah. Thus it happened so. Even after being appointed as a Caliph of Islam he used to sell clothes as a hawker and managed the affairs of the Muslims as well. His sole aim from the Caliphate was to seek reward in the Hereafter and Pleasure of Allah.

Next he named Umar Ibn Khattab (may Allah be pleased with him) and said that if he be appointed as the *Amir* after me, he will prove strong and straightforward in all the affairs undaunted by any opponent, render the rights of others, manage the affair without caring who says what. And it happened accordingly. There was nothing to fear in his period and hundreds of countries were conquered and Islam spread far and wide, and rights of the Muslims were paid in full.

Thereafter, he named Ali (may Allah be pleased with him) and said that if he be appointed as *Amir* after me; although he does not think they will do so because of his tender age in comparison to Abu

Bakr and Umar (may Allah be pleased with them), he will play his role as a guide to the straight path.

When the Messenger of Allah (peace and blessings of Allah be upon him) made final departure, Ali (may Allah be pleased with him) was only 33, while Abu Bakr Siddiq (may Allah be pleased with him) was 61 years old, and Umar (may Allah be pleased with him) was 50 years old. May be the Apostle would have come to know about the state of affairs through revelation or he would have told so in order to cast a soothing effect on Ali (may Allah be pleased with him).

In short, from the above *hadith*, good traits of all the three came to light.

Tirmidhi reports from Hadrat Ali (may Allah be pleased with him) that the Messenger of Allah (peace and blessings of Allah be upon him) said:

رحم الله ابا بكر زوجتي ابنته وحملني الى

دار الهجرة وصحبني فى الغار واعتق بلا لا من ماله

> "May Allah show mercy to Abu Bakr that he gave his daughter to me in marriage, led me on his mount to the place of migration, accompanied me in the Cave, purchased Bilal from his own money and set him free.

رحم الله عمر يقول الحق وان كان مرا تركه الحق

وماله من صديق رحيم رحم ناالله عثمان يستحيى منه

الملائكة رحم الله عثمان يستحيى منه الملائكة رحم

الله عليا اللهم ادار الحق معه حيث دار –

> May Allah show mercy to Umar that whenever he speaks, he speaks the truth, even if the truth is bitter; his plain

speaking deserted his friends; may Allah show mercy to Uthman that even angels are ashamed of him; may Allah show mercy to Ali; O Allah! let truth follow Ali which way he turns."

Hadrat Abu Bakr Siddiq (may Allah be pleased with him) sacrificed his life and property in the way of Allah, the Almighty. He gave his daughter to the Prophet of Allah (peace and blessings of Allah be upon him) in marriage keeping his Prophethood in view; when the pagans of Arab started troubling and torturing the Apostle and Believers, they were permitted to migrate to Madinah; Abu Bakr Siddiq got the Apostle mounted on his back and carried him for some distance, walking on the fingers of his feet so that no trace of feet is imprinted on the earth. When they reached the cave of a mountain, Abu Bakr entered the cave to cleanse it. Thereafter, he carried the Apostle into the cave. Therein he saw a hole and he put his thumb on the hole and he was bitten by a snake. Later on, a camel was brought to the cave and the Messenger of Islam (peace and blessings of Allah be upon him) mounted on it with Abu Bakr and left for Madinah. Bilal was the slave of an infidel. Abu Bakr purchased him in return for two thousand guineas and a strong Roman slave and set him free. He was always at the service of the Apostle. Hence he praised the good traits of Abu Bakr and sought Allah's mercy for him.

Thereafter, the Apostle says that Umar speaks the truth, although his plain speaking antagonised and deserted his friends. May Allah show mercy to him.

The Apostle then referred Uthman and sought mercy of Allah, the Almighty for him because he was so modest and shameful that the angels were ashamed at his shame. That is, he is superior even to the angels in this respect. Thus nobody saw Uthman naked; he himself never saw parts of his body below the *navel* out of shame.

For Ali, the Apostle sought mercy of Allah because he will face people of different nature, each group treading on its own chosen path. Hence, the Apostle invoked Allah to place truth on the side of Ali.

Tirmidhi reports form Jabir (may Allah be pleased with him): that the Messenger of Allah (peace and blessings of Allah be upon him) looked at Talha bin Ubaidullah and remarked:

من سره ان ينظر الى شهيد يمشى على
وجه الارض فلينظر الى طلحة ابن عبيدالله –

"Anyone who wants to see a martyr walking on earth should see Talha bin Ubaidullah."

Shaheed (martyr) is one who lays down his life and property in the way of Allah. Same was the condition of Talha He looked like a martyr even during his lifetime with his appearance, gestures and yearnings. And he died a martyr too.

Bukhari and Muslim report from Jabir (may Allah be pleased with him) that the Holy Prophet (peace and blessings of Allah be upon him) said:

ان لكل نبى حواريا وحوارى الزبير–

"Every Prophet has some pure-hearted friends; my pure-hearted friend is Zubair."

Tirmidhi reports from Ali (may Allah be pleased with him) that he heard the Messenger of Allah (peace and blessings of Allah be upon him) say:

طلحة والزبير جاراى فى الجنة –

"Talha and Zabair are both my neighbour in the Heaven."

Tirmidhi reports from Abu Hurairah (may Allah be pleased with him) that the Holy Prophet (peace and blessings of Allah be upon him) was on Mount. Hira with Abu Bakr, Umar, Uthman, Ali,

Talha and Zubair (may Allah be pleased with them). Meanwhile, the stone moved a little. The Messenger of Allah (peace and blessings of Allah be upon him) asked:

اهدء فما عليك الانبى اوصديق اوشهيد -

"keep motionless, for there are a Prophet and *Siddiq* and *Shaheed* on you."

The Apostle referred to himself as Prophet; Abu Bakr as Siddiq; Umar, Uthman, Ali, Talha and Zubair as *Shaheed.*

Bukhari and Muslim report from Anas (may Allah be pleased with him) that the Holy Prophet (peace and blessings of Allah be upon him) said:

لكل امة امين وامين هذه الامة عبيدة ابن الجراح:

"Every *Ummah* has a trustee and Ubaida bin Jarrah is the trustee of my *Ummah.*"

Muslim reports from Abi Mulaika that some people asked Hadrat Aisha (may Allah be pleased with her) whom would the Messenger of Allah (peace and blessings of Allah be upon him) appoint caliph if he so wanted?"

ابوبكر فقيل ثم من بعد ابى بكر قال عمر قيل من بعد
عمر قالت ابوعبيدة ابن الجراح -

Hadrat Aisha (may Allah be pleased with her) said in reply :

"To Abu Bakr."

"Whom after Abu Bakr?" they asked.

"To Umar," she replied.

"Whom after Umar?" they asked.

"To Ubaida bin Jarrah," she replied.

Bukhari and Muslim report from Ali (may Allah be pleased with him) to have said:

ما سمعت النبی صلی الله علیه وسلم جمع ابویه لاحد

الالسعدبن مالك فانی سمعته یقول یوم احد یاسعد ارم

فداك ابی وامی :

> "I have never heard the Messenger of Allah (peace and blessings of Allah be upon him) collecting his parents for anyone other than Sa'd bin Malik. That day the Apostle said:
>
> "Shoot arrows O Sa'd! may my father and my mother be sacrificed on you."

It was the practice with the Arabs that they used to say 'may my father or mother be sacrificed on you' and the Messenger of Allah (peace and blessings of Allah be upon him) maintained the same practice. But on the day of the Battle of Uhad, he said to Sa'd:

> "O Sa'd! go on shooting arrows at the infidels; may my father and mother be sacrificed on you."

It means the Apostle loved Sa'd most.

Tirmidhi reports Hadrat Aisha (may Allah be pleased with her) that the Holy Prophet (peace and blessings of Allah be upon him) used to say to his wives:

ان امرکن مما یهمنی من بعدی ولن یصبر علیکن الا

الصا برون الصدیقون

> "I am anxious about your future course of life. Certainly, only one keeping patience and forebearance could come to

your help."

Hadrat Aisha (may Allah be pleased with her) addressing Abi Salma bin Abdur Rahman remarked:

قالت عائشة يعنى المتصدقين

قالت عائشة لابى سلمة بن عبدالرحمن سقى الله اياك من سلسبيل الجنة وكان ابن عوف قد تصدق على امهات المومنين بحديقة بيعت باربعين الفا -

"May Allah make your father Abdur Rahman bin Auf drink water from the 'Salsabil Canal' of the Heaven that he gifted a garden to the Mothers of the Believers that was sold at forty thousand (Dirham or guineas)."

Tha case of women is very delicate, paticularly if it is the case of purdah-observing women. They need servants and attendants for day to day work. But they cannot have them if they have no means to pull on. But they can be economically stabilized if a helping hand is extended to them. Abdur Rahman rose to render economic help to the consorts of the Apostle by gifting a garden to them. Hence Hadrat Aisha (may Allah be pleased with her) told Abu Salma that his father, Abdur Rahman, will be given water from the canal of Heaven in return for his exemplary service done to the Mothers of the Believers.

Bukhari reports Hadrat Umar (may Allah be pleased with him) to have said:

ما احد احق بهذا لامر من هولاء النفر الذين توفى رسول الله صلى الله عليه وسلم وهو عنهم راض فسمى عليا وعثمان وزبير وطلحةوسعدا وعبدالرحمن

"None has any claim to the Caliphate with respect to ability other than those with whom the Messenger of

> Allah (peace and blessings of Allah be upon him) continued to be pleased till his end." Thereafter, he named Ali, Uthman, Zubair, Talha, Sa'd bin Abi Waqqas and Abdur Rahman bin Auf."

When death approached, Hadrat Umar ibn Khattab (may Allah be pleased with him) said:

> "Those persons had better claim to the Caliphate with respect to ability."

It is clear from this *hadith* that after Hadrat Abu Bakr Siddiq and Hadrat Umar bin Khattab (may Allah be pleased with them), six persons had very high status to the Messenger of Allah (peace and blessings of Allah be upon him) and to his holy Companions (may Allah be pleased with them).

Tirmidhi reports Abdur Rahman bin Auf (may Allah be pleased with him) that the Messenger of Allah (peace and blessings of Allah be upon him) said:

ابوبكرٍ فى الجنة وعمر فى الجنة وعثمان فى الجنة وعلىٌّ فى الجنة وطلحة فى الجنة وزبيرٌ فى الجنة وعبد الرحمن بن عوفٍ فى الجنة وسعد بن ابى وقاصٍ فى الجنة وسعيد بن زيدٍ فى الجنة وابو عبيدة ابن الجراح فى الجنة :

> "Abu Bakr in the Heaven; Umar in the Heaven; Uthman in the Heaven; Ali in the Heaven; Talha in the Heaven; Zubair in the Heaven; Abdur Rahman in the Heaven; Sa'd bin Abi Waqqas in the Heaven; Sayeed bin Zaid in the Heaven; and Ubaidullah bin Jarrah in the Heaven."

These ten persons belong to the Heaven beyond any doubt.

Tirmidhi reports from Burida (may Allah be pleased with him) that the Messenger of Allah (peace and blessings of Allah be upon him) said:

ان اللـه تبـارك تعـالى امرنـى بحـب
اربعةٍ واخبرنى انه يحبهم قيل يا رسـول اللـه سـمهم
قـال علـىٌ منهـم يقـول ذلـك ثلاثـاً وابـوذرٍ والمقـداد
وسلمان امرنى يحبهم واخبرنى انه يحبهم :

"Allah, the Almighty ordained me to love four persons because Allah, the Almighty loves them."

O'Prophet of Allah, tell us their names." the Companions requested.

"Ali is one of them," he said and repeated his name thrice.

He further added the names of Abu Dhar. Miqdad and Salman to the list saying that Allah too loves them."

That is, Allah, the Almighty said to the Messenger of Allah (peace and blessings of Allah be upon him) that He loved those four persons and the Apostle should also do so. Glory be to Him! What a status! Allah, the Almighty loves these four and ordains His Beloved too, to love them.

Ali bin Abi Talib reports that the Messenger of Allah (peace and blessings of Allah be upon him) said:

ان لكل نبيٍ سبعة نجبـاء رقبـاء واعطيت انـا اربعـة
عشـر قلنـا مـن هـم قـال انـا وابنـاى وجعفـر وحمـزة
وابوبكر وعمر ومعصب بـن عميرٍ و بـلالٌ وسـلمان
وعمارٌ وعبد الله بن مسعودٍ وابوذرٍ ومقدادٌ :

"Every Prophet has seven noble guards, but I have got fourteen."

"Who are they?" I asked.

They are Ali; my two sons Hasan and Husain; Jafar, Hamza, Abu Bakr, Umar, Mus'ab bin Umayr, Bilal, Salman, Ammar, Abdullah bin Mas'ood, Abu Dhar and Miqdad."

Jafar was the brother of Ali and Hamza was the son of Abdul Muttalib.

Bukhari and Muslim report from Jabir (may Allah be pleased with him) that he heard the Messenger of Allah (peace and blessings of Allah be upon him) said:

اهتز عرش الرحمان بموت سعد بن معاذٍ

"The Empyrean of Allah moved at the death of Sa'd ibn Muadh."

Those who are loved by Allah, the Almighty, are adored by all except Satan. They seek blessings of Allah for them till they live in this world; all the creatures of Allah mourn their death. But the abode where their souls stay and the angels express their joys for their arrival. Thus when Sa'd bin Muadh (may Allah be pleased with him) passed away, his soul reached the Empyrean, it expressed joy and moved to greet the soul.

Bukhari and Muslim report from Bra'a bin Azib (may Allah be pleased with him) that he heard the Messenger of Allah (peace and blessings of Allah be upon him) say about the Ans'ar:

للانصار لايحبهم الا مؤمن ولايبغضهم الا منافقٌ فمن
احبهم احبه الله ومن ابغضهم ابغضه الله :

"A Believer will love them and one keeping Unbelief will keep malice towards them. Thus, one who loves them will be loved by Allah; and those who keep malice towards them will be paid in the same coin by Allah, the Almighty."

The Messenger of Allah (peace and blessings of Allah be upon him) has denoted the love for the Ansar as the sign of Iman and malice towards them as the sign of infidelity. Thus it is clear from this *hadith* that those loving the Ansar are Believers, while those showing malice towards them are hypocrites.

Bukhari reports from Abu Hurairah (may Allah be pleased with him) that the Holy Prophet (peace and blessings of Allah be upon him) said:

لو لا الهجرة لكنت امرءٍ من الانصار ولو سلك النـاس وادياً و شعبا لسلكت وادى الانصار وشعبها الانصـار شعار والناس دثار :

"Had there been no Hijrat (migration) I would have been one of the Ansar; if all people walk along one way or ravine and the Ans'ar on others, I shall be with them. The Ans'ar are like the clothe stuck to the body while others are like the clothes worn outside."

That is, the Ansar have such a great status and virtuosity that the Messenger of Allah (peace and blessings of Allah be upon him) had remarked that if *hijrat* (migration) was not destined, he would have been among the Ans'ar. Moreover, if the whole world would follow one way and the Ans'ar any other, he would have joined them. To him the Ansar were like the lining sticking to the body while others were like outside clothes like the sheet etc. Thus the excellence of the Ansar was recognised beyond doubt.

Muslim reports Abu Hurairah (may Allah be pleased with him) that the Holy Prophet (peace and blessings of Allah be upon him) said:

انی عبد اِلله ورسوله هاجرت الی الله واليكم المحيا محياكم والممات مماتكم :

"I am the slave of Allah and His Messenger; I migrated with my attention towards Allah, my place of living and demising is the same as that of yours."

That is, the Apostle told the Ans'ar that he had with them a relation of life and death; and that, he would not desert them.

Bukhari reports Anas bin Malik (may Allalh be pleased with him) that the Messenger of Allah (peace and blessings of Allah be upon him) said to the Ans'ar:

اللهم انتم من احب الناس الی اللهم انتم من احب الناس الی اللهم من احب الناس الی -

"Allah bears witness to the fact that you are the dearest to me; you are the dearest to me; you are the dearest to me."

Bukhari reports from Anas bin Malik (may Allah be pleased with him) that the Messenger of Allah (peace and blessings of Allah be upon him) once came out with a piece of cloth wrapped round his head and mounted on the pulpit for the last time and said after praising the glory of Allah, the Almighty:

اوصيكم بالانصار فانهم كرشی وعيبتی قد قضو الذی عليهم وبقی الذی لهم فاقبلوا من محسنهم وتجاوزوا عن مسيئهم :

"I bequeath you concerning the Ans'ar that they are my belly i.e., my confidants and my bale i.e., my secret-keepers. They did all that they were obliged to do. But so far their rights are concerned they can be rendered by accepting their virtues and forgiving their wrongs."

That is, you should accept whatever virtues come from the Ansar and forgive whatever vices emerge from them. It is clear from this *hadith* that even if some evil is caused by the Ans'ar, they must not be censured for this.

Muslim reports from Zaid bin Arqam that the Messenger of Allah (peace and blessings of Allah be upon him) said:

اللهم اغفر الانصار والابناء الانصار والابناء ابناء الانصار:

"May Allah pardon the Ans'ar, their children and their offsprings."

Bukhari and Muslim report from Ali (may Allah be pleased with him) that the Holy Prophet (peace and blessings of Allah be upon him) said:

لعل الله اطلع على اهل بدرٍ فقال اعملوا ما شئتم وجبت لكم الجنة :

"Perhaps Allah, the Almighty was fully conscious of the people of Badr that He decreed for them that they could do whatever they liked for Heaven had already been bestowed on them."

That is, Allah, the Almighty said about those who accompanied the Holy Prophet (peace and blessings of Allah be upon him) in the Battle of Badr that the Heaven had already been conferred on them and hence any sin committed by them was supposed to be pardoned. Hence the Apostle said that Allah, the Almighty knew fully well that they would not commit a sin of such a nature that would send them to Hell. In short, this *hadith* makes it clear that the people who took part in the Battle of Badr had a high place among the Companions.

Bukhari reports from Refa'a bin Rafe (may Allah be pleased with him) that the Holy Prophet (peace and blessings of Allah be upon him) was asked by Jibril:

ماتعدون اهل بدرٍ فيك قال من افضل المسلمين او كلمة نحوها وقال كذالك من شهد بدرًا من الملائكة :

"Do you know about the status of your companions of the Battle of Badr?"

"Best of all the Muslims!" said the Apostle, or he said something similar to this.

"This angels of Badr among the angels enjoy the same status," Jibril revealed.

Some angels had also accompanied the Messenger of Allah (peace and blessings of Allah be upon him) and fought against the infidels of Mak'kah. Hence Jibril told that the angels participating in the Battle of Badr were superior to other angels as was the case with the Companions of Badr.

Muslim reports from Lady Hafsah, the daughter of Umar (may Allah be pleased with him) and the consort of the Messenger of Allah (peace and blessings of Allah be upon him) that the Apostle said:

انى لارجوا ان لايدخل النار ان شآء الله تعالى احدٌ شهدبدرًا والحديبية :

"I hope the person who was present during the Battle of Badr and the Treaty of Hudaibiya would not go to Hell"

Bukhari and Muslim report from Jabir (may Allah be pleased with him) that on the Day of Hudaibiya there were one thousand four hundred Companions and the Messenger of Allah (peace and blessings of Allah be upon him) affirmed:

انتم اليوم خير اهل الارض :

"Today you are best of all on the earth."

The thirteen *ahadith* that have been cited above are taken from Mish'kat in the chapter on 'Comprehensive Virtues", which establish that these Companions are far superior to others in status.

In fine, the above-mentioned *ayah* and *ahadith* establish it beyond doubt that all the Companions of the Apostle, whether *Muhajir* or *Ansar* were superior to all other Muslims and were beloved of Allah, the Almighty; their status was higher than all the jinns and human beings; thereafter those who participated in the Battle of Badr and Uhad and the Treaty of Hudaibiya, followed by the four Caliphs of Islam.

Bukhari and Muslim report from Miswar bin Makhramah that the Messenger of Allah (peace and blessings of Allah be upon him) said:

فاطمة بضعة منى فمن اغضبها اغضبنى يريبنى ما ارابها :

"Fatima is a part of my body and one who causes her angry makes me angry and I am annoyed at what teases her."

Bukhari and Muslim report from Lady Aisha (may Allah be pleased with her) that the Messenger of Allah (peace and blessings of Allah be upon him) said:

يا فاطمة الا ترضين ان تكونى سيدة نسآء اهل الجنة

"O Fatima! Are you not happy that you are to be appointed the chief of the women of Heaven?"

Tirmidhi reports from Lady Aisha (may Allah be pleased with her) that the most beloved of all to the Messenger of Allah (peace and blessings of Allah be upon him) was Lady Fatima (may Allah be pleased with her).

Bukhari and Muslim report from Bra'a (may Allah be pleased with him):

رأيت النبى صلى الله عليه وسلم والحسن بن على على عاتقه يقول

> "I saw the Messenger of Allah (peace and blessings of Allah be upon him) with Hasan, the son of Ali (may Allah be pleased with him) on his shoulder and he was saying:

اللهم انى احبه فاحبه :

> "O' Allah! I love him so You too love him."

Bukhari and Muslim report from Abu Hurairah (may Allah be pleased with him) :

خرجت مع رسول الله صلى الله عليه وسلم فى طآئفة من النهار حتى اتى خباء فاطمة فقال اثم لكعٌ اثم لكعٌ يعنى الحسن فلم يلبث ان جآء يسعى حتى اعتنق كل واحدٍ منهما صاحبه فقال رسول الله صلى الله عليه وسلم اللهم انى احبه فاحبه واحب من يحبه

> "Once I went out with the Holy Prophet (peace and blessings of Allah be upon him) and when he came to the house of Fatima (may Allah be pleased with her) and asked:
>
> "Where is my son, i.e., Hasan?" The Apostle had said this twice that Hasan came running and both of them put their hands round the neck of each other and the Apostle said:

'O' Allah! I love him and You too love him and love him also who loves him."

Bukhari reports from Abi Bakr (may Allah be pleased with him) that he saw the Messenger of Allah (peace and blessings of Allah be upon him) on the pulpit and Hasan bin Ali beside him; the Apostle was looking once towards us and twice towards Hasan saying:

ان ابنی هذا سیدٌ ولعل الله ان

یصلح به بین فئتین عظیمتین من المسلمین :

"This is my son, Hasan, and I hope that the two groups of Muslims will get united through him."

Thus, it happened that Hadrat Imam Hasan (may Allah be pleased with him) handed over the Caliphate to Hadrat Mua'wiyyah and brought peace to the Muslims without any confrontation.

Tirmidhi reports from Yala bin Murrah (may Allah be pleased with him) that the Messenger of Allah (peace and blessings of Allah be upon him) said:

حسینٌ منی و انا من حسینٍ احب الله من احب حسیناً

حسینٌ سبطٌ من الاسباط :

"Husain is from me and I from Husain. May Allah love one whom I love. He is among my children."

'Sibt' means offspring; 'asbat' were the offsprings of Hadrat Yaqub (peace be on him) who had twelve sons and each of them had many offsprings. This was the indication that Husain (may Allah be pleased with him) will have a big race.

Tirmidhi reports from Ibn Abbas (may Allah be pleased with him):

كان رسول الله صلى الله عليه وسلم حامل الحسن بن عليٍ على عاتقه فقال رجلٌ نعم المركب ركبت يا غلام فقال النبى صلى الله عليه وسلم نعم الراكب هو۔

"The Messenger of Allah (peace and blessings of Allah be upon him) was once keeping Husain ibn Ali on his shoulder."

Thereupon someone remarked:

"What a good riding it is!"

At this, the Holy Prophet (peace and blessings of Allah be upon him) remarked:

"What a good rider it is!"

Imam Ahmad reports from Ibn Abbas (may Allah be pleased with him):

رأيت النبى صلى الله عليه وسلم فيما يرى النائم ذات يومٍ بنصف النهار اشعث اغير بيده قارورة فيها دمٌ فقلت بابى انت وامى ما هذا قال هذا دمٌ الحسين واصحابه لم ازل التقطه منذ اليوم فحصى ذلك الوقت فاجد قتل ذلك الوقت۔

"I saw the Holy Prophet (peace and blessings of Allah be upon him) in a state that he saw a man sleeping in the noon with his hair scattered and a cup of blood in his hand.

'What is this?' may my father and mother be sacrificed on you.

"This is the blood of Husain and his Companions.

From that on I wait for the day on which he will be martyred."

This dream was seen by Ibn Abbas before the battle of Karbala. Hence he was waiting for the day when he will be martyred with Husain.

This *hadith* indicates that the soul of the Holy Prophet (peace and blessings of Allah be upon him) was highly disturbed and expressed deep sorrow over the tragic incident. Hence the Muslims should express sorrow over what happened. They should also feel that Abdullah ibn Zeyad, Umar bin Sa'd, Shimr etc. grieved the Imam by the permission of Yazid, the accursed.

The Muslims should refrain from putting the Apostle and the members of his House of grief, and, hence, to remember this tragic incident every year means to add to the grief of the Apostle.

Tirmidhi reports from Osama bin Zaid (may Allah be pleased with him) that the Messenger of Allah (peace and blesssings of Allah be upon him) said about Hasan and Husain (peace be on them):

هذان ابناءى وابناء ابنتى اللهم انى احبهما فاحبهما
واحب من يحبهما

"These two are my sons and sons of my daughter. O` Allah, I love both of them and You too love them and those who love them."

Tirmidhi reports from Hudhaifah (may Allah be pleased with him) that the Holy Prophet (peace and blessings of Allah be upon him):

هذا ملـك لـي ينـزل الـى الارض قـط قبـل هـذه الليلـة استاذن ربه ان يسلم على ويشـرنى بـان فاطمـة سـيدة نسآء اهل الجنة وان الحسن والحسين سيد شباب اهـل الجنة :

"This is the angel who never descended on earth before this night that he sought permission from his Lord to salute me and give me good tidings that Lady Fatima is the Chief of all Heavenly women and Hasan and Husain are the chiefs of the youths of the Heaven."

Tirmidhi reports from Zaid bin Arqam (may Allah be pleased with him) that the Holy Prohet (peace and blessings of Allah be upon him) said:

لعلى وفاطمة والحسن والحسين انا حربٌ لمن حاربهم وسلمٌ لمن سالمهم :

"I would like to fight against those who fight against Ali, Fatima, Hasan and Husain, and keep peace with those who are at peace with them."

Muslim reports from Lady Aisha (may Allah be pleased her) that one morning the Holy Prophet (peace and blessings of Allah be upon him) came out putting on small blanket with prints of hair on it. In the meantime Hasan appeared and he (the Apostle) took him in; then Husain came and he was also taken in; the same happened with Fatima and Ali all inside his small blanket. Thereafter, he said:

إِنَّمَا يُرِيْدُ اللّٰهُ لِيُذْهِبَ عَنْكُمُ الرِّجْسَ اَهْلَ الْبَيْتِ وَيُطَهِّرَكُمْ تَطْهِيْراً :

> "Allah wants to remove pollution from you O' members of (my) house and get you cleaned with purity."

The Holy Qur'an says that Allah, the Almighty wants to get your (the Apostle's) wives and members of the House cleaned and make them pious.

This *ayah* makes it clear that it is related to the wives of the Apostle. Since the Messenger of Allah (peace and blessings of Allah be upon him) took Imam Hasan, Imam Husain, Ali and Lady Fatima in his small blanket and recited this *ayah*, it meant that he was supplicating Allah for them. He also made it clear that not only his wives but all these five also comprised the members of the House.

Muslim reports from Sa'd ibn Abi Waqqas:

قال لما نزلت هذاه الآية ندعُ اَبْنَاءنَا وَاَبْنَاءكُمْ وَنِسَاءنَا وَنِسَآءكُمْ وَاَنفُسَنَا وَاَنفُسَكُم ثُمَّ نَبتَهِل فَنَجعَلَ لَعنَةَ اللهُ عَلَىَ الكَذِبِينَ دعا رَسول الله صلى الله عليه وسلم علياً وفاطمة وحسناً وحسيناً فقال اللهم هؤلاء اهل بيتى:

> "When this *ayah* was revealed, the Holy Prophet (peace and blessings of Allah be upon him) called Ali, Fatima, Hasan and Husain and said:
>
> "O'Allah! These are members of my house."

The Christians considered Hadrat Isa (Jesus) (peace be on him) to be the son of God. When Allah, the Almighty said in the Qur'an that Hadrat Isa (peace be on him) is the slave of Allah, and as He Created Adam (peace be on him) with father and mother out of His command alone, so He Created Hadrat Isa (peace be on him) without a father. But the Christians refused to accept this and declared the religion of the Last Prophet (peace and blessings of Allah be upon him) wrong and their own to be right. Thereupon this *ayah* was revealed and became a part of Surah A'le-Imran which says that Allah, the Almighty observes:

> "O, Prophet! tell those Christians to call their sons and you also call your sons; tell them to call their women and you also call your women together with yourself and they should also include themselves; thereafter, both the groups should curse the liars."

When this *ayah* was revealed, the Prophet of Allah (peace and blessings of Allah be upon him) called Ali, Fatima, Hasan and Husain (may Allah be pleased with all of them), took them with himself and submitted:

> "O'Allah! these are members of my house."

This *hadith* makes it clear that the Holy Prophet (peace and blessings of Allah be upon him) considered Ali, Hasan and Husain (may Allah be pleased with them) as his sons.

Tirmidhi reports from Abdul Muttalib bin Rabia that Abbaas came to the Messenger of Allah (peace and blessings of Allah be upon him) in anger.

> "What made you angry?" asked the Apostle.
>
> "O' Prophet of Allah! When the Quraish meet among themselves, they express joy, but when they meet me they express no joy." Abbas revealed.

Hearing this, the Holy Prophet (peace and blessings of Allah be upon him) fell in anger so much so that his face turned red, and he said:

> "By One in Whose hands lies my life, Iman (Faith) will never enter the heart unless they love you for Allah and for His Messenger, and further said:
>
> "O'people! one who troubles my uncle, troubles me; an uncle is equal to father."

Abbas (may Allah be pleased with him) was the uncle of the Holy Prophet (peace and blessings of Allah be upon him). When the people did not behave properly, he complained to the Apostle against them. Thereupon, the Apostle said:

والذى نفسى بيده لا يدخل قلب الرجل الايمان
حتى يحبكم لله ولرسوله ثم قال. وايها الناس من آذى
عمى فقد آذانى فانما عم الرجل صنو ابيه :

> "One who doesn't love my uncle and members of my house, he has no Iman; one who troubles my uncle, troubles me, for the uncle is like the father and hence he should be held in esteem."

Razin reports from Ibn Abbas that the Holy Prophet (peace and blessings of Allah be upon him) said to Abbas:

> "Come to me with your son on the morning of Monday so that I pray for the welfare of both of you." Next morning Abbas and I appeared before the Apostle and covering both of us with his sheet, he supplicated:

اللهم اغفر للعباس وولده مغفرة ظاهرة وباطنة
لاتغادر ذنباً اللهم احفظه فى ولده وجعل الخلافة باقية
فى عقبه :

> "O' Allah! Forgive Abbas and his son; save them from sins, big or small; and allot caliphate his offsprings.

Bukhari and Muslim report from Abdullah bin Umar (may Allah be pleased with him):

ان زيد بن حارثة مولى رسول الله صلى الله عليه

وسلم ما كنا ندعوه الا زيد بن محمدٍ حتى نزل القرآن

ادعوهم لآبائهم:

"We would call the boy of the Prophet of Allah as "Zaid bin Muhammad," unless this *ayah* was revealed:

"Call the adopted sons with the name of their fathers."

Zaid was a boy whom the Holy Prophet (peace and blessings of Allah be upon him) had adopted and hence called his son. Hence this *ayah* was revealed to suggest that any boy be called after his real father and not after one who adopts him. Thereafter the Companions ceased to call him Zaid bin Muhammad and he was then came to be called Zaid bin Harith. This *hadith* shows that the Companions considered Zaid to be among the members of the Prophet's house.

Tirmidhi reports from Lady Aisha (may Allah be pleased with her):

اراد النبى صلى الله عليه وسلم ان ينهى مخاط اسامة

قالت عائشة دعنى حتى انا الذى افعل

"The Holy Prophet (peace and blessings of Allah be upon him) intended to clean the nose of Osama." Thereupon I (Aisha) asked him to leave it to me.

At this the Apostle said:

يا عآئشة احبه فانى احبه :

"O' Aisha, I love him and you too love him." Zaid was the adopted son of the Prophet of Allah.

Tirmidhi reports from Osama (may Allah be pleased with him):

يا رسول الله جئناك نسألك اى اهلك احب اليك قال
احب اهلى الى من قد انعم اللّٰه عليه وانعمت عليه
اسامة بن زيدٍ قال ثم من قال على ابن ابى طالبٍ :

"Abbas and Ali once came to the Messenger of Allah (peace and blessings of Allah be upon him) and submitted:

"Who among the males is more loving to you?"

"One who is shown mercy by Allah and myself and he is Osama, the son of Zaid," he replied.

"Who after that?" they asked.

"The son of Abi Talib," replied the Apostle.

These 19 *ahadith* have been written in Mish'kat in the chapter on "virtues of the Members of the House of Muhammad" (peace and blessings of Allah be upon him). This *hadith* clarifies that the Apostle loved Osama too much.

Bukhari and Muslim report from Ali (may Allah be pleased with him) that the Holy Prophet (peace and blessings of Allah be upon him) said:

خير نسائها مريم ابنةُ عمرانَ وخير نسآءها خديجة
ابنةُ خويلدٍ :

"The best among the women of all the *Ummahs* is lady Maryam, the daughter of Imran and the best among the women of this *Ummah* is Khadija, the daughter of Khawalid."

Lady Maryam was the mother of Hadrat Isa (Jesus) (peace be on him) and Lady Khadija is the wife of the Apostle.

Tirmidhi reports from Lady Aisha (may Allah be pleased with her):

> "Jibril came with the face of Aisha in a green silken cloth and said to the Holy Prophet (peace and blessings of Allah be upon him):
>
> هذا زوجتك فى الدنيا والاخرة :
>
> "This is your wife in this world and the Hereafter."

This *hadith* clarifies that Allah, the Almighty had Himself selected Lady Aisha (may Allah be pleased with her) for His Messenger (peace and blessings of Allah be upon him) for this world and the Hereafter.

Bukhari and Muslim report from Lady Aisha (may Allah be pleased with her):

ان الناس يتحرون بهداياهم يوم عآئشة يبتغون بذالك
مرضات رسول الله صلى الله عليه وسلم فكلمت ام
سلمة رسول الله صلى الله عليه وسلم ان يقول من
اراد ان يهدى الى رسول الله صلى الله عليه وسلم
فليهد اليه حيث كان فقال لها لايؤذننى نى عائشة فان
الوحى لم يأتنى وانا فى ثوب امرأء ة الا عائشة قالت
اتوب الى الله من اذاك يا رسول الله

> "People would generally send their gifts to the Prophet (peace and blessings of Allah be upon him) on the day when he happened to be with Lady Aisha, just for the sake of his pleasure. However, Umme Salma requested the Apostle to tell the people that whoever wanted to send a gift to him, he or she should do it irrespective of where

the Apostle stayed at night".

Thereupon the Messenger of Allah (peace and blessings of Allah be upon him) said:

> 'O' Salma, trouble me not in regard to Aisha, 'Revelation' is not caused to me when I had slept with any other wife other than Aisha.'
>
> She (Umm Salma) said"
>
> "I seek forgiveness of Allah for the trouble inflicted on you."

Thereafter, the consorts of the Apostle sent Lady Fatima to the Apostle who talked to him in this matter. Thereupon the Apostle replied:

يا بنية الا تحبين مـا احـب قالت بلى قالت فاحبى هذه :

> "My dear daughter, do you not like what I like?"
>
> "Why not?" Lady Fatima submitted.
>
> "Then love her (Aisha)," he said.

It was the practice of the Messenger of Allah (peace and blessings of Allah be upon him) to stay with every wife of his at night by turns. But, however, he loved Lady Aisha (may Allah be pleased with her) most. Anyone who sent any gift to the Apostle was consumed by the wife with whom the Apostle would stay. Hence, most people sent their gifts to the Apostle on the night he would stay with Lady Aisha so that she could consume that to the pleasure of Allah. Lady Umm Salma, who was also a consort of the Apostle, therefore, objected to this practice of the people. But the Apostle was annoyed at this objection and asked his wives not to grow jealous at Aisha. She was superior to others in the eyes of Allah too because Revelation was caused to him when he stayed with none other than Aisha. Thus, the wives sent Lady Fatima to the Apostle for seeking forgiveness.

Bukhari and Muslim report from Abu Musa (may Allah be pleased with him) that the Holy Prophet (peace and blessings of Allah be upon him) said:

فضل عائشة علـى النسآء كفضـل الـثريد علـى سـائر الطعام :

> "The virtue of Aisha upon other women was like that of *Tharid* on other foods."

Tharid is a kind of food which is eaten by the Arab with much fondness.

Muslim report from Zaid bin Arqam (may Allah be pleased with him):

> "One day the Messenger of Allah (peace and blessings of Allah be upon him) rose to address us at a place between Mak'kah and Madina. At first, he praised Allah, the Almighty, admonished us," and warned:

يـا ايهـا النـاس

انما انا بشر يؤشك ان ياتينى رسول ربى فاجيب وانـا تاركٌ فيكم الثقلين اولها كتاب الله فيه هدىً ونورٌ هـو حبل الله من اتبعه كان على الهدى ومـن تركـه كـان على الضلالة فخذوا بكتاب الله واستمسـكوا بـه فحث على كتاب الله ورغب فيه ثم قال واهل بيتى اذكر كم الله فى اهل بيتى وفـى روايـةٍ وعـترتى واهـل بيتـى ولويتفرقا حتى يـردا علـى الحـوض فـا نظـروا كيـف تخلفونى فيهما

> "O' people! I am just a man and shall obey the messenger of death sent by Allah. Hence, I leave for yor two things—— one is the Book of Allah which is a string from Allah; one who holds it follow the right path and one who leaves it, goes astray. Hence follow the Book which bears virtue and Light and hold it fast. Thereafter he added:
>
> I remind you of members of my house. They are my honour, and those who look forward to join me at *Hauz-e-Kausar* should see that they are not mal-treated."

In another narrative the Messenger of Allah (peace and blessings of Allah be upon him) is reported to have said:

يا ايها الناس انى تركت فيكم ما ان اخذتم به لن

تضلوا كتاب الله وعترتى:

> "O' people! I leave two things for you; if you adopt them you will never go astray one is the Book of Allah and another ones are my family members."

From this *hadith* it is clear that the members of the Apostle's house should be held in high esteem.

Tirmidhi reports from Ibn Abbas (may Allah be pleased with him) that the Holy Prophet (peace and blessings of Allah be upon him) said:

احبوا الله لما يغذوكم من نعمه واحبونى لحب الله

واحبوا اهل بيتى لحبى :

> "Love Allah because He feeds you; love me for the sake of your love for Allah; and love the members of my house for the sake of your love for me."

Imam Ahmad reports from Abu Dhar (may Allah be pleased with him) that the Holy Prophet (peace and blessings of Allah be upon him) said:

الا ان مثل اهل بيتی فيكم مثل سفينة نوحٍ من ركبها نجی ومن تخلف عنها هلك :

> "Beware! the example of members of my house is like the Ark of Noah that those who mounted on it were saved and those left were ruined."

It is clear from this *hadith* that those who love and follow the ways and modes of the *ahle-bait* (members of the Prophet's house) are saved from Unbelief and Hell, like those who were saved by mounting on the Ark of Noah. Those who refused to be in the Ark were ruined, including a son of Noah who was also among the Unbelievers. As the *ahle-bait* were made a source of salvation so the Companions of the Holy Prophet (peace and blessings of Allah be upon him) were declared as the source of peace.

. Muslim reports from Abu Burdah that his father Abu Musa transmitted that the Holy Prophet (peace and blessings of Allah be upon him) said:

النجوم امنةٌ للسمآء فاذا ذهبت النجوم اتی السمآء ما توعدُ وانا امنةٌ لاصحابی فاذا ذهبت انا اتی اصحابی مایوعدون اصحابی اتی امتی مایوعدون :

> "The stars are safely studded in the sky, so when they are no more, the sky will get what is promised. Similarly, I am the saviour of my Companions, and when I am gone, they will get their due. In the same way my Companions are the saviour of my *Ummah*, so when they depart, my *Ummah* will get what is promised."

Allah, the Almighty reveals that in the Last Day's battles, riots and innovations will erupt. The Holy Prophet (peace and blessings of Allah be upon him) observed that when his Companions would be no more, his *Ummah* whould get what was destined by Allah, the Almighty. It is the same as my Companions will become victim of dissensions when I am no more. It is like the sky without stars as it will turn lightless without them and will succumb to ruination and thus the Day of Ressurrection will be caused.

Anas (may Allah be pleased with him) reports from the Messenger of Allah (peace and blessings of Allah be upon him) said:

مثل اصحابی فی امتی کالملحِ فی الطعام الا بالملحِ :

"The example of my Companions in my *Ummah* is like salt without which food becomes tasteless."

Tirmidhi reports from Ubaidullah bin Buraidah that his father heard from the Holy Prophet (peace and blessings of Allah be upon him) say:

ما من اصحابی یموت بارضٍ الا بعث قائداً ونوراً

لهم یوم القیامةِ :

"Whoever among my Companions will remain alive will lead others to Heaven and will serve as a light for the people, and they will be a source of salvation on the Day of Resurrection too."

Tirmidhi reports from Jabir (may Allah be pleased with him) that the Holy Prophet (peace and blessings of Allah be upon him) said:

لا تمس مسلماً من رانی او رای من رانی:

"Hell-Fire will not touch that Muslim who saw me or one who saw him."

This *hadith* makes it clear that the Companions of the Apostle held such a high status that even seeing their face will save one from Hell-Fire.

Nasa'i reports from Umar (may Allah be pleased with him) that the Holy Prophet (peace and blessings of Allah be upon him) said:

اكرموا اصحابی فانهم خيارکم ثم الذين يلونهم ثم الذين يلونهم :

> "Show respects to my Companions for they are better than you. They are followed by those who are nearer to them i.e. *tabeyeen* and thereafter *taba'tabeyeen.*"

That is, from the lifetime of the Holy Prophet (peace and blessings of Allah be upon him) to those who will be born till the Doomsday, the Companions of the Apostle were better than all. These Companions remained alive till 170 H. *Tabeyeen* remained alive till 170 H. followed by 260 H. They should all be respected and followed.

Bukhari and Muslim report from Abu Sa'eed Khudri (may Allah be pleased with him) that the Holy Prophet (peace and blessings of Allah be upon him) said:

لا تسبو اصحابی فلو ان احدکم انفق مثل احدٍ ذهباً ما بلغ مد احدهم ولا نصيفه

> "Don't reproach my Companions for if anyone of you spend gold equal to Mount. Uhad, it will not be equal to a *mud* in reward nor half of it."

Mud is a container for measuring grain and it measures, perhaps, a 'ser' (800 kg). Thus the Apostle said that if anyone spends gold equal to Mount. Uhad in the way of Allah, he will get not so much reward as his Companions will get by spending a *mud* or half of it. Thus, if the Companions of the Holy Prophet (peace and blessings of Allah be upon him) had such a high status, they must not be reproached.

Tirmidhi reports from Abdullah bin Mughaf'fal that the Holy Prophet (peace and blessings of Allah be upon him) said:

الله الله فى اصحابى الله الله فــى اصحـابى اللــه اللـه فى اصحـابى لاتتخذوهم غرضاً من بعدى فمن احبهم فبحبى احبهم ومن ابغض هم فبعضــى ابغضـهم ومـن اذاهم فقد اذانى ومن اذانى فقد اذى الله ومن اذى الله فيوشك ان ياخذه :

> "Fear Allah, and fear in matter of my Companions; make not target of reproach after me. One who loves them, it is because of his love for me; if one harbours malice against them, it is because of his malice against me; one who troubles them, troubles me, and one who troubles me, troubles Allah, and one who troubles Allah will soon be caught for punishment."

Thus, the Holy Prophet (peace and blessings of Allah be upon him) laid utmost emphasis to show respects to his Companions. Hence, they must not be reproached. They should, rather, be loved.

Those who love the Companions, love the Holy Prophet (peace and blessings of Allah be upon him) and those who love the Apostle, love Allah, the Almighty. Same is the case with giving trouble to them.

Tirmidhi reports from Ibn Umar (may Allah be pleased with him) that the Holy Prophet (peace and blessings of Allah be upon him) said:

اذا رأيتهم الذين يسبون اصحابى فقولو لعنة الله على شرهم

"Whenever you see some persons reproaching my Companions, curse the evils of those persons."

This *hadith* shows the Companions of the Holy Prophet (peace and blessings of Allah be upon him) must not be reproached at any cost. And one who does so invites curse and wrath from Allah.

Razin reports from Umar (may Allah be pleased with him) that he heard the Holy Prophet (peace and blessings of Allah be upon him) said:

"I asked my Lord about the differences among my Companions. Allah, the Almighty sent His Revelation saying:

يامحمد ان اصحابك عندى بمنزلة النجوم فى السماء بعضها اقوى من بعض ولكل نور من اخذ بشىء مما هم عليه من اختلافهم فهو عندى هدى

"O' Muhammad! Your Companions are to Me like stars in the sky; some are more bright than others. But each of them has light with him. Thus one who followed the way of the Companions follow the right path before Me.

The Holy Prophet (peace and blessings of Allah be upon him) is reported to have said:

اصحابى كالنجوم بايهم اقتديتم اهتديتم

"My Companions are like the bright stars in the sky, hence whoever you follow, you will attain slavation."

The Companions of the Holy Prophet (peace and blessings of Allah be upon him) were more than one lakh in number. They were different in taste and temperament and had various kinds of engagements and activities. Naturally, they have difference of opinion too. Hence, Allah, the Almighty said, ignoring their differences, that each of them was like a bright star and whoever would follow any of them would get the right path. Hence, in spite of differences of opinion, each Companion is virtuous before Allah.

Baihaqi reports from Ibn Abbas (may Allah be pleased with him) that the Holy Prophet (peace and blessings of Allah be upon him) said:

احبو العرب لثلث فانى عربى والقران عربى وكلام
اهل الجنه عربى

> "Love the Arabs for three reasons: I am an Arab; the Qur'an is in Arabic; and the language of the Paradise is Arabic."

It is very common that one who loves anyone loves his village, city and country too. he enjoys even the mention of those places. The Holy Prophet (peace and blessings of Allah be upon him) asked the Muslim to love the Arabs for he was an Arab, the Book of Allah has been revealed in Arabic, and the language of Paradise would be Arabic. Hence those who have a desire to be in Paradise must love the language of the Paradise. May Allah infuse this love in the heart of all the Believers.

Chapter - Five

Innovations Concerning Graves

فِي ذِكْرِ بِدْعَاتِ الْقُبُوْرِ

This chapter mentions *ayahs* and *hadiths* which show the evils of innovations which belong to graves. Visiting graves by males without any specification of date, year and particular congregation is desirable, rather the *sunnah*. The sole intention should be to remember his own death and the Heareafter. But to make long journeys to visit a grave with the specification of date, day and time, to organise a fair or hold congregation, to light a lamp there, to build a mosque in the graveyard because of that grave, visiting of the grave by a female, to write down the obituary and some verses of the Qur'an on the grave or mausoleum, to say prayer near the grave thinking it to be better act etc. are all *haram* (unlawful) *makruh* (undesirable) and *bid'at* (innovation). They perform such acts because they consider their saints or dead ones to be the purveyors of rewards, but, in fact, Allah alone has such a unique power. All the saints and pious men were themselves needy and asked Allah, the Almighty to fulfil their needs.

Allah, the Almighty says in Surah A'le-Imran of the Holy Qur'an:

قُل يَا اَهلَ الكِتَابِ تَعَالَوا اِلَى كَلِمَةٍ سَوَآءٍ بَينَنَا وَبَينَكُم اَلاَّ نَعبُدَ اِلاَّ اللهَ وَلاَنُشرِكَ بِهِ شَيئاً وَلاَيَتَّخِذَ بَعضُنَا بَعضاً اَربَاباً مِّن دُونِ اللهِ فَاِن تَوَلَّو فَقُولُوا وَاشهَدُوا بِاَنَّا مُسلِمُونَ :

"Say: O people of the Book! come to common terms as between us and you: that we worship none but Allah; that we associate no partners with Him; that we erect not, from among ourselves. Lords and patrons other than Allah.:
(Q. 3:64)

The Jews took Hadrat Aziz as the son of Allah, and at the helm of affairs. They would bow down before him and worshipped the graves of their saints and elders, religious guides and scholars. They were all declared men committing polytheism.

Allah, the Almighty also asked the Muslims not to worship anyone other than Allah nor invoke anybody to fulfil your needs. Thus both the Qur'an and the Books of the Jews and the Christians are quite one in this matter. Thus they were asked to refrain from worshipping graves of their Prophets, religious guides, friends of Allah, jinn, ghosts, trees, graves and not to associate any partner with Allah. None should be considered as Lord and nourisher.

This *ayah* makes it amply clear that to consider anyone as the fulfiller of need and to be the trouble-shooter is against the teachings of all Books of Allah and, is therefore, an act of *shirk* (polytheism) which is the invention of the Jews and the Christians. But, unfortunately, some of the ignorant Muslims have also joined ranks with them. They put forward nonsense pleas to justify their perversions.

Allah, the Almighty says in Surah Al-Imra'n of the Holy Qur'an:

مَا كَانَ لِبَشرٍ اَن يُوتِيَهُ اللهُ الكِتَابَ وَالحُكمَ وَالنُّبُوَّةَ ثُمَّ يَقُولُ لِلنَّاسِ كُونُوا عِبَاداً لِّي مِن دُونِ اللهِ وَلَكِن كُونُوا رَبَّانِيينَ بِمَا كُنتُم تَعلَمُونَ الكِتَبَ وَبِمَا كُنتُم تَدرُسُونَ:

> "It is not (possible) that a man, to whom is given the Book, and Wisdom. And the Prophetic Office, should say to people: "Be ye my worshippers rather than Allah's: on the contrary (He should say): "Be ye worshippers of Him (Who is truly the Cherisher of all) for ye have taught the Book and ye have studied it earnestly."
>
> (Q: 3:79)

The one who has been conferred upon Prophethood and wisdom is not expected to ask people to worship him, keeping Allah aside. Thus, the Prophets and Wisemen have been saying through the ages that all men should turn to Allah and be God-fearing. No Prophet or wiseman is expected to say anything against the Will and Pleasure of Allah.

Allah, the Almighty says in Surah Al-Ma'ida of the Holy Qur'an:

وَاِذْ قَالَ اللهُ يَاعِيسَى بنِ مَريَمَ ءَاَنتَ قُلتَ لِلنَّاسِ اتَّخِذُونِي وَاُمِيَّ اِلَهَينِ مِن دُونِ اللهِ ط قَالَ سُبحَانَكَ مَا يَكُونَ لِي اَن اَقُولَ مَا لَيسَ لِي بِحَقٍ اِن كُنتَ قُلتُهُ فَقَد عَلِمتَهُ تَعلَمُ مَا فِي نَفسِي وَلَا اَعلَمُ مَا فِي نَفسِكَ اِنَّكَ اَنتَ

عَلاَّمُ الغُيُوبِ ـ مَا قُلتَ لَهُم اِلاَّ مَا اَمرتَنِى بِهٖ اَنِ اعبُدُوا اللّٰهَ رَبِّى وَرَبَّكُم وَكُنتُ عَلَيهِم شَهِيداً مَا دُمتُ فِيهِم فَلَمَّا تَوَفَّيتَنِى كُنتَ اَنتَ الرَّقِيبَ عَلَيهِم وَاَنتَ عَلٰى كُلِّ شَىءٍ شَهِيدٌ اِن تُعَذِّبهُم فَاِنَّهُم عِبَادَكَ وَاِن تَغفِرلَهُم فَاِنَّكَ اَنتَ العَزِيزُ الحَكِيمُ :

> "And behold! Allah will say: "O Jesus the son of Mary! didst thou say unto men, 'take me and my mother for two gods besides Allah?" He will say: "Glory to Thee! never could I say what I had no right (to say). Had I said such a thing, Thou wouldst indeed have known it. Thou knowest what is in my heart, though I know not what is in Thine. For Thou Knowest in full all that is hidden.
>
> Never said I to them aught except what Thou didst command me to say, to wit, 'Worship Allah, my Lord and your Lord': And I was a witness over them whilst I dwelt amongst them; when thou didst take me up thou wast the Watcher over them, and Thou art a witness to all things. If Thou dost punish them, they are Thy servants: if Thou dost forgive them, Thou art the Exalted in power, the Wise."
>
> (Q. 5: 116-118).

Hadrat Isa (peace be on him) was born without father just by the Power of Allah, and he brought the dead to life, restored eyesight to born-blind and cured the lepers. Having seen these miracles the Christians claimed him to be the son and his mother Maryam, the wife of God. They thought that those two could do anything at will. The Jews sent the Christ to gallows and the Christians started holding the cross in high esteem, thinking that Allah would be happy with their action. Allah, the Almighty said that He would ask Hadrat Isa (peace be on him) on the Day of Judgment whether he had asked his people to declare you His son your mother, His wife. Thereupon Hadrat Isa (peace be on him) would say how could he make such a high claim while he had neither power nor position to make such a claim. How could he ask people to worship and bow down before him. Had he told so it had been written in His Records. He had told the people what he had been asked to say to the people by Him. He asked them to worship the Lord both of Isa and Maryam. But after his going up to heaven they started worshipping him and his mother.

It is clear from this *ayah* that none of the Prophets or saints have the power, position and authority to ask people to worship him. Worshipping the graves has been approved neither by the Qur'an nor *Hadith*, nor Hadrat Ali (may Allah be pleased with him) nor Hadrat Muhiuddin Jilani (Mercy of Allah be upon him).

Allah, the Almighty says in Surah Yunus of the Holy Qur'an:

وَيَعْبُدُونَ مِن دُونِ اللَّهِ مَا لَا يَضُرُّهُمْ وَلَا يَنفَعُهُمْ وَيَقُولُونَ
هَٰؤُلَاءِ شُفَعَاؤُنَا عِندَ اللَّهِ قُلْ أَتُنَبِّئُونَ اللَّهَ بِمَا لَا يَعْلَمُ فِي
السَّمَاوَاتِ وَلَا فِي الْأَرْضِ سُبْحَانَهُ وَتَعَالَىٰ عَمَّا يُشْرِكُونَ

> "They serve, besides Allah, what can hurt them not nor profit them, and they say: 'These are our intercessors with Allah.' Say: 'Do ye indeed inform Allah of something He knows not, in the hevens or on earth? Glory to Him.' and far is He above the partners they ascribe (to Him)."
>
> (Q. 10:18).

That is, those who worship pictures, idols, images, tombs, sign, house or soul etc. of their elders and saints, get no good in return. It is quite wrong to think they are intercessors with Allah, the Almighty.

Allah, the Almighty says in Surah Al-Ma'ida of the Holy Qur'an:

قُلْ يَا أَهلَ الكِتَابِ لَاتَغلُوا فِى دِينِكُم غَيرَ الحَقِّ وَلَاتَتَّبِعُوا أَهوَاءَ قَومٍ قَد ضَلُّوا مِن قَبلُ وَأَضَلُّوا كَثِيراً وَضَلُّوا عَن سَوَاءِ السَّبِيلِ :

> "Say: 'O people of the Book! Exceed not in your religion the bounds (of what is proper), trespassing beyond the truth, nor follow the vain desires of people who went wrong in times gone by,——who misled many, and strayed (themselves) from the even way."
>
> (Q. 5:77).

Religion should be followed as ordained, neither more nor less. If anything is added to the religion, it is not an act of righteousness. Hence the Jews and the Christians, saints and religious leaders have done the same -- they added something and curtailed others.

It means the religious guide or scholar must not be followed if he distorts or changes the text of the Qur'an and *Hadith*. A large number of people have gone astray by following them. Worshipping the graves and tombs is a grave sin and the root of many sins.

Bukhari and Muslim report from Abu Sa'eed Khudri (may Allah be pleased with him) that the Holy Prophet (peace and blessings of Allah be upon him) said:

لا تشد الرحالُ الا الى ثلثة مساجدٍ المسجد الحرام و المسجد الاقصى و مسجدى هذا

> "Journey must not be made except for three Mosques - the Mosque of Ka'abah, Mosque of Aqsa, and my Mosque at Madina."

That is, one must not make a long journey for visiting any house but for the Ka'abah, the Mosque of Aqsa and Mosque of the Prophet at Madinah. People in the past used to make long journeys for visiting Mount Tur, portrait of Isa and the tomb of Yuhena. This practice is being forbidden according to this *hadith*. Thus Makkanpur, Ajmer, Bahraich, Baghdad, Karbala, Najaf Ashraf etc. as a pilgrim is forbidden.

Nasa'i reports from Abu Hurairah (may Allah be pleased with him) that he heard the Holy Prophet (peace and blessings of Allah be upon him) say:

لا تجعلوا قبری عیدًا و صلوا علی فان صلوتکم

تبلغنی حیث کنتم

> "Don't make my grave a place of festivity; send Darud (peace of Allah) to me for it is made to reach me."

When the Messenger of Allah (peace and blessings of Allah be upon him) saw that the Jews and the Christians visited the graves of their saints once in a year and organised fair and congregation on that occasion and placed their needs before the graves, he forbade his *Ummah* to treat his grave like them. However, if any reward for me lies in mind, the better and the desirable way is to send *Darud* to me. And for sending *Darud* it is not at all necessary to be near the grave. This exercise may be performed from a distance of thousand miles. Allah, the Almighty has appointed some angels just for conveying *Darud* to the Apostle.

This *hadith* makes certain things clear: it is not permissible to organise congregation of any kind annually at the grave of the Holy Propeht (peace and blessings of Allah be upon him). Now when it is forbidden for the grave of the Apostle, how can it be valid for the graves of others? Moreover, any source of song, music and means of joys are not permitted near a grave, as it is done during *urs*. Now if the purpose is to send reward to the dead, the better way is to seek forgiveness of Allah for them or make some charity for them. Thus if the position is that some angels have been appointed by Allah, the Almighty to convey the *Daruds* to the Holy Prophet (peace and blessings of Allah be upon him), why should he come to the congregations to receive *Daruds*? Thus all these notions are false and figment of mind.

Imam Ahmad, Tirmidhi and Ibn Majah report from Abu Hurairah (may Allah be pleased with him) that the Holy Prophet (peace and blessings of Allah be upon him) said:

لعن الله زورات القبور

"Allah curses the female visitors of graves."

This *hadith* makes it clear beyond doubt that visiting of graves by women is *haram* (unlawful).

Imam Malik reports from Ata bin Yasar (may Allah be pleased with him) that the Holy Prophet (peace and blessings of Allah be upon him) said:

اللهم لا تجعل قبرى و ثنا يعبد اشتد غضب الله تعالى

على قومِ ا تخذو واقبور انبيا ئهم مساجد

> "O Allah! Make not my grave an object of worship; wrath of Allah fall on those who made the graves of their Prophets place of worship.

That is, to say prayers in the mosque, to observe *itikaf* there for the mosque is meant for these acts to be performed. Moreover, it is rewarding to sweep the mosque, to spread carpets etc. to keep water containers for the comfort of the people who come to say prayers, to light the lamp etc. inside the mosque. Now what is done for a mosque must not be done for a grave for it invites wrath and terrible punishment from Allah. Hence, the Messenger of Allah (peace and blessings of Allah be upon him) invoked Allah to save his grave from becoming a place of worship.

Bukhari and Muslim report from Aisha (may Allah be pleased with her) that the Messenger of Allah (peace and blessings of Allah be upon him) said during his last illness:

الذی لم یقم منه لعن الله الیهود و النصاری اتخذو قبور ا نبیا ئهم مساجد

> "The Jews and the Christians be cursed by Allah that they turned the graves of their Prophets into mosques."

That is during his last illness, the Apostle, in order to warn his *ummah*, said that the Jews and the Christians be cursed that they made the graves of their Prophets into mosques for doing all what is generally done in a mosque. They started building shrines like mosques, light the lamps and say prayer there.

It is unfortunate that some people of his *ummah* started doing the same for which he cursed the Jews and the Christians.

In fine, when the Holy Prophet (peace and blessings of Allah be upon him), who is better of all the saints and religious leaders and guides, invoke curse of Allah for the worshippers of shrines, what to speak of his followers.

Muslim reports from Jundub (may Allah be pleased with him) to have heard the Holy Prophet (peace and blessings of Allah be upon him) say:

الا ان من کان قبلکم کا نو یتخذون قبور انبیا ئهم وصا لحیهم مسا جد فلا تتخذوالقبور مساجد انی انهکم عن ذلك

> "Be warned that the people before you had turned their shrines into mosques, but you must not do so."

Muslim reports from Abi Marsad Ghanawi that the Holy Prophet (peace and blessings of Allah be upon him) said:

لا تجلسو على القبور ولا تصلو ا اليها

"Sit neither on the grave nor pray towards it."

If prayer is said towards a grave for paying respects it is infidelity; if it is for engaging attention of one in the grave, it is *haram*.

Muslim reports from Abi Hayyaj Asadi that Ali (Allah be pleased with him) said: Should I not send you on a mission that the Holy Prophet (peace and blessings of Allah be upon him) had once sent me.

الا تدع تمثا لا الا طمسته ولا قبرًا الا سويته

"I should not leave any idol unbroken nor leave any grave high without levelling it."

This *hadith* makes it clear that the Muslims not make a grave higher by one cubit, and if it is made so it should be levelled if power permits. Hence the Messenger of Allah (peace and blessings of Allah be upon him) asked Ali who ordered Abu Hajjyaj to do the same.

Muslim reports from Jabir (may Allah be pleased with him) that the Holy Prophet (peace and blessings of Allah be upon him) forbade us from whitewashing the grave from constructing any building on the grave and from sitting on the grave,

Tirmidhi reports from Jabir (may Allah be pleased with him) that the Holy Prophet (peace and blessings of Allah be upon him) forbade us from whitewashing the graves, from writing on the grave and from trampling it.

Bukhari and Muslim reports form Lady Aisha (Allah be pleased with her) to have narrated that "When the Holy Prophet (peace and blessings of Allah be upon him) fell ill, some of his wives made a mention of a church called Maria. Lady Umme

Salma and Lady Umme Habiba (wives of the Apostle) had visited the church in Abyssinia". They were talking about the beauty of the church, about pictures etc. Having heard this the apostle raised his head and said:

اولئك اذا مات فيهم الرجل الصالح بنوا على قبره مسجدًا ثم صور فيه تلك الصور اولئك شرار خلق الله

> "Whenever any male among them would die, they built a mosque over his grave; they were very wicked, worst of all the creatures."

That is, Lady Umm Salma and Lady Umm Habiba (may Allah be pleased with them) had gone to Abyssinia where there was a church of the Christians named Maria. It had pictures. When they made a mention of this to the Apostle, the Apostle, despite his illness, raised his head to explain to them what the Jews and Christians would do after the demise of a virtuous man among them.

Bukhari and Muslim report from Lady Aisha (may Allah be pleased with her) that the Holy Prophet (peace and blessings of Allah be upon him) once went out for *jihad*. In his absence I made a curtain out of *namt* (a kind of cotton cloth) and hung it over the door. When the Apostle came back he pulled the curtain and almost tore it saying:

ان الله لم يأمر نا ان نكسو الحجارة و الطين

> "Allah the Almighty did not permit us to cover stone and soil with cloth."

It is clear from this *hadith* that to cover the grave with a sheet or any other cover is not at all permissible. The Apostle would dislike it.

Abu Dawud, Tirmidhi and Nasai report from Ibn Abbas (may

Allah be pleased with him) that the Messenger of Allah (peace and blessings of Allah be upon him) said:

لعن الله زائرات فى القبور والمتخذين عليها المساجد والسراج

> "Allah cursed those women who visited the graves; those who built mosques over the graves, and those who lighted lamps on the graves."

Lighting lamps on the graves is something to be cursed and unwise. Lamp is for removing darkness for persons who work, it serves no purpose to the dead. However, if the dead person is pious and virtuous, he gets light from Allah and the worldly light is useless for him. If the dead person is a sinner and transgresser, he is passing through the state of punishment, and, therefore, needs no light at all. Moreover, this lighting is a sort of extravagance.

Imam Malik Reports :

ان على ابن ابى طالب يتوسد القبور و يضتجع عليها

> "Ali (may Allah be pleased with him) would lean against the grave and lay on it."

This *hadith* denotes that sitting beside a grave or leaning against it at times is not prohibited. What is forbidden is to become a *'mojawir'* (an attendant of a shrine) or to hold an assembly or to sit in meditation or to seek help from the dead.

Abu Dawud, Tirmidhi and Darmi report from Abu Sa'eed (may Allah be pleased with him) that the Holy Prophet (peace and blessings of Allah be upon him) said:

الارض كلها مسجد ا لا المقبرة والحمام

> "The whole of earth is a mosque i.e. liable to say prayer, except the graveyard and the bathroom."

Ibn Majah reports from Ibn Mas'ud (may Allah be pleased with him) that the Holy Prophet (peace and blessings of Allah be upon him) said:

نهيتكم عن زيارة القبور فذوروها فا نها تزهد فى الدنيا وتذكر الاخرة

> "I had forbidden you from visiting graves; but now you visit graves for it makes one detached from the world and reminds of the Hereafter."

At first, the Messenger of Allah (peace and blessings of Allah be upon him) had forbidden from visiting graves but permitted it later, saying that it has two benefits: one, it makes one detached from the world; two, it reminds one of death and the Day of Resurrection.

When a person visits a grave, he recalls that the dead person was, once alive; he would walk on the earth, eat and drink, hold talks with the friends and acquaintances; what lofty thoughts he had. But now he is unnoticed and uncared for; none comes to his rescue. He is now alone to face Allah, the Almighty. But visiting a grave does not mean to pray there, to hold assemblies and fair etc, to seek help from the dead, to organise festivities there, to light lamps and to offer sweetmeats on the grave etc. When these shrines became centres of festivals, even women, young and old made a practice to visit such places. The '*mujawirs*' and '*molvis*' happened to be worshipped and they concocted many false stories to attract the masses for visiting graves with precious offerings and huge amounts for the attendants.

Chapter - Six

Rejection of Innovation Concerning Blind Following

فِى رَدِّ بِدْعَةِ التَّقْلِيْدِ

This chapter mentions *ayahs* and *hadiths* which prove the blind following of others as rejected. Some people consider sayings and actions of their religious guides as totally authentic and follow them blindly, without trying to know whether they were right or wrong. Now, if *ayahs* and *hadiths* are cited against the sayings and actions of the so-called religious guides, their followers refuse to accept them as true. And instead of knowing the truth they raise disputes in this matter. They are so simple that they even don't know that they have lost their 'Faith' by rejecting the truths borne by the Qur'an and *hadiths*. They may consult the religious guides and scholars in religious matters, but they must not treat anything absolutely authentic. They should turn to the Qur'an first in all matters; if the Qur'an does not give detail about the matter, they should turn to *Hadith* for the guidance; and if even *ahadith* don't make the matter clear, they should practise according to the unanimity of the Companions, for we have been asked to follow the Companions of the Apostle. Although the Companions had been constantly in the company of the Holy Prophet (peace and blessings of Allah be upon him); they listened to what he said and saw how he acted; they were pious and righteous. However, they were not innocent. But they had better position in comparison to the *'mujtahids'* (religious directors) and most often they apply their conjectures. Hence we find that they have sometimes committed mistakes and had to revise their opinion. Then how religious men of lesser degree can be relied upon. Thus the Muslims should follow their *'mujtahids'* unless the matter doesn't go against the Qur'an and *Hadith*, but he should keep himself constantly engaged in objective study and research of various religious matters. In fine, blind following of the religious guides without knowing the authenticity of the matter is *taqleed-e-bid'at* and is, therefore, *haram*.

Allah, the Almighty says in Surah Al-An'am of the Holy Qura'n:

إِنِ الْحُكْمُ إِلاَّ لِلَّهِ

"The Command rests with none but Allah."

(Q. 6:57).

None has power and status to issue orders for the creation nor the creation are bound to follow their orders, for the Creator and Master of all His creation is Allah and hence He alone should be worshipped and obeyed.

It is clear from this *ayah* that commands of any religious guide or scholars cannot be imposed on the people but what are according to the injunctions of Allah, the Almighty. Such orders are supposed to be from Allah. For instance, when Allah enjoins upon people to follow His Messenger; the subjects to obey their king; the women to obey their husbands; the children to obey their parents; the slaves to follow their masters - but, in fact, these are all from Allah, the Almighty. A Prophet is an innocent person and cannot say anything of his own. However, what the prophet says by way of advice, it may or may not be followed. Thus to obey or follow any religious scholar or guide against the will of Allah is an act of polytheism.

Allah, the Almighty says in Surah Bara'at (Tauba) of the Holy Qur'an.

اِتَّخَذُوا اَحبَارَهُم وَرُهبَانَهُم اَربَابًا مِّن دُونِ اللّٰهِ وَالمَسِيحَ
ابنَ مَريَمَ وَمَا اُمِرُوا اِلَّا لِيَعبُدُوا اِلٰهًا وَّاحِدًا لَا اِلٰهَ اِلَّا
هُوَ سُبحٰنَهُ عَمَّا يُشرِكُونَ

"They take their priests and their anchorites to be their lords besides Allah. And (they take as their Lord) Christ the son of Mary; yet they were recommended to worship but One God: there is no god but He. Praise and glory to Him: (Far is He) from having the partners they associate (with Him)."

(Q. 9:31).

That is, they consider Allah as the Great Master, but Jesus Christ, Molvis, Dervesh etc. are supposed to be the masters of lesser degree and hence they obey them also like Allah which is not binding on them. Hence they commit polytheism. Allah, the Almighty says in Surah Ash-Shura of the Holy Qur'an:

اَم لَهُم شُرَكٰٓؤُا شَرَعُوا لَهُم مِنَ الدِّينِ مَا لَم يَأذَن بِهِ اللّٰهُ
وَلَولَا كَلِمَةُ الفَصلِ لَقُضِيَ بَينَهُم وَاِنَّ الظّٰلِمِينَ لَهُم
عَذَابٌ اَلِيمٌ

"What! Have they partners (in godhead), who have established for them some religion without the permission of Allah? Had it not been for the Decree of Judgment, the matter would have been decided between them (at once). But varily the wrong-doers will have a grievous chastisement."

(Q.42:21)

It is the height of injustice to interfere with the Soveregnty of the Administration of Allah. Hence, to create loopholes or new avenues in religious matters which do not have the approval of Allah, the Almighty, is to associate partners with Him which is great injustice indeed. Had Allah not fixed the Day of Judgment, they would have been punished right now for their wrong-doings.

It is clear from this that whoever creates new paths in religion and those who follow them are all polytheists. They will face terrible punishment on the Day of Resurrection.

Allah, the Almighty says in Surah An-Nisa'a of the Holy Qur'an:

يَا أَيُّهَا الَّذِينَ آمَنُوا أَطِيعُوا اللهَ وَأَطِيعُوا الرَّسُولَ وَأُولِي الأَمْرِ مِنكُمْ فَإِن تَنَازَعْتُمْ فِي شَيْءٍ فَرُدُّوهُ إِلَى اللهِ وَالرَّسُولِ إِن كُنتُمْ تُؤْمِنُونَ بِاللهِ وَالْيَوْمِ الآخِرِ ط ذَلِكَ خَيْرٌ وَأَحْسَنُ تَأْوِيلاً

> "O ye who believe! obey Allah, and obey the Messenger, and those charged with authority among you. If ye differ in anything among yourselves, refer it to Allah and His Messenger, if ye do believe in Allah and the Last Day: That is best, and most suitable for final determination."
>
> (Q. 4:59)

That is, one has to follow the path set by Allah and His Messenger. You have to obey your master, ruler and judge also. But, wherever difference of opinion arises, you have to turn to the Qur'an and *Sunnah* and do accordingly.

This *ayah* denotes that in matters of difference, one has to consult the Qur'an and *Sunnah*

Abu Dawud and Ibn Majah report from Abdullah ibn Umar (may Allah be pleased with him) that the Messenger of Allah (peace and blessings of Allah be upon him) said:

العلم ثلثة اية محكمة اوسنة قائمة او فريضة عادلة

وما كان سوى ذلك فهوفضلٌ

> "Knowledge lies in three things: The Qur'an, the *Hadith* and the unanimity among the *Ummah*, all are useless other than these."

That is, religious principles are formulated only through three things i.e. the Qur'an *Hadith* and unanimity among *Ummah*. Everything other than these are futile and worthless.

Baihaqi reports from Ibrahim bin Abdur Rahman Udhri (may Allah be pleased with him) that the Holy Prophet (peace and blessings of Allah be upon him) said:

يحمل هذالعلم من كل خلفٍ عدو له ينفون عنه

تحريف الغالين وانتحال المبطلين وتاويل الجاهلين

> "Some people learn but distort the meaning; some persons make a mess of what they learn; others add false meaning to the learning material; and still others will be there to misguide the learners in the name of putting the matter right."

That is, some people in future will exaggerate the meaning of the Qur'an and *Sunnah*; some persons will add to the meaning from their own behalf; some foolish persons will misguide others in the name of guidance; still others will appear in the end who will put all matters right and remove all falsehood, distortion and misguidance. True and righteous religious persons belong to the last category.

Daremi reports from the son of Zeyad bin Judair that Umar (may Allah be pleased with him) said to him:

هل تعرف ما يهدم الاسلام قلت لا قال يهـد مـه زلـت العالم وجدال المنافق بالكتاب وحكم الأئمة المضلين

> "Do you what gets demolished 'Faith'? I replied in the negative. Thereupon he said: The religious scholars' deviation in understanding true meaning of religious tenets; disputing of the hypocrites with the Qur'an, and the injunctions of the perverted rulers to the subjects."

That is, to get deviated under the guidance of the deviated religious scholars. Some persons raise disputes with the meaning of Quranic verses out of ignorance. In fact, they are Muslims in name only and Islam has not entered their heart. The perverted rulers also lead their subjects astray and thousands of people thus deviate from the right path. The Muslims should not pay heed to such persons nor follow them.

Bukhari and Muslims report from Ibn Umar (may Allah be pleased with him) that the Messenger of Allah (peace and blessings of Allah be upon him) said:

السمع و الطاعة علـى المـر ء المسـلم فيمـا حـب وكـر ه مالم يؤمر بمعصية فـاذا امـر بمعصيـة فـلا سـمع و لا طاعة

> "Listening and obeying are obligatory on the Muslims unless they are not commanded to follow the wrong path; wrong guidance is neither to be accepted nor obeyed."

That is, the ruler must be obeyed until he commands to do the wrong.

Sharhe Sunnah reports from Nawwas bin Sāman that the Messenger of Allah (peace and blessings of Allah be upon him) said:

لا طاعة لمخلوقٍ فى معصية الخالق

> "Obedience is not liable for one among the creation who disobeys his Creator."

This *hadith* denotes that whoever speaks against the Qur'an and whatever he says, he must not be paid any heed to. Similarly, what has been forbidden by the Qur'an must not be acted upon however much emphasis is laid upon its doing.

Tirmidhi reports from Adi ibn Hatim (may Allah be pleased with him) that once he came to the Holy Prophet (peace and blessings of Allah be upon him) with a cross of gold round neck. He said to him:

يا عدى اطرح عنك الوثن وسمعته يقرأ فى سورة البراءة

> "O Adi! Throw this idol off."
>
> I have also heard this *ayah* of surah Bara'at being recited by the Messenger:

اِتَّخَذُوا اَحبَارَهُم وَرُهبَانَهُم اَربَابًا مِّن دُونِ اللّٰه

> "They take their priests and their anchorites to be their lords besides Allah."

The Messenger further said:

وَقَالَ اِنَّهُم لَم يَكُونُوْ وَيَعبُدُونَهُم وَلٰكِنَّهُم كَانُوا اِذَا حَلُّوا لَهُم استَحِلُّو وَاِذَا حَرَّمُوا عَلَيهِم شَيئاً حَرَّمُوهُ ○

> "They did not worship them but accepted their verdicts on *halal* and *haram*.

Jews had hanged Jesus Christ of their own, hence the Christians pay respects to the gallows in the form of Cross. They put the Cross of gold or silver round their neck. Hence, the Messenger of Allah (peace and blessings of Allah be upon him) called it an idol and asked to throw it off. And since their religious guides and leaders were followed by them blindly without any consultation with the Gospel and Torah, they were blamed by Allah to have declared their religious guides as their Lord and Master.

Chapter - Seven

Concerning Rejection of Rituals

فِي ذِكْرِ رَدّ الرُّسُومِ

What is in practice among the common people without being objected or condemned is called ritual, It becomes the part of common practice and usage and nobody wonders at it nor anyone looks down upon it. Gradually these baseless rituals and practices become an integral part of religion. But, in fact, they are either innovation or undesirable or unlawful or polytheism or infidelity according to circumstances.

They sacrifice animals only on the Eid-day by way of practice alone. Similarly, charities in food or cash are performed on the day someone has passed away and this practice continues as far as possible and some rituals are performed on the day of demise or for three days or on the seventh day or fortieth day or on the annual day etc. Although to give food or cash in charity on behalf of the dead person is valid, but the selection of particular days for this purpose is wrong. In the same way, a widow cannot re-marry in spite of her need for a male or for fulfilling her household and other social needs; one has to spend lavishly on food and other items on the occasion of marriage, circumscision and beginning of lesson etc. for fear of being condemned by society, are all wrong and hence be discarded and rejected.

Some wise and virtuous persons had started something in a particular cirumstances, but later on, it became a permanent ritual for all circumstances. In all such rituals and practices, what is important is the social side rather than the religious aspect.

Moreover, some Muslims celebrate Diwali and Holi at their house with their relatives and neighbours. They celebrate the birthday of Jesus Christ and are, therefore, condemned. But the Muslims also celebrate the birthday of the Messenger of Allah in the form of *milad sharif*.

In short, when practice converts into ritual, it is accepted without any objection. When someone objects to these pratices and rituals they answer in the medium of the pagans of the past.

Allah, the Almighty says in Surah Al-Baqarah of the Holy Qur'an :

وَاِذَا قِيلَ لَهُمُ اتَّبِعُوا مَا اَنزَلَ اللّٰهُ قَالُوا بَلْ نَتَّبِعُ مَا اَلْفَيْنَا
عَلَيهِ اٰبَاءَنَا اَوَلَوْ كَانَ اٰبَاۤؤُهُمْ لَا يَعقِلُونَ شَيْئًا وَّلَا يَعتَدُونَ

"When it is said to them "Follow what Allah hath revealed:"

They say: Nay! we shall follow the ways of our fathers."

What! even though their fathers were void of wisdom and guidance?

(Q.2:170).

Whenever the Messenger of Allah (peace and blessings of Allah be upon him) would ask the Pagans of Makkah to abandon *shirk* (polytheism) and *bid'at* (innovation) and follow the Qur'an revealed by Allah, the Almighty, they used to say that they were quite foolish for they were following their ancestors who had neither wisdom nor any knowledge of the Book. Common sense says that the son would not adopt a business which failed his father. How should they follow their perverted forefathers. Now what to speak of the rituals and practices of the Muslims who consider the rituals of their ancestors as correct and follow in their footsteps, keeping aside the path of Allah and His Messenger. And in spite of all these shortcomings they claim to be Muslims. They follow their forefathers even in what was committed by any of them once in life in a particular circumstance. They should, however, not follow their forefathers who were a deviated lot and try to hold fast the Qur'an and Hadith.

Allah, the Almighty says in Surah Az-Zukhruf of the Holy Qur'an:

وَكَذٰلِكَ مَا اَرسَلنَا مِن قَبلِكَ فِي قَريَةٍ مِّن نَّذِيرٍ اِلاَّ قَالَ
مُتَرَفُوهَا اِنَّا وَجَدنَا اٰبَاءَنَا عَلٰى اُمَّةٍ وَّاِنَّا عَلٰى اٰثَارِهِم
مُقتَدُونَ قَالَ اَوَلَو جِئتُكُم بِاَهدٰى مِمَّا وَجَدتُّم عَلَيهِ
اٰبَاءَكُم قَالُوا اِنَّا بِمَا اُرسِلتُم بِهِ كٰفِرُونَ فَانتَقَمنَا مِنهُم فَا
نظُر كَيفَ كَانَ عَاقِبَةُ المُكَذِّبِينَ

"Just in the same way, whenever We sent a Warner before thee to any people, the wealthy ones among them said: "We found our fathers following a certain religion, and we will certainly follow in their footsteps." He said: "What! even if I brought you better guidance than that which ye found your fathers followings?" They said: "For us, we deny that which ye (Prophets) are sent with." So We exacted retribution from them: now see what was the end of those who rejected (Truth)!"

(Q. 43: 23-25)

That is, all the Prophets got the same reply from the perverted persons that they were following the path of their fathers. When they were made to surrender before the righteous pleas of the Holy Prophet (peace and blessings of Allah be upon him) they refused to accept what was said to them in spite of the fact that his path was more righteous than the path of their fathers. When the wickedness and ignorance of the infidels touched its height, Allah, the Almighty took revenge from them. They were inflicted open punishment in the form of showers of stones and fire; others were ruined by devastating hurricane, by being sunk into earth, by being drowned into river. Hence, they should see what happened to the followers of their fathers. They were all ruined leaving no trace behind.

This *ayah* denotes that the *Ummah* of all the Prophets answered the call of the Prophets in almost the same language. None of them agreed to abandon the religion of their fathers and embrace the religion of their Prophets. Moreover, it is a common experience that most often the well-to-do and satiated persons put forward such arguments and they find it very hard to break away with the rituals and practices of their fathers. Thus, this class, should first of all accept the Truth. The Muslim should fear the wrath and torment of Allah and keep from the Path of Satan.

Allah, the Almighty says in Surah Al-Hajj of the Holy Qur'an:

وَمِنَ النَّاسِ مَن يُجَادِلُ فِى اللهِ بِغَيرِ عِلمٍ وَ يَتَّبِعُ كُلَّ شَيطَانٍ مَّرِيدٍ ط كُتِبَ عَلَيهِ اَنَّهٗ مَن تَوَلَّاهُ فَاِنَّهٗ يُضِلُّهٗ وَيَهدِيهِ اِلٰى عَذَابِ السَّعِيرِ

"And yet among men there are such as dispute about Allah, without knowledge, and follow every Satan obstinate in rebellion! About whom (Satan) it is decreed that whoever turns to him for friendship, Him will he lead astray, and he will guide him to the Chastisement of the Fire."

(Q. 22: 3-4).

That is, some persons are in the habit of raising disputes regarding the Commands of Allah and hold the rope of Satan fast. Thus they go astray in this world and will face Hell-Fire in the Hereafter. They are the men of Satan and hence they follow the path shown by him.

This *ayah* denotes that some people who raise ifs and buts regarding the Commands of Allah and place the pleas taught by their friend Satan, they will have to face Hell-Fire. Hence to follow the rites and rituals of the Pagan past leaving aside the Qur'an and Hadith is the practice of the men of Satan.

Rites and rituals lead to corruption and perversion of many kinds. Some of them follow:

First Practice

Song and Music

سَمَاعِ الغَنَا وَالمعَازِف

First Practice is to organise song and music concerts in marriage ceremonies, festivities, *urs* etc. Some ignorant persons argue that a marriage cermony without song and music gives no pleasure and looks like the assembly of sorrow. Some persons consider it a prayer although the Qur'an and *Hadith* condemn this practice in strong words.

Allah, the Almighty says in Surah Luqman of the Holy Qur'an:

وَمِنَ النَّاسِ مَن يَّشتَرِى لَهوَالحَدِيثِ لِيُضِلَّ عَن سَبِيلِ اللّٰهِ
بِغَيرِ عِلمٍ وَ يَتَّخِذَ ها هُزُوًا ط اُولٰئِكَ لَهُم عَذَابٌ مُّهِينٌ

"But there are, among men, those who purchase idle tales, without knowledge (or meaning), to mislead (men) from the Path of Allah and throw ridicule (on the Path): for such there will be a humiliating chastisement."

(Q. 31:6).

Unwise persons spend lavishly on songs, music and dance and purchase Fire of Hell in return. Such concerts make one forget his prayers and other obligations and turn him ecstatic and out of control behaving in ridiculous manner and making others laugh at him. Thus the time and money which should have been spent in the way of Allah, is spent in the way of Satan. Those who consider the tenets of Islam as playthings will face terrible punishment.

Allah, the Almighty says in Surah Al-Israa of the Holy Qur'an:

وَاستفزِ ز مَنِ استَطَعتَ مِنهُم بِصَوتِكَ وَ ا جلِب عَلَيهِم بَخَيلِكَ وَ رَجِلِكَ وَشَارِكهُم فى الاَموَالِ و الاَولاَدِ وَعِدهُم وَمَا يَعِدُ هُمُ الشَّيطٰنُ اِلاَّ غُرُورًا

> "And arouse those whom thou canst among them, with thy (seductive) voice; make assaults on them with thy cavalry and thy infantry: matually share with them and with their children; and make promises to them. But Satan promises them nothing but deceit."
>
> (Q. 17:64).

When Satan was cursed by Allah, the Almighty, he invoked Allah to keep him alive till the Doomsday so that he could mislead His servants, his prayer was granted. Allah said to him to go and mislead the people but keep in mind that His virtuous servants would never go astray. He was permitted to apply all the devices of deviations from the right path. He chalked out various attractive programmes which might make men to lose time and money with loss in return. Thus offerings in the name of Shaikh Saddo, Zain Khan, Bale Mian, Bibi Otawali, Lal Pari, etc., naming their sons as Bhawani Bux, Ganga Bux, Madar Bux, Salar Bux etc., teaching songs, music and dancing, etc. are all Satanic acts. Spending money on such filthy activities means to extend support to Satan in his scheme. The children who are taught such things go to share Satanic functions. Satan puts such thoughts into heart that such and such acts lead to the pleasure and favour of Allah, such acts make the soul of the saints happy, such acts bring name and fame. These are all Satanic acts, the result of which is tragic.

Baihaqi reports from Jabir (may Allah be pleased with him) that the Holy Prophet (peace and blessings of Allah be upon him) said:

الغناء ينبت النفاق فى القلب كما ينبت الماء الزرع

"Song creates hypocrisy in heart as water grows harvest."

Hypocrisy means to claim to be a Muslim in appearance and having divine feeling at heart. Thus the Messenger of Allah (peace and blessings of Allah be upon him) said that singing creates hypocrisy in heart as water grows harvest.

Imam Ahmad and Abu Dawud report from Nafe (may Allah be pleased with him):

كنت مع ابن عمر فى طريقٍ فسمع مزماراً فوضع اصبعيه فى اذنيه ونا ء عن الطريق الى الجانب الاخرى ثم قال لى بعد ان بعد يا نا فع هل تسمع شيئاً قلت لا فرفع اصبعيه عن اذنيه قال كنت مع رسول الله صلى الله عليه وسلم فسمع صوت يراعٍ فصنع مثل ما صنعت قال نا فع رضى الله تعالى عنه وكنت اذ ذاك صغيراً

"Once I was passing by a thoroughfare alongwith Ibn Umar (may Allah be pleased with him) we heard music and saw him inserting his fingers in both the ears. When we walked a long distance, he asked me:

"O Nafe, do you hear anything?"

"I replied in the negative. He then pulled his fingers out of ears and said:

"Once I was with the Messenger of Allah (peace and blessings of Allah be upon him) that we heard the sound of flute and he did as I did.' 'I was then a boy', said Nafe.

This *hadith* denotes that the Messenger of Allah (peace and blessings of Allah be upon him) and his Companions (may Allah be pleased with all of them) avoided music so much that if ever they heard they would shut their ears. How unfortunate are those who hold concerts of music and song at their houses.

Baihaqi reports from Ibn Abbas (may Allah be pleased with him) that the Messenger of Allah (peace and blessings of Allah be upon him) said:

ان الله تعالى حرم الخمر والميسر والكوبة وقال كل مسكر حرام

"Allah, the Almighty declared wine, gambling and koba *haram*," and added: 'What intoxicates is *haram*.'

'Koba' is that musical instrument which is covered from both ends like drum etc.

Imam Ahmad reports from Abu Omamah (may Allah be pleased with him) that the Messenger of Allah (peace and blessings of Allah be upon him) said:

ان الله بعثنى رحمةً للعالمين وهدىً للعالمين و امرنى ربى عز و جل بمحق العازف والمزامير والاوثان والصلب وامر الجاهلية

"Allah, the Almighty sent me as a Prophet for the whole world for mercy and guidance and my Lord, the Exalted commanded me to do away with musical instruments with strings, flute, idols and cross and all acts of Ignorance".

That is, when Allah, the Almighty looked upon His creation with Mercy and wanted to guide the people and save from wrong-doings, He appointed His Messenger and commanded him to do away with musical instruments with strings like *sitar* (a kind of guitar with three strings), tambour, *sarod* (a song), *sarangi* (a musical instrument) etc. and flute like musical instruments, the idols, cross, rites of paganism.

This *hadith* denotes that not only the Prophet of Allah (peace and blessings of Allah be upon him) was commanded to do away with this practice but also to erase it from face of society.

Bukhari reports form Abi Amir and Abi Malik Ash'ari (may Allah be pleased with him) that they heard the Messenger of Islam (peace and blessings of Allah be upon him) say:

ليكونن من امتى اقوام يستحلون الخزو الحرير والخمر والمعازف

"Some people from my *Ummah* will take as *halal* (lawful) *khazz*, *daryai*, wine and musical instruments."

The prophecy of the Messenger came true. Most of them consider it *halal* to wearing silken clothes, listening and playing music. Some of the ignorant people consider it *halal* too. Gradually musical instruments of all kinds came to be played and listened openly in various functions and parties. But the Qur'an and *Hadith* go against these Satanic displays. These ignorants call it the illumination of Allah. What a wonder! a Satanic exercise is called the illumination of Allah. Had there been anything like the illumination of Allah, it would have been with the recital of the Qur'an and the hearing of *hadiths*. Drum beating is permitted during the *Jihad* for spreading news, while it is desirable to beat 'daf' (tambourine) for giving news of marriage. However, this exercise is not necessary where a considerable number of people are present and bear witness to what is going on.

Second Practice

Pride in Genealogy

اِفْتِخَارْ بِالْاِنْسَابِ

Second Practice is to take pride in genealogy. Some people are proud of being Shaikh, Syed, Pathan etc. and son of a molvi or saint etc. They must bear in mind that all are the offsprings of Adam and Eve and have born of the same parents. They adopted different professions to earn a livelihood. Even the Prophets had various occupations. Hadrat Adam would spin cloth and do agriculture; Hadrat Idris would sew clothes; Hadrat Nuh would work as a carpenter; Hadrat Ibrahim and Hadrat Lut were cultivators; Hadrat Saleh and Hadrat Hud were traders; Hadrat Dawud was an ironsmith; and Hadrat Shuyab would rear goats and sheep. When the offsprings of Adam (peace be on him) spread in other corners of the land, every section of men adopted the names of their respective heads of the family and were known with that name. This practice gave birth to various castes. The Prophet Hadrat Yaqub's name was Israil and hence his children were known as Bani Israil; the children of Ismail were known as Bani Ismail; our Prophet Muhammad was called as Syed, hence his offsprings were called Syed; Abu Bakr was entitled Siddique and Umar had the title of Farooq, hence their descendents were known as Shaikh

Siddiqui and Shaikh Farooqui, respectively. Later on, some people made someone their religious guide and named themselves after them like the disciples of Shaikh Abdul Qadir Jilani became Qadiri; the disciples of Bahauddin Naqshbandi and that of Shahabuddin Suhrawardi were named Suhrawardi. Similarly, some sections of people were called Hanafi, Shafei, Hambali and Maliki etc. Thereafter some ignorant people adopted some titles for attaching honour and status with themselves and for bragging and boasting. Thus they made themselves venerable by attaching themselves to some saint or religious guide.

This pride in on their ancestors and religious guides naturally make them look down upon sects. A syed, however immoral and characterless he be, thinks himself higher than non-Syeds even if they are men of character and morals. Similarly, the Shaikhs consider themselves the descendants of the Quraish, Siddiq Akbar, Umar Farooq, Uthman Zinnurain and hence superior to others, although they have no liking for following those pious souls. The Pathans consider themselves the descendants of Bani Israil and take pride in this attachment, for thousands of Prophets and Kings belonged to this nation and they had been noted for valour and courage. Most of the Friends of Allah and saints were born among them. The same happened with the Mughals.

But the Qur'an and Hadith have nothing to do with such wrong and baseless practices. To consider oneself higher and superior is the practice with the Unbelievers.

Allah, the Almighty says in Surah Al-Hujurat of the Holy Qur'an:

يَا أَيُّهَا النَّاسُ إِنَّا خَلَقْنٰكُم مِّن ذَكَرٍ وَّ أُنثٰى وَجَعَلْنٰكُمْ
شُعُوباً وَّ قَبَائِلَ لِتَعَارَفُوا إِنَّ أَكْرَمَكُمْ عِندَ اللهِ
أَتْقٰكُمْ إِنَّ اللهَ عَلِيمٌ خَبِيرٌ

> "O mankind! We created you from a single (pair) of a male and a female; and made you into nations and tribes, that ye may know each other (not that ye may despise each other). Verily the most honoured of you in the sight of Allah is (he who is) the most righteous of you. And Allah has full knowledge and is well acquainted (with all things)."
>
> (Q. 49:13).

That is, high caste does not mean virtue, greatness and righteousness. Castes are meant for acquaintances. It is the piety and fear of Allah which is recognised by Him. One who is not righteous has no status to Allah, the Almighty. Hence a shoemaker or a weaver or a comber of cotton who is righteous is better than Syed, Shaikh, Mughal and Pathan who are transgressors and sinners. Some people argue that *kufu* to marry in low caste. This notion is based on misunderstanding. Such a thing is kept in view with the sole intention of keeping balance and affinity between husband and wife and to avoid differences of opinion, standard and standpoint. If the hand of a girl, who has not yet attained her puberty, is given to a man of a mean and immoral person without the consent of her guardian, the latter has a right to cancel the marriage.

But this action cannot be taken by the guardian in case the girl has been married to someone with her consent and after attaining puberty.

Allah, the Almighty says in Surah Al-Muminun of Holy Qur'an:

فَإِذَا نُفِخَ فِى الصُّورِ فَلَآ أَنسَابَ بَيْنَهُمْ يَوْمَئِذٍ وَّلَا يَتَسَآءَلُونَ

> "Thou when the Trumpet is blown, there will be no more relationships between them that day, nor will one ask after another!"
>
> (Q. 23:101).

That is, there will be no consideration of geneology and caste on the Day of Judgement. Thus the notion that they are the descendants of so and so will be of no help to them. Nobody will come to their rescue on that Day. All connections of geneology, caste and relation will be severed. Hence it is sheer ignorance to take pride in caste and geneology.

Allah, the Almighty says in Surah An-Najm of the Holy Qur'an:

فَلَا تُزَكُّوا أَنفُسَكُمْ

"........therefore hold not yourselves purified."

(Q. 53:32).

That is, only Allah is faultless, otherwise everyone of us is at fault more or less. Why should they be proud of their fathers and forefathers? This is all nonsense and unwise.

Allah, the Almighty says in Surah An-Najm of the Holy Qur'an:

لَا تَزِرُ وَازِرَةٌ وِزْرَ أُخْرَىٰ وَأَن لَّيْسَ لِلْإِنسَانِ إِلَّا مَا سَعَىٰ ۝
وَأَنَّ سَعْيَهُ سَوْفَ يُرَىٰ ثُمَّ يُجْزَاهُ الْجَزَاءَ الْأَوْفَىٰ

"Namely, that no bearer of burdens can bear the burden of another; that man can have nothing but what he strives for; that (the fruit of) his striving will soon come in sight; then will he be rewarded with a reward complete."

(Q. 53: 38-41).

That is, nobody will bear the burden of another. It means nobody will get punishment for the fault of any other person. A person will get what he earns. As one sows so will he reap. Parents are not punished for the crimes of their sons and daughters. Similarly, sins of pupils and disciples will not be attached to their religious guides and teachers. Everybody will have to bear the brunt of his doings. Hence one's claim to belong to so and so father and forefathers, saints and guides will not save one from Hell-Fire.

Muslim reports from Abu Hurairah (may Allah be pleased with him) that the Holy Prophet (peace and blessings of Allah be upon him) said:

من ابطا به عمله لم يسرع به نسبه

> "Family lineage will be of no help to one whose deeds are unacceptable (to Allah)."

That is, only the deeds come to help instead of caste, however high he be with respect to caste. If a person belongs to high caste but his deeds are low, he is quite worthless. Hadrat Bilal (may Allah be pleased with him) was a Negro slave but he was dear to Allah because of his piety, purity and reghteousness. Abu Jahl was of noble birth but his misdeeds made him low in the eyes of the noble souls and to Allah, the Almighty. Caste system is, therefore, something useless and futile for this world as well as the Hereafter. It should be discarded and rejected outright as something impure and uncivilized. To be a Muslim is itself a matter of pride.

Muslim reprts from Abu Malik Ash'ari (may Allah be pleased with him) that the Messenger of Allah (peace and blessings of Allah be upon him) said:

اربع فى امتى من امر الجاهلية لا يتركون هن الفخـر فـى الاحسـاب والطعـن فـى الا نسـاب والاستسـقاء بـا لنجوم والنيا حة

> "Four things in my *ummah* belong to the deeds of Ignorance, - these are describing the greatness of family lineage; casting aspertions on other castes; begging water from *nachhattar* (star); and weeping loudly at the dead person."

That is, these four practices are going on among the Muslims and they are not prepared to abandon them. One is to be proud of the deeds of his fathers, their richness, bravery, courage and deeds, Secondly, they cast aspersions on other castes and their fathers, family lineage and status. Thirdly, begging water from *nachhattars* and thinking that it cannot rain unless such and such *nachhattar* reaches a certain stage. Fourthly, to cry loudly over the dead. A Muslim should keep away from all these practices because it is a matter of shame to follow the Unbelievers.

Bukhari and Muslim report from Abu Hurairah (may Allah be pleased with him) that the Messenger of Allah (peace and blessings of Allah be upon him) was once asked:

"Who is more respectable?"

ای الناس اکرم قال اکرمهم عند الله اتقهم

"The most respectable to Allah is one who is most pious," the Apostle replied.

"We don't ask you this," the people said.

Thereupon the Apostle said:

قال فاكرم الناس يوسف نبی الله ابن نبی الله ابن خليل الله

"The most respectable among all men is Yusuf, (peace be on him) the Prophet of Allah and the son of a Prophet i.e. Yaqub (peace be on him), the Prophet of Allah; the son of the Friend of Allah, Ibrahim (peace be on him),"

"We don't ask you this," the people said.

"Do you ask then about the root of the Arabs?" the Apostle said.

"Yes," they submitted.

فخيـاركم فـى الجاهليـة خياركم فى الاسلام اذا فقهوا

"One who is pious in the state of unbelief is pious in the state of Islam also," the Messenger of Allah replied.

That the greatness in man lies in the fact that he either be pious or a Prophet, particularly a hereditary one, for instance, Yusuf (peace be on him) who was himself a Prophet, son of Hadrat Yaqub was son of Hadrat Ishaq whose father was Hadrat Ibrahim, the Friend of Allah (peace be on all of them). In short, greatness lies either in piety or Prophethood. Thus, it is sheer ignorance to be proud of family lineage.

Muslim reports from Ayaz bin Hemar al-Majashul (may Allah be pleased with him) that the Holy Prophet (peace and blessings of Allah be upon him) said:

ان اللـه اوحـى الـى ان تواضعو حتـى لا يفتخـر احـد
على احدٍ ولا يبغى احدُ على احدٍ

"Allah, the Almighty commanded me to practise humility so that nobody is proud of others or sing praise of other."

That is, men have born of one father and mother and have to go to earth after death from where they have been raised. Hence, it is quite futile to be proud of oneself or one's fathers.

Tirmidhi and Abu Dawood report from Abu Hurairah (may Allah be pleased with him) that the Holy Prophet (peace and blessings of Allah be upon him) said:

لينتهين اقوام يفتخرون با با ئهم الذيـن مـاتوا انمـا هـم
فحم من جهنم اوليكونـن اهـون علـى اللـه مـن الجعـل

الذى يد هدع الخـرء بـا نفـه ان اللـه قـد اذهـب عنكـم
عبية الجاهلية وفخرها بـا لاباء انمـا هـو مومـن تقـى
وفاجر شقى كلهم بنو ادم و ادم من ترابٍ

"Certainly the people should refrain from taking pride in their fathers for they were mere coal of Hell, otherwise they will become worms of cowdung which moves it with its nose. Allah removed the pride of the Age of Ignorance and being proud of their fathers; a man would either be a Believer, pure and pious or a sinner and transgressor. All are the offsprings of Adam and Adam was born of earth."

That is, in fact, all men have born of earth, hence, they should refrain from being proud of anything. Since all of them are offsprings of Adam and hence they are brother of one another: To be proud of one's father is nonsense because some of the fathers had been unbelievers, the coal of Hell. Why should one be proud of one's forefathers; it is a matter of shame and disgrace to mention the names of such persons. Hence the Holy Prophet (peace and blessings of Allah be upon him) asked the people to refrain from doing so, otherwise Allah, the Almighty would convert them into worms of cowdung which go on moving it through their nose. People think that their bragging would make them great but, in fact, they are the most wretched and shameless to Allah. To take pride in the practices of the pagans of the past which Allah purgated from His religion and forbade the Believers from following such a practice. A man would be either a pure and pious Believer or a wretched and sinner. In case of being a Believer it is enough to be proud of being pious, while a sinner may be proud of his wretchedness.

Tirmidhi and Ibn Majah report from Samura (may Allah be pleased with him) that the Messenger of Allah (peace and blessings of Allah be upon him) said:

الحسب المال والكرم التقوى

"Piety is the only honour and greatness lineage is money."

That is, piety is the only source of greatness and the virtuous person is the only one who practise piety, whichever caste he belongs to. Nobody talks about the caste when the person is wealthy. They find fault only with the poor.

Imam Ahmad and Baihaqi report from Uqbah bin Amir (may Allah be pleased with him) that the Holy Prophet (peace and blessings of Allah be upon him) said:

انسابكم هذه ليست بمسبة على احدٍ كلكم بنو ادم طف
الصاع باالصاع لم تملأ ليس لاحد فضل الا بدين
وتقوى كفى بالرجل ان يكون بذياً فا حشا بخيلاً

"These castes of yours are not meant for abusing others. All of you are the progeny of Adam; you should share the loss of one another; none is better than others but in piety; the evil-doers are those who talk nonsense and are miser."

That is, none has a bad lineage to be reproached and none has a good lineage to be proud of. Both of these concepts are nonsensical.

Once Hadrat Yusuf (may peace be upon him) was sold to an unbelieving slave. Since a famine broke out and that remained continued for seven long years, each of them had sold himself to other person. Thus all of them were passing the life of a slave. Moreover, the mother of Prophet Hadrat Ismail (peace be on him) was a maidservant and the Quraish belong to her. Thus one who reproaches, reproaches his forefathers. Similarly, if one looks down upon persons of various castes formed on the basis of professions as we have already described, he reproaches the

Prophets and pious persons.

But, however, they are reproached and taunted till they are weak and poor. The day they achieve wealth or power, nobody tries to know their lineage.

Third Practice

Esteemed Respect

اِفْرَاطُ التَّعْظِيْم

Third Practice is the abundance of esteemed showered upon an individual. Such an extremity of honour for one another is tantamount to disgrace Allah, the Almighty, but they are quite oblivious to its evil. For instance, prostration of reverence is confined to Allah and to do it for anyone other than Allah is an affront to Him. Similarly, it is particular for Allah to show respects to Him by standing silent and bow down in *ruku*, for He is the Creator of the universe and king of kings, only one liable to be worshipped, purveyor of reward and punishment to one and all. Now to bow before anybody else, to stand before anyone with folded hands or to call anyone king of kings etc. is to show disrespects to Allah, the Almighty. All these sayings and gestures are against the dictates of the Qur'an and *Sunnah* and hence they must be discarded and the right path be followed. Moreover, everybody should be paid respects according to his status.

Allah, the Almighty says in Surah Bara'at of the Holy Qur'an:

فَإِن تَابُوا وَأَقَامُوا الصَّلَوٰةَ وَءَاتَوُا الزَّكَوٰةَ فَإِخْوَانُكُمْ فِي الدِّينِ

"But (even so), if they repent, establish regular prayers, and pay *Zakat* they are your brethren in Faith." (Q. 9:11).

This *ayah* tells that the Muslims have been commanded to treat as their brethren who repent for evil doings and refrain from doing so in future, establish prayer and pay *Zakat*. One should neither stand in esteem for another person nor prostrate for him nor call him king of kings etc. One should say 'Assalam-o-alaikum' to another in a simple and dignified manner.

The *ayah* also denotes that one should not be treated as brother who commits sin, ignores prayer and evades paying of *Zakat* even if he is his blood brother, what to speak of unbelievers and transgressers.

Allah, the Almighty says in Surah Bara'at of the Holy Qur'an:

وَالْمُؤْمِنُونَ وَالْمُؤْمِنَٰتُ بَعْضُهُمْ أَوْلِيَاءُ بَعْضٍ

"The Believers, men and women, are protectors, one of another."

(Q. 9:71).

If a Muslim imparts some benefit to his Muslim brother, it should be considered from Allah and his Muslim brother was just a helper. He, therefore, does not deserve any undue thanksgiving, bowing and prostration from one who has been helped. No authority in any form or shape deserves respect beyond his status and capacity.

Allah, the Almighty says in Surah Al-Hujurat of the Holy Qur'an

إِنَّمَا الْمُؤمِنُونَ إِخوَةٌ

"The Believers are but a single Brotherhood."

(Q. 49:10).

Hence one who is greater in Islamic activities is the real "big brother", one who is weak in Islamic activities is the "younger brother", and one who performs no Islamic act is not at all a brother, whether he be a ruler, king, or saint.

Tirmidhi reports from Anas (may Allah be pleased with him) that a certain person submitted:

يا رسول الله الرجل منا يلقى اخاه او صديقه اينحنى له قال لا قال افيلتزمه ويقبله قال لا قال افيا خذه ويصا فحه قال نعم

"O Prophet of Allah, should anyone while meeting his friend or a Muslim bow before him?"

"No," the Prophet of Allah said.

"Should one embrace and kiss him?" he asked.

"No," the Apostle said.

"Should one hold him for a handshake?" he asked

"Yes," the Prophet of Allah said.

Thus this *hadith* tells that while meeting a brother or friend or a Muslim, one should not go beyond handshaking. Bowing, embracing, holding one's hands or touching his feet are all acts of Unbelievers and Hypocrites.

Tirmidhi reports from Anas (may Allah be pleased with him).

لم يكن شخص احب اليهم من رسول اللـه صلـى اللـه عليه وسلم وكانو اذا رأوه لم يقوموا لمـا يعلمـون مـن كراهية لذلك

"None was dearer to the Companions of the Apostle than the Messenger of Allah (peace and blessings of Allah be upon him). But they would never stand up to welcome him because of his displeasure at this act."

This *hadith* tells that the Messenger of Allah (peace and blessings of Allah be upon him) would show his displeasure at the getting up of one to greet another, hence the Companions would not pay respect to the Apostle in such a manner. Then why should the Muslims do so when the Messenger disliked it.

Tirmidhi and Abu Dawud report Muawiyyah (may Allah be pleased with him) that the Holy Propeht (peace and blessings of Allah be upon him) said:

من سره ان يتمثل لـه الرجـال قيامـاً فليتبوامقعـده مـن النار

"Those who like to that people keep standing before him like a picture, should find his place in Hell."

That is, one who likes others to keep standing before him out of regard without moving like a statue is Hellish.

Abu Dawud reports from Abi Umamah (may Allah be pleased with him):

خرج رسول الله صلـى اللـه عليـه وسـلم متكئـاً علـى عصاً فقمنا له

"Once the Messenger of Allah (peace and blessings of Allah be upon him) came out with the aid of a stick and we got up to pay our respects to him. Thereupon he said:

لا تقومو كما يقوم الاعاجم يعظم بعضهم بعضاً

'Don't get up like the Persians to pay regard to one another."

It was practice of the Persians and non-Arabs to get up to pay respects to their superiors and this is the practice with these countries even today.

Abu Dawud reports from Mutarrib bin Abdullah bin As'shakhir (may Allah be pleased with him):

انطلقت فى و فد بنى عامرٍ الى رسول الله صلى الله عليه وسلم فقلنا انت سيدنا فقال السيد هو الله فقلنا وافضلنا فضلاً واعظمنا طولاً فقال قولوا قولكم او بعض اقولكم ولايستجرءنكم الشيطان :

"Once I came to the Messenger of Allah (peace and blessings of Allah be upon him) with the emissaries of Bani Amir and submitted:

"You are our chief."

"The chief is Allah alone," he replied.

"You are our superior and a generous person,"

we submitted.

"Say a little than or other Satan may make you disrespectful."

That is, one should speak cautiously in praise of one's superiors. Hence to say to someone that he is the master, chief, best of all etc. is wrong and forbidden.

Bukhari and Muslim report from Umar (may Allah be pleased with him) that the Messenger of Allah (peace and blessings of Allah be upon him) said:

لاتطرونى كما اطرت النصارى ابن مريم فان مـا انـا عبده فقولوا عبد الله ورسوله :

"Don't enhance my status beyond a certain limit as the Christians did in case of Isa bin Maryam. I am His Slave so call me the Slave and Messenger of Allah."

That is, describe only those traits which Allah has confined on him. To eulogize his Prophethood is enough for nothing for man could be greater than this status and all others go below it. However, a slave is a slave even after being appointed a Messenger. So the Messenger of Allah has forbidden from doing what the Christians did with Isa (peace be on him).

Muslim reports from Miqdad bin Aswad (may Allah be pleased with him) that the Messenger of Allah (peace and blessings of Allah be upon him) said:

اذا رأيتم المدّاحين فاحثوا فى وجوههم التر ابُ :

"When you see someone praising you highly, fill his mouth with dust."

That is, those who praise their superiors and wealthy persons beyond all limits tell a lie and the one who is praised turns proud. Hence the one who praises is liable to be filled dust in his mouth.

Bukhari and Muslim report from Abi Bakrah (may Allah be pleased with him): A certain person eulogized another one in presence of the Messenger of Allah (peace and blessings of Allah be upon him). The Messenger said thrice:

قطعت عنق اخيك ثلاثاً من كان منكم مادحاً

لامحالةَ فليقل احب فلاناً والله حسيبه ان كان يرى انه

كذالك ولايزكى على الله احداً :

'May you be condemned that you cut the neck of your brother; one who wants to anybody should only say:

'I love so and so; and Allah knows well what he feels."

That is, Allah alone knows the truth about everything. He alone knows both the inside and the outside of every person. A person eulogizes another seeing his appearance without knowing his inward traits. Hence if he praises one against the reality, it goes against what Allah knows about him. In this way, he declares good what is evil to Allah. Now to save such a situation, the Messenger of Allah asked the people to say, 'I love you,' if they want to express their appreciation for anyone.

Baihaqi reports from Anas (may Allah be pleased with him) that the Holy Prophet (peace and blessings of Allah be upon him) said:

اذا مدحَ الفاسقُ غضبَ الربُ تعالى اهتزّ له العرشُ :

"When a transgresser is eulogized, Allah, the Almighty grows so angry that His Throne trembles."

This *hadith* denotes that those who praise the clean-shaved person, the person who refrains from saying prayers, observing fasts, performing Hajj, a drunkard, a debauch, one who considers song and music and worshipping of graves as valid or flatter someone vacally or by writing eulogy for him - are all victim of Allah's wrath and punishment. Now to eulogize such evil persons is so much disliked by Allah that His Throne trembles with His fear when He falls in wrath by hearing such eulogies:

Muslim Reports from Abu Hurairah (may Allah be pleased with him) that the Holy Prophet (peace and blessings be upon him) said:

اغيظ رجلٍ على الله يوم القيامةِ واخبثه رجلٌ كان يسمى ملك الاملاك :

"On the Day of Judgement, Allah will curse those who are so wicked to be xalled the king of kings."

That is, to call a person king of kings emperor of the world is a hellish act and the person who utters these words will also be under the divine wrath on the Day of Judgement because Allah is the King of kings and the Cherisher of the worlds.

Muslim reports from Abu Hurairah (may Allah be pleased with him) that the Messenger of Allah (peace and blessings of Allah be upon him) said:

لا يقل العبد ربى ولكن ليقل سيدى

"Let not the slave call his master his Lord but his chief."

Another tradition says:

لايقل العبد لسيده مولاءى فان مولكم الله :

"Let not the slave call his master his Lord for his master is none but Allah."

That is, the slave must not call his master his Lord because Allah is the Lord of all. Similarly, it is undesirable and nonsense to call anybody "Cherisher of slaves or servants".

Sharhe Sunnah reports from Hudhaifah (may Allah be pleased with him) that the Messenger of Allah (peace and blessings of Allah be upon him) said:

لاتقولوا ماشاء الله ومحمدٌ وقولوا ماشاء الله وحدهُ :

> "Don't say what Allah and Muhammad want, rather say, what Allah wants."

This *hadith* makes it clear that to say someone 'As you like, so will it be," is tantamount to *shirk*.

Abu Dawud reports from Hudhaifah (may Allah be pleased with him) that the Messenger of Allah (peace and blessings of Allah be upon him) said:

لاتقولوا للمنافق سيداً فانــه ان يك سيداً فقد اسخطتم ربكم:

> "Don't call the hypocrite your chief because if you say so, you displease your Lord most."

That is, one who calls chief to one who is a Muslim in name, annoys Allah; what to speak of those who attach titles to sinners, transgressers and Unbelievers.

Fourth Practice

Extravagance in Marriage etc.

مُغَالَاةٌ فِى الْمُهُوْرِوَالْاِسْرَافُ

To settle excessive dower and to show extravangance once on the occasion of marriage ceremony and many other such practices are quite against the simple and righteous nature of Islam. Some of such practices are as follows:

To serve food to the brotherhood or community before marriage; relatives of the bride serve food to this brotherhood and those present in the cermony even if they belong to the same city or locality; marriage cermony is celebrated with song, dance and music, crackers are supposed to be a must for the occasion; to wear 'sehra' (a garland worn on the fore-head by the bride and the bridegroom at the marriage ceremony); to settle excessive dower etc. Some of these rites belong to Unbelievers. These are all *bid'ats* (innovations) and lead to deviation from the right path and invite displeasure and wrath of Alla'ı, the Almighty.

Allah, the Almighty says in Surah Al-Isra'a of the Holy Qur'an:

وَلَاتُبَذِّرْ تَبْذِيْرًا. اِنَّ الْمُبَذِّرِيْنَ كَانُوْٓا اِخْوَانَ الشَّيَاطِيْنِ وَ

كَانَ الشَّيْطَانُ لِرَبِّهِ كَفُوْرًا :

"But squander not (your wealth) in the manner of a spendthrift. Verily spend thrifts are brothers of the Satans. And the Satan is to his Lord (Himself) ungrateful."

(Q. 17: 26-27).

That is, wealth is the blessings of Allah. It makes one praceful during prayer, gives advantage to the Muslims, stabilises the religion. Allah gives wealth to be spent according to His Will and Pleasure. Thus extravagance is ungratefulness. Hence those who are spendthrift are brothers of Satan. Some persons borrow money on interest to spend on Satánic rites. Both the taking and giving of interest are *haram*. Some persons even beg for spending on marital rites, although begging is *haram* if need be fulfilled with any other means. To some religious scholars, a dying person should eat from the dead animals like crow or dog if available instead of begging. Such a begging is a matter of disgrace too. To some it is *haram* and one should give alms to such a beggar. Such persons invite the displeasure of Allah for the pleasure of Satan.

Allah, the Almighty says in Surah Al-An'am of the Holy Qur'an:

وَلَاتُسْرِفُوْا اِنَّهُ لَا يُحِبُّ المسْرِفِيْنَ .

"But waste not by excess: for Allah loveth not the wasters."

(Q. 6:141).

Reckless spending of money is *haram* and one who does so displeases Allah. Hence the marriage which is celebrated with extravagance is deprived of the blessings of Allah. Morever, such spendthrifts are counted among the rebels of Allah.

Baihaqi reports from Lady Aisha (may Allah be pleased with her) that the Messenger of Allah (peace and blessings of Allah be upon him) said:

ان اعظم النكاح بركةً ايسره مؤنةً :

"Most blessing is the matrimony which is simple and free from trouble."

That is, that matrimony is full of blessings in which there is no trouble in collecting resources and the woman agrees with small dower. More the trouble less is the blessing. Since they do not wish to pay the dower, they accept any amount as a dower. The relatives of the bride settle an excess amount in the hope that if not during lifetime, it will be taken from the property of the dead.

Muslim reports from Abu Salma (may Allah be pleased with her) that she asked Lady Aisha (may Allah be pleased with her) how much was her dower settled with the Messenger of Allah (peace and blessings of Allah be upon him)?"

Lady Aisha (may Allah be pleased with her) explained :

كان صداق ازواجه ثنتى عشرة اوقيةً ونشٌ قالت اتدرى ما النش قال لا قالت نصف اوقية فتلك خمس مائة درهمٍ :

"Twelve Oqiah and one *nash*" and enquired

"Do you know what is *nash* ?"

"It is equal to half an Oqiah ie. 500 dirhams."

Less and less dower should be settled and quite within the pecuniary circumstances. Had excessive dower been a matter of reward, the Messenger of Allah (peace and blessings of Allah be upon him) would have settled the dower more and more.

Tirmidhi, Abu Dawud, Nasa'i, Ibn Majah and Darimi report that Umar ibn Khattab (may Allah be pleased with him) said:

الا لاتغالوا صدقة النساء فانها لوكانت مكرمة فى

الدنيا وتقوى عند الله لكان اولكم بها نبى اللـه صلـى
الله عليه وسلم ما عملت رسول الله صلى اللـه عليـه
وسلم نكح شيئاً من نسائه ولا انكح شيئاً من بناته على
اكثر من اثنتى عشر اوقية :

"Beware, and do not settle excessive dower of women. Had there been any superiority and piety in this matter in this world, the Messenger of Allah (peace and blessings of Allah be upon him) was the most priviledged of this. I don't know that the Messenger had married to any woman or had given any of his daughter in marriage on more than twelve Oqiah."

A Prophet is the most virtuous and pious man on the earth. Our Prophet (peace and blessings of Allah be upon him) is superior to all other Prophets. That is why if it had been a matter of virtue and reward he would settled excessive dower of his wives and daughters.

Abu Dawud reports from Umme Habiba (may Allah be pleased with her):

انها كـانت تحـت عبـد اللـه بـن جحـشٍ فمـات بـارض
الحبشة فزوجها النجاشى النبى صلى الله عليـه وسـلم
وامهرها عنه اربعة آلاف درهمٍ :

"I was married to Abdullah bin Jahash. After his demise in Abyssinia, Negus gave me in the marriage of the Messenger and settled four thousand dirham as dower."

Excessive dower is a debt and it should be said in this world otherwise it will be considered like other debts and will be settled in the Hereafter by taking virtues from her husband, otherwise he will not go to Heaven.

Bukhari and Muslim report from Anas (may Allah be pleased with him) who said:

ما اولم رسول الله صلى الله عليه وسلم على احدٍ من نسآئه ماأولم على زينب اولم بشاةٍ :

> "The Messenger of Allah (peace and blessings of Allah be upon him) gave more food in the *walima* (marriage feast) of Lady Zainab (may Allah be pleased with her) than any other wife, and it was a goat."

That is, the Apostle served the feast of *walima* with the meat of a goat. Never before he served so much and so better a feast. It means one should serve feast of *walima* according to the economic condition at the time. *Walima* is the feast served after marriage and hence any feast served before marriage is futile and spendthriftness which is against *Sunnah*.

Bukhari and Muslim report from Anas (may Allah be pleased with him):

ان رسول الله صلى الله عليه وسلم اعتق صفية وتزوجها وجعل عتقها صداقها واولم عليها بحيسٍ :

> "The Messenger of Allah (peace and blessings of Allah be upon him) set Safia free and married her setting her freedom as her dower and served *hais* as marriage feast."

Hais is a kind of food like *halwa* (a kind of sweet dish made of flour, ghee and sugar). It means to serve a particular kind of food according to the standard of the community is nonsensical.

Whatever is available at the time should be served.

Bukhari reports from Lady Safia (may Allah be pleased with her) that the Messenger of Allah (peace and blessings of Allah be upon him) served two mud of barley as the feast of marriage for some of his wives.

اولم النبى صلى اللـه عليـه وسـلم عـلى بعـض نسـآئه مدين من شعيرٍ :

Two mud of *Sattu* (barley parched and ground and made into a paste drunk) make about two *sers*. In short, the Apostle would serve whatever was available at the time. He was never found anxious to serve a better food and putting himself to trouble. Hence the Muslim should follow in the footsteps of their Prophet. Morever, marriage feast should be served after marriage as a result of pleasure achieved by marriage. To serve delicious food for name and fame is nonsensical.

Tirmidhi reports from Ibn Ma'sud (may Allah be pleased with him) that the Holy Prophet (peace and blessings of Allah be upon him) said:

طعـام اول يـومٍ حـقٌ وطعـام يـوم الثـانى سـنة وطعـام الثالث سمعة ومن سمع سمع الله به :

> "Serving food on the first day is right; on the second day is a custom; and on the third day, for name and fame, is to be put to disgrace by Allah, the Almighty."

That is, when the bride is brought to bridegroom's house, the latter should serve marriage feast to his friends and relatives to express pleasure for the achievement. Serving marriage feast on the second day of the marriage is a general custom. But to serve the marriage feast on the third day is just for the name and fame and hence it is disgraceful for the host. One should refrain from attending such a feast.

Ahmad reports from Abu Hurairah (may Allah be pleased with him) that the Messenger of Allah (peace and blessings of Allah be upon him) said:

المتباريان لايحابان ولايؤكل طعامها :

> "Those who serve food as a return and for name and fame should not be acceptable to the invitees."

It has now become a practice to serve food as a token of rivalry or for the sake of achieving reputation. Now to achieve this purpose a person sells his garden or gets his house mortgaged or borrow money from someone or begs and gets entangled in a number of troubles. Hence one is asked to avoid such marriage parties.

Fifth Practice

To Keep Away Widows from Remarriage

مُمَانَعَةُ النِّسَآءِ عَنِ النِّكَاحِ الثَّانِیْ :

It has become a custom that the widow is prevented from second marriage after the death of her first husband. Gradually, second marriage of a widow has become a matter of disgrace. Hence a young widow keeps away from second marriage for fear of reproachment from relatives and members of society, even if she is passing a life of poverty and grief. This practice has been taken from the Hindus, for it is invalid for a Hindu widow to remarry after the death of her first husband. This custom is against wisdom as well as religious tenets. Allah, the Almighty has created sexual need both in male and female and to deny this need is injustice from every point of view. Moreover, it is quite strange and a matter of sheer injustice that a male is permitted to remarry after the death of his first wife but a widow is denied this right.

Allah, the Almighty says in Surah Al-Baqarah of the Holy Qur'an:

وَاِذَا طَلَّقْتُمُ النِّسَآءَ فَبَلَغْنَ اَجَلَهُنَّ فَلَا تَعْضُلُوا لَهُنَّ اَنْ

يَّنْكِحْنَ اَزْوَاجَهُنَّ اِذَا تَرَاضَوْا بَيْنَهُمْ بِالْمَعْرُوْفِ ط ذَالِكَ
يُوْعَظُ بِهٖ مَنْ كَانَ مِنْكُمْ يُؤْمِنُ بِاللّٰهِ وَالْيَوْمِ الْآخِرِ ذَالِكُمْ
اَزْكٰى لَكُمْ وَاَطْهَرُ وَاللّٰهُ يَعْلَمُ وَاَنْتُمْ لَا تَعْلَمُوْنَ :

"When ye divorce women, and they fulfil the term of their ('Iddat), do not prevent them from marrying their (former) husbands, if they mutually agree on equitable terms. This instruction is for all amongst you, who believe in Allah and the Last Day. That is (the course making for) most virtue and purity amongst you. And Allah knows, and ye know not."

(Q. 2:232).

'Iddat is fixed for three monthly courses or three months. Now if a widow plans to marry after completing her *'iddat*, her guardians must not prevent her from doing so, if they believe in Allah and the Doomsday. If one goes against the dictate of Allah, he is liable to be punished severely. If she is permitted to remarry, she is saved from perverted ideas and adultery. Allah the Almighty know it well and hence He has laid emphasis on the remarriage of the widow. The guardians should rather persuade her to remarry. Hence one who goes against the dictates of Allah, the Almighty is bound to taste the severity of Hell Fire.

Allah, the Almighty says in Surah An-Nur of the Holy Qur'an:

وَاَنْكِحُوْا الْاَيَامٰى مِنْكُمْ وَالصَّالِحِيْنَ مِنْ عِبَادِكُمْ وَاِمَائِكُمْ
ط اِنْ يَّكُوْنُوْا فُقَرَآءَ يُغْنِهِمُ اللّٰهُ وَاسِعٌ عَلِيْمٌ :

"Marry those among you who are single, and the virtuous one among your slaves, male or female: If they are in poverty, Allah will give them means out of His grace: for Allah is Ample-giving, and He knoweth all things."

(Q. 24:32).

That is, those women who become widow may easily be wedded to someone in their own families. If slave men and women are pious and virtuous, they should also be married among themselves. It is Allah Who will turn them wealthy by His Grace. There is no want of anything with Allah, the Almighty. He is above all needs.

This *ayah* makes it clear that the guardians should give the hands of the widows in marriage themselves without waiting for the widows to make such a demand. Moreover, Allah, the Almighty will, according ot this *ayah*, make the destitute widow well-to-do by His Grace. It means re-marriage of the widow is the most liked act to Allah, the Almighty. Hence, poverty must not be allowed to stand in the way of re-marriage of the widows. The Messenger of Allah (peace and blessings of Allah be upon him) also, therefore, liked this too much.

Tirmidhi reports from Ali (may Allah be pleased with him) that the Messenger of Allah (peace and blessings of Allah be upon him) said:

يا علىُ ثلاثٌ لاتؤخرها الصلوة اذا انت والجنازة اذا

حضرت والايّمُ اذا وجدت لها كفواً :

> "O Ali, make no delay in three things: in saying prayer when it is time for saying it; in saying prayer of the dead body when it is available; and in re-marrying the widow when her pair is there."

This *hadith* tells that the widow of the marriageable age should be married without delay to a man of agreeable nature and behaviour. Similarly, the dead body must not be left unburied for a longer period. Re-marriage of widows must be expedited. This has been the custom in Islamic societies and countries. This has been the practice during the days of the Messenger of Allah (peace and blessings of Allah be upon him). His daughter Hadrat Ruqaiyya (may Allah be pleased with her) was first married to Utbah, the son of Abu Lahab. Later on, she was married to Hadrat Uthman (may Allah be pleased with him). The second daughter of the Messenger named Umm Kulthum was first married to Atibah, the son of Abu Lahab, but, later on, she was given to Hadrat Uthman in marriage. Umm Kulthum, the daughter of Hadrat Fatima (may Allah be pleased with her) and the granddaughter of the Messenger was married to Hadrat Umar (may Allah be pleased with him) first, but after his death, she was married to Awn, the son of Hadrat Jafar (may Allah be pleased with him). When Awn passed away, she was married to Muhammad, the second son of Jafar and after the death of Muhammad too, she was married to the third son of Jafar. The daughter of Hadrat Zainab (may Allah be pleased with her), and the granddaughter of the Messenger was married to Hadrat Ali after the death of Hadrat Fatima and she was married to Mughira bin Naufal after the death of Hadrat Ali according to his will. All the wives of the Messenger of Allah (peace and blessings of Allah be upon him) save Hadrat Aisha (may Allah be pleased with her) were such that either first, second or third husbands had died before being married to the Messenger of Allah (peace and blessings of Allah be upon him).

This is the condition of the wives, and daughters of the Messenger of Allah (peace and blessings of Allah be upon him). There was one lady Roman, the mother-in-law of the Messenger, who was first married to Abdullah bin Manjarah, then to Hadrat Abu Bakr Siddiq (may Allah be pleased with him) who gave birth to Lady Aisha and Abdur Rahman. Lady Asmaa bint Umais (may Allah be pleased with her) was first married to Jafar bin Abi Talib, then to Hadrat Abu Bakr who gave birth to Muhammad bin Bakr. She was married to Hadrat Ali after the death of Hadrat Abu Bakr. This is how great and virtuous souls passed their lives and those who opposed it is certainly the enemies of Allah and His Messenger. Had the second, third and fourth marriages of the widows been a shameful act, the Messenger and his Companions would have never practised it.

Sixth Practice

Crying Over the Dead

فِى النُّوحَةِ وَالْإِحْدَادِ هـ

When a person passes away, his or her friends and relatives cry over him or her. The women, in particular, beat their chest and others join them in this exercise. This exercise goes on for three or seven or forty days. Women stand in circle, eulogize the dead and beat their face and knees and cry in loud voice. Thus more the mourning and lamentation more it is commendable. In case, mourning in such a style is absent, mourners are made the target of raproachment. One should bear in mind that crying loudly and mourning in such a style is quite unlawful. They also cease to wear fine clothes, apply perfume and collyrium, attend marriage ceremony and remain confined to house; all these are unlawful acts. Only the widow is permitted to avoid adorning for four months and ten days. Relatives of the deceased may avoid adorniing for three days, but they are not permitted to sit in mourning for more than three days.

But the common practice goes that the widow cannot wear red and coloured clothes, *nath* (a large nose ring worn by women) and other ornaments. Friends and relatives have it a duty to console the widow and her relatives and ask them to keep patience. But the general practice is contrary to this.

Allah, the Almighty says in Surah Baqarah of the Holy Qur'an:

يَاأَيُّهَا الَّذِيْنَ آمَنُوْا اسْتَعِيْنُوْا بِالصَّبْرِ وَالصَّلٰوةِ ط اِنَّ اللّٰهَ مَعَ الصَّابِرِيْنَ :

"O ye who believe! seek help with patient Perserverance and Prayer· for God is with those who patiently perservere."
(Q. 2:153)

When a relative is dead or any calamity befalls, the person concerned is embarrassed and cries out in frustration and impatience. Hence, Allah, the Almighty says that one should seek help with patience and perseverance and rely on Allah, for Allah is with those who keep patience. Thus the Believers should seek forebearance and firmness with prayer and patience.

Allah, the Almighty says in Surah Baqarah of the Holy Qur'an:

وَبَشِّرِ الصَّابِرِيْنَ.الَّذِيْنَ اِذَا اَصَابَتْهُمْ مُّصِيْبَةٌ قَالُوْا اِنَّا لِلّٰهِ وَاِنَّا اِلَيْهِ رَاجِعُوْن اُولٰئِكَ عَلَيْهِمْ صَلَوَاتٌ مِّنْ رَّبِّهِمْ وَرَحْمَةٌ وَاُولٰئِكَ هُمُ الْمُهْتَدُوْنَ :

"........give glad tidings to those who patiently persevere, ...who say, when afflicted with calamity: "To Allah we belong, and to Him is our return."
(Q. 2: 155-157).

That is, Allah, the Almighty appreciates those who claim to be the property of Allah Who created them, have unchallenged authority on them and they have to go back to Him. Allah tells the Messenger to give glad tidings of Allah's Favour and Mercy to those who keep patience in calamity without complaining against it

Allah, the Almighty says in Surah Al-Hadid of the Holy Qur'an:

مَا اَصَابَ مِن مُّصِيبَةٍ فِى الاَرضِ وَلاَ فِى اَنفُسِكُم اِلاَّ فِى كِتٰبٍ مِّن قَبلِ اَن نَّبرَأَهَا اِنَّ ذٰلِكَ عَلىَ اللهِ يَسِيرٌ لِكَيلاَ تَأسَوا عَلٰى مَا فَاتَكُم وَلاَتَفرَحُوا بِمَا آتَاكُم وَاللهُ لاَ يُحِبُّ كُلَّ مُختَالٍ فَخُورٍ :

"No misfortune can happen on earth or in your souls but is recorded in a Book before We bring it into existence: that is truly easy for Allah. In order that ye may not despair over matters that pass you by, nor exult over favours bestowed upon you. For Allah loveth not any vainglorious boaster."

(Q. 57:22-23).

That is, Allah, the Almighty has already recorded all the weal and woes, comforts and sufferings and all the happenings with a man before his birth and the decrees of fate cannot be avoided. He should neither express sorrow over calamities nor be proud of Favours conferred upon by Allah, the Almighty. Thus, if one dies, it should be considered that he has lived his life in full. Moreover, beating and crying cannot restore his life. Allah, the Almighty does not like the proud and haughty.

Abu Dawud reports from Abu Sa'eed Khudri (may Allah be pleased with him):

لعن رسول الله صلى الله عليه وسلم النآئحة والمستمعة

"The Messenger of Allah (peace and blessings of Allah be upon him) cursed the woman who cries and those who hear."

This *hadith* makes it clear that both the criers and the listeners are cursed.

Bukhari and Muslim report from Abdullah bin Umar (may Allah be pleased with him) that the Messenger of Allah (peace and blessings of Allah be upon him) said:

الا تسمعون ان الله لا يعذب بدمع العين ولابحزن القلب ولكن يعذب بهذا واشار الى لسانه او يرحم وان الميت ليعذب ببكاء اهله عليه :

"Don't you listen that Allah, the Almighty doesn't punish for shedding tears nor at the grief of heart, but of course, for complaining against Allah or for crying over the dead."

That is, to mourn at heart or to shed tears over the death of anyone is but natural, hence it does not invite anger and punishment from Allah, the Almighty. But if he shows patience and looks for the Mercy of Allah, he is shown Mercy and Favour from Him.

Bukhari and Muslim report from Abdullah bin Mas'ud (may Allah be pleased with him) that the Messenger of Allah (peace and blessings of Allah be upon him) said:

ليس منا من ضرب الخدود وشق الجيوب ودعى بدعوى الجاهلية :

"One who slaps his face, tears his garment to pieces and cries loudly does not belong to my group."

Before the advent of the Messenger of Allah (peace and blessings of Allah be upon him) it was the Age of Ignorance and it was a custom with the pagans that their women would cry loudly over the dead and eulogize his virtues.

Bukhari and Muslim report from Abu Barda (may Allah be pleased with him) that the Holy Prophet (peace and blessings of

Allah be upon him) said:

انا برءى ممن حلق وصلق وخرق :

"I am disgusted at the one who tears his hairs, and garment and cries loudly".

That is, one who tears his hair and clothes and cries loudly is one with whom the Messenger is displeased and one who invites displeasure of the Messenger must know whether he is a Muslim or not.

Muslim reports from Abu Malik Ash'ari (may Allah be pleased with him) that the Messenger of Allah (peace and blessings of Allah be upon him) said:

اربع فى امتى من امر الجاهلية لا يتركون هن فذكر منها النياحة وقال النائحة اذا لم تتب قبل موتها تقام يوم القيامة و عليها سربال من قطرانٍ ودرع من جربٍ :

"Four things in my *ummah* belong to unbelief and people do not refrain from them; crying loudly is one of them."

The Messenger added:

"If such a woman did not cease to do so before her death, she will be raised on the Day of Resurrection wearing dress of 'cheeda' oil and 'Orhni' (small sheet) of scabies."

That is, the woman who mourns the dead loudly, if dies unrepented, she will be raised on the Doomsday wearing the garment of 'cheeda' oil and 'Orhni' (smaller sheet worn by women) of scabies so that she gets burnt deeply and severely.

Bukhari and Muslim report Mhugira bin Shuba (may Allah be pleased with him) that the Messenger of Allah (peace and blessings of Allah be upon him) said·

من نيح عليه يعذب بما نيح عليه يوم القيامة :

> "The dead person who is lamented loudly will be punished on the Day of Judgment of what was narrated about him."

That is, the dead person on whom women cry loudly will be punished according to the words used for him.

Tirmidhi reports from Abu Musa (may Allah be pleased with him) that the Messenger of Allah (peace and blessings of Allah be upon him) said:

ما من ميتٍ يموتُ فيقوم باكيهم فيقوّل واجبلاه واسيداه ونحو ذالك الا وكل الله به ملكين يكهزانه ويقولان ا هكذا كنت :

> "The dead person on whom somebody cries loudly saying, 'O my mountain; o my Chief etc.' will find two angels appointed by Allah, the Almighty to give blows on his breast saying, 'Had you been so?"

That is, the angels punish the dead person at the same words used by the mourner for him. Thus, every Muslim should save the dead person from the torments, and keep all away from beating the breast and cry loudly over the body.

Imam Ahmad reports from Ibn Abbas (may Allah be pleased with him):

> "When the women cried loudly over the dead body of the daughter of the Messenger of Allah (peace and blessings of Allah be upon him), Hadrat Umar (may Allah be pleased with him) started lashing at them. The Messenger stopped Umar with his hands and observed:
>
> "Save yourselves from Satanic voice."

Thereafter he added:

انه مهما كان من العين ومن القلب فمن اللـه عزوجـل ومـن الرحمـة وماكـان مـن اليـد ومـن اللسـان فمـن الشيطان :

"What come out of eyes and heart, they are from Allah's Mercy and what result from hands and tongue are from Satan."

That is, if the heart is grieved and tears come out of one's eyes, there is no harm because he or she is helpless in this matter. Hence it is supposed to be Mercy on the part of Allah, the Exalted. But beating the breast, narrating about the dead and crying loudly are all from Satan. Hence every Muslim man and woman should desist from such acts displeasing to Allah. Such persons seem to be entrapped by Satan and hence they should be beaten if possible.

Imam Ahmad and Ibn Majah report from Ibn Umar (may Allah be pleased with him):

نهى رسول الله صلى الله عليه وسلم ان تتبـع جنـازة معها دانة :

"The Messenger of Allah (peace and blessings of Allah be upon him) has forbidden from accompanying the funeral procession of such a body which has mourning women with it."

That is, it is forbidden to accompany the funeral procession carrying women beating their breasts and crying loudly and to attend the feast playing song, dance and music.

Tabarani reports that the Messenger of Allah (peace and blessings of Allah be upon him) said:

ان هذاه النوائح يجعلن يوم القيامـة صفيين فـى جهنـم

صف عن يمينهم وصف عن يسارهم فينحن على اهل
النار كما يتنح الكلاب :

"Women beating their breasts will be divided into two tows in Hell......one on the right and another on the left, mourning the Hellish persons like the barking dogs."

That is, these women will go to Hell barking like dogs and beating their breasts as they used to beat and cry over the dead bodies.

Bukhari reports:

لما مات الحسن بن الحسن بن عليٍ ضربت امرأته
القبة على قبره سنة ثم رفعت فسمعت صالحا يقول
الاهل وجدوا ما فقدوا فاجابه آخر بل يئسوا فانقلبوا

"When Hasan, the grandson of Hadrat Ali (may Allah be pleased with him) died, his wife erected a tent near his grave for the whole year. During this period a voice sounded:

"Did you get what you had lost?"

Another voice replied:

"She went back getting nothing."

That is, a voice was sounded from the unseen that she could not get back one for whom she kept sitting for the whole year. At last she returned hopeless and frustrated. The dead cannot be restored to life even if one passes one thousand years waiting and lamenting for him. Hence, it is better to sit in prayer than to sit in mourning.

Lady Zainab (may Allah be pleased with her) reports:

> "I called at Lady Umme Habiba (may Allah be pleased with her) when her father Abu Sufyan passed away. She asked for perfume having yellowish colour of saffron or something else. She rubbed it on her face saying:
>
> "By Allah I need no perfume but I have heard the Messenger of Allah (peace and blessings of Allah be upon him) say: لا يحل

لامرأة تؤمن بالله واليوم الآخر ان تحد على ميتٍ

فوق ثلاثة ايامٍ الا على زوج اربعة اشهر وعشراً :

> 'It is not lawful for a woman who believes in Allah and the Day of Judgment to sit in mourning for a dead person more than three days except her husband for four months and ten days."

This *hadith* clarifies that to mourn anybody other than the husband more than three days is prohibited. It is not permitted for women to mourn the death of any relative other than husband for a long time and go without red and coloured garments, refrain from applying antimony, chewing betel, wearing bangles, using perfume, attending marriage ceremonies. All these practices are futile and nonsensical.

Imam Ahmad and Ibn Majah report from Imran bin Husain and Abu Hurairah (may Allah be pleased with them):

> "We went out alongwith the Messenger of Allah (peace and blessings of Allah be upon him) and joined a funeral procession. We found the people walking in their garments without sheets. Thereupon, the Messenger remarked:

الفعــل الجاهلية تاخذون او بصنيع الجاهلية تشبهون لقد
همـمـت ان ادعو عليكم دعــوة ترجعـون فــى غـير صور
كـم قــال فاخذوا ارديتهم و لم يعودوا لذالك :

> "Don't adopt rites of the people of *Jahiliah* or resemble it. I decided to curse you so that you would have been disfigured, but changed my mind because you covered yourselves with your sheets." ·

This *hadith* makes it clear that it is not permitted to uncover one's body or head or feet. Moreover, a Muslim is forbidden to follow the practice of the unbelievers to put off sheets while joining a funeral procession. Since some Muslims also imitated the Unbelievers out of ignorance, the Messenger of Allah (peace and blessings of Allah be upon him) grew so much angry with them that he decided to curse them. But he changed his mind because those Muslims corrected their mistake then and there. Hence the Muslim should refrain from adopting the rites and practices of the Unbelievers.

Seventh Practice

Excessive Decoration

اِفْـرَاطُ فِی التّزیین هــــ

Adoring oneself with fine and precious clothes or the house with delicious food and costly utensils or ride on better mount is not unlawful provided it is done with permissible income. However, to do so out of pride and arrogance is undesirable and unlawful. Moreover, if such exercises show no amount of pride and arrogance but resemble those of innovators and transgressers, they are forbidden. These days people do all these out of a desire to excel others and achieve name and fame in the community. This undue desire has erased the difference between lawful and unlawful. Moreover, when the mind remains preoccupied with the thought of running after pomp and show, one keep way from divine feelings and practices.

Allah, the Almighty says in Surah Al-Imra'n of the Holy Qur'an:

زُيِّنَ لِلنَّاسِ حُبُّ الشَّهَوَاتِ مِنَ النِّسَآءِ وَالبَنِينَ وَالقَنَاطِيرِ

الْمُقَنطَرَةِ مِنَ الذَّهَبِ وَالفِضَّةِ وَالخَيلِ الْمُسَوَّمَةِ وَالاَنعَامِ وَالحَرثِ ط ذَلِكَ مَتَاعُ الحَيَاةِ الدُّنيَا وَاللّٰهُ عِندَهُ حُسنُ الْمَآبِ :

> "Fair in the eyes of men is the love of things they covet: women and sons: heaped-up hoards of gold and silver; horses branded (for blood and excellence); and (wealth of) cattle and well-tilled land. Such are the possessions of this world's life; but with Allah is the best of the goals (to return to)."
>
> (Q. 3:14).

That is, people hanker after women, sons, a lot of money, horses, cattle, camels, goats and sheep, land etc. day in and day out and consider these commodities the source of respect in society. They build towering houses, elegantly designed and decorated with the latest items of luxuries. They pass a greater part of their precious life in collecting money and items of luxuries and depart from this mortal world empty-handed taking with them only the displeasure of Allah, the Exalted. They should, rather strive for Pleasure and Favour of Allah more and more. This is the real purpose of life.

Allah, the Almighty says in Surah Yunus of the Holy Qur'an:

اِنَّمَا مَثَلُ الحَيَاةِ الدُّنيَا كَمَآءٍ اَنزَلنَاهُ مِنَ السَّمَآءِ فَاختَلَطَ بِهِ نَبَاتُ الاَرضِ مِمَّا يَاكُلُ النَّاسُ وَالاَنعَامُ ط حَتّٰى اِذَا اَخَذَتِ الاَرضُ زُخرُفَهَا وَازَّيَّنَت وَظَنَّ اَهلُهَا اَنَّهُم قَادِرُونَ عَلَيهَا اَتَاهَا اَمرُنَا لَيلاً اَو نَهَاراً فَجَعَلنَهَا حَصِيداً كَاَن لَم تَغنَ بِالاَمسِ ط كَذٰلِكَ نُفَصِّلُ الآيَاتِ لِقَومٍ يَتَفَكَّرُونَ :

"The likeness of the life of the Present is as the rain which We send down from the skies: By its mingling arises the producing of the earth, which provides food for men and animals: (it grows) till the earth is clad with its golden ornaments and is decked out (in beauty): the people to whom it belongs think they have all powers of disposal over it: there reaches it Our command by night or by day; and We make it like a harvest clean-mown, as if it had not flourished only the day before! Thus do We explain the Signs in detail for those who reflect."

(Q. 10:24).

That is, as rain falls on the dry land and fields grow green and food for men and animals. Those green fields add to the beauty of earth which looks adored. Farmers also look happy. But all of a sudden an army invades and plunders the harvests or a storm uproots it in no time or the burning sun makes the fields dry.

That is also the condition of human life on earth. A man comes to life and flourishes but all of a sudden he passes away by the Command of Allah, the Exalted and he disappears as if he had never born. All the physicians put together cannot keep him alive. All the treasures of life cannot save his life. Thus all sorts of decorations and adorations, pomp and luxuries, and worldly comforts and riches are all worthless and unwise.

Allah, the Almighty says in Surah Az-zukhruf of the Holy Qur'an:

وَلَولاَ اَن يَّكُونَ النَّاسُ اُمَّةً وَّاحِدَةً لَّجَعَلنَا لِمَن يَّكفُرُ
بِالرَّحمٰنِ لِبُيُوتِهِم سُقُفاً مِّن فِضَّةٍ وَّمَعَارِجَ عَلَيهَا يَظهَرُونَ
وَلِبُيُوتِهِم اَبوَاباً وَسُرُراً عَلَيهَا يَتَّكِئُونَ وَزُخرُفاً ط وَ اِن كُلُّ
ذٰلِكَ لَمَّا مَتَاعُ الحَيَاةِ الدُّنيَا وَالاٰخِرَةُ عِندَ رَبِّكَ لِلمُتَّقِينَ :

> "And were it not that (all) men might become one community we would provide, for everyone that blasphemes against The Most Gracious, silver roofs for their houses, and (silver) stair- ways on which to go up, and (silver) doors to their houses, and couches (of silver) on which they could recline, and also adornments of gold. But all this was nothing but enjoyment of the present life: the Hereafter, in the sight of thy Lord, is for the Righteous."
> (Q. 43: 33-35).

That is, the unbelievers roll in luxuries in this world without thinking that they will be severely punished in the Hereafter. But some Muslim follow the course of the Unbelievers because of their material advancements and comforts. But, however, their material advancements also has a certain limit otherwise they had silver roofs of their houses and stair- ways also of silver, shining white and golden gates. But all these luxuries are limited to this mortal world. If the Unbeliever fail to understand this bitter reality of life, the Muslim should know it well and act accordingly.

Abu Dawud reports from Abu Umama (may Allah be pleased with him) that the Messenger of Allah (peace and blessings of Allah be upon him) said:

الا تسمعون الا تسمعون ان البـذازة مـن الايمان :

> "Listen! wearing old clothes and avoid excessive adornment is the matter of Faith, and to wear old clothes and refrain from excessive consist of the acts of Faith."

That is, one who has a desire for the Blessings and Favours of Allah, the Almighty, in the Hereafter and cares the least for worldly luxuries, is the most successful.

Abu Dawud reports from Suwaid bin Wahb (may Allah be pleased with him) that one of the Companions of the Messenger would say after having heard from the Messenger of Allah (peace and blessings of Allah be upon him) say:

من ترك لبس ثوب
جمالٍ تواضعاً كساه الله حلة الكرامة :

"One who abandons wearing decorative clothes out of humility, Allah will make him wear respectable dress."

Imam Ahamd, Nasa'i and Ibn Majah report from Amr bin Shu'aib that his father would say that the Messenger of Allah (peace and blessings of Allah be upon him) said:

كلوا واشربوا وتصدقوا والبسوا ما لم يخالط
اسراف ولا مخيلة :

"Eat, drink, dress and give charity to the extent that you don't indulge in extravagance and pride."

That is, eating, drinking and giving charity must also be within a certain limit and with permitted source of income, all these acts are wrong.

Abu Dawud reports from Abdullah bin Buraida (may Allah be pleased with him) that Fudala bin Ubaid was told by someone why he appeared with unruly hairs?

ان رسول
الله صلى الله عليه وسلم نهنا عن كثير من الارفاة

"The Messenger of Allah (peace and blessings of Allah be upon him) has forbidden from various superficial exercises," he replied.

"Why are you bare-footed?" he asked.

"The Messenger of Allah (peace and blessings of Allah be upon him) has said:

يامرنا ان نحتفى احيانا :

"We would sometimes remain bare-footed." he replied.

The Messenger of Allah (peace and blessings of Allah be upon him) has laid emphasis on plain living in spite of being well-to-do. Formalities may be avoided at times.

Imam Ahmad and Ibn Majah report from Lady Safina that Lady Fatima (may Allah be pleased with her) invited the Messenger of Allah (peace and blessings of Allah be upon him) on feast. The Messenger called at Fatima and stopped at the door putting his both hands on two doors of the houses and saw a curtain hung at the corner of her house. Thereafter he went back followed by Fatima asking the reason of his going back." Thereupon the Messenger said:

انـه ليس لى او لنبى ان يدخل بيتا مزوقا :

'It does not behove of me or any other Prophet that he takes a seat in a decorated house.'

This *hadith* clarifies that it is not worthy of a Prophet to enter a house having luxurious items. Hence the Muslims should also follow their Prophet.

Tirmidhi reports from Lady Aisha (may Allah be pleased with her) that the Messenger of Allah (peace and blessings of Allah be upon him) said:

يا عائشة ان اردت اللحوق فيكفيك من الدنيا كزاد الراكب وإياك ومجالسة الاغنياء ولا تستخلقى ثوبا حتى ترقعيه :

"O Aisha, if you want to keep company with me, it is sufficient for you to take as much as from the provisions of this world as a riding traveller and save yourself from the company of the wealthy persons and think not your clothes old unless it requires patches."

That is, the garments should be taken as old only when it is patched. Similarly, the Messenger advised Aisha (may Allah be pleased with her) not to have contacts with the wealthy persons; she should consume as little from the earthly provisions as the mounting travellers have because of their running. The Messenger put these as conditions for her company with the Messenger. Adorement has a resemblance with the style of life of Unbelievers.

Abu Dawud and Nasa'i report from Abi Raihana (may Allah be pleased with her) that the Messenger of Allah (peace and blessings of Allah be upon him) has forbidden ten things:

عن الوشر والوشم النتف وعن مكامعة الرجل الرجل
بغير شعار وعن مكامعة المرأة المرأة بغير شعار
وان يجعل الرجل فى اسفل ثيابه حريرا مثل الاعاجم
او يجعل على منكبيه حريرا مثل الاعاجم وعن النهى
وعن ركوب النمور ولبوس الخاتم الا لذى سلطان :

"Filing of teeth by women; pulling out hairs of her beard or forehead; sleeping of two males together in a nude state; sleeping of two females together without dress; males stitching silken piece under the garment like the Persians; stitching of silken piece on the shoulders like the Persians; wearing of the skin of leopard; and from wearing ring except for the ruler."

Some people use silken piece on the shoulders for displaying elegance; some of them skin of leopard as a cover for riding; pull out hairs of the beard and forehead, filing of teeth in order to beautify them; sleeping of two nude males or females together etc. are strongly forbidden.

Abu Dawud and Nasa'i report from Ibn Mas'ud (may Allah be pleased with him) that the Messenger of Allah (peace and blessings of Allah be upon him) disliked

يكره الصفرة يعنـــى الخلـوق وتغـير الشيب وجر الازار والتختم بالذهب والتبرج بالزينة بغـير محلها :

> "applying yellow *sâlarga* by males, colouring the white hairs, hanging of trouser-string, wearing of gold ring, adoring of women for showing others."

Arabs have a practice of preparing yellow *salarga* by collecting perfumes of saffron etc. Hence applying of *salarga* or blackening of white hair, hanging of trouser-string up to knees, wearing of gold ring, adoring of women to show other men etc. were something highly disliked by the Messenger of Allah (peace and blessings of Allah be upon him). Hence all the Muslims should keep away from all these exercises. Moreover, some of these practices resemble those of the Unbelievers, hence the Muslims should desist from these acts. However, the question of resemblance with the Unbelievers does not arise in eating and drinking, sleeping, awakening, marrying etc.

Imam Ahmad and Abu Dawud report from Ibn Umar (may Allah be pleased with him) that the Messenger of Allah (peace and blessings of Allah be upon him) said:

من تشبه بقوم فهو منهم

"One who resembles any other community is one of them."

Thus, one who resembles any other nation or community, whether they are Christians, Jews, Magi, Hindus, males or females, will be bracketed with them.

Tirmidhi reports from Rukana that the Messenger of Allah (peace and blessings of Allah be upon him) said:

فرق ما بيننا وبين المشركين العمائم على القلانس :

"The difference between the polytheists and ourselves lies in the fact that we tie our turbans on caps."

That is, the polytheists of Makkah would wear turban without cap below it. It means the Muslims should make difference with Unbelievers in dress also.

Bukhari and Muslim report from Abu Hurairah (may Allah be pleased with him) that the Messenger of Islam (peace and blessings of Allah be upon him) said:

ان اليهود والنصارى لا يصبغون فخالفوهم :

"The Jews and the Christians do not colour their beards hence you do it to oppose them."

The *hadith* tells that the Muslim should oppose the Unbelievers in fashion and appearance also. The sum and substance of the three *hadiths* is that the Muslims should avoid resemblance with the Unbelievers in all walks of life. Thus, celebrating Holi and Diwali, distributing sweetmeats on these occasions, visiting various fairs of the non-Muslims, paying regards to cow, Ganges, *pepal* trees etc., avoiding beef, wearing *dhotis*, thinking cowdung clean, entitling themselves Raja, Kunwar, Thakur, etc., making boys wear ornaments, decorating houses profusely, bowing to salute someone, displaying magnificence and splendour, bowing before anyone to pay regards. All these acts resemble those of non-Muslims and hence must be totally discarded.

Tirmidhi and Nasa'i report from Abu Musa (may Allah be pleased with him) that the Messenger of Allah (peace and blessings of Allah be upon him) said:

إحل الذهب والحرير للاناث من امتى وحرم على ذكورها:

"Permitted are gold and silk to the women and prohibited to the men of my *ummah*."

Bukhari and Muslim report from Ali (may Allah be pleased with him)

Someone sent a dress to the Messenger of Allah (peace and blessings of Allah be upon him) with silken stripes. He (the Messenger) sent it to me and I appeared before him in the same dress.

I found sign of anger on his face, and he remarked:

انى لم ابعث بها اليك لتلبسها انما بعثت بها اليك لتشققها خمرا بين النساء :

"I had not sent that to you for wearing but for tearing it into pieces of *'Orhni'* (a smaller sheet used by a girl to cover her head) for women and not to be worn by you."

In spite of the fact that the cloth was not pure silk but had silken stripes only and hence Hadrat Ali (may Allah be pleased with him) had worn it, the Messenger of Islam (peace and blessings of Allah be upon him) grew angry.

Bukhari and Muslim report from Umar (may Allah be pleased with him)

نهى عن لبس الحرير الا هكذا ورفع رسول الله

صلى الله عليه وسلم اصبعيه الوسطى والسبابة وضمهما :

The Messenger of Allah (peace and blessings of Allah be upon him) forbade from wearing silken dress but this much, he pointed out by joining two middle fingers.

انما يلبس الحرير فى الدنيا من لا خلاق له فى الآخرة

"That very person will wear silk in this world who has nothing for him in the Hereafter."

That is, the male who wears silk in this world will remain deprived of the blessings in the Hereafter. It means that a male is forbidden to use silk, otherwise he will get nothing in the Hereafter.

Tirmidhi and Abu Dawud report from Abdullah bin Umar (may Allah be pleased with him):

مر رجل وعليه ثوبان احمران فسلم على النبى صلى الله عليه وسلم فلم يرد عليه :

"Once a certain person passed by the Messenger of Allah (peace and blessings of Allah be upon him) in red garments and saluted him; but the Messenger did not make any reply."

This *hadith* tells that wearing of red clothes for a man is so much prohibited for a man that the Messenger of Allah (peace and blessings of Allah be upon him) did not respond to the salutation of the man in red dress. It means responding to the salutation of a transgresser is not valid so that he correct his manners.

Bukhari and Muslim report from Lady Aisha (may Allah be pleased with her):

"I purchased a small carpet with pictures printed on it. When the Messenger of Allah (peace and blessings of Allah be upon him) saw it he kept standing at the door and did not enter the house. Then I read expression of his displeasure over his face and said:

"I repent before Allah and His Messenger and want to know what sin have I committed?"

Thereupon the Messenger (peace and blessings of Allah be upon him) asked:

'What is this small carpet?'

'I have bought this for you to sit on and use it as a pillow' I replied.

Thereupon, the Messenger of Allah (peace and blessings of Allah be upon him) said:

ان اصحاب هذه الصور

يعذبون يوم القيامة و يقال لهم احيو ما خلقتم وقال

ان البيت الذى فيه الصور لاتدخل الملائكة

"Certainly those having pictures will be punished; they will be asked to put life into these pictures;" and he further said: 'The house having picture does not have entry of the angels."

This *hadith* tells that one should not have pictures in one's house even for the sake of decoration. One should also avoid to be in a house where pictures are found.

Tirmidhi reports from Abu Hurairah (may Allah be pleased with him) that the Messenger of Allah (peace and blessings of Allah be upon him) said:

اتانى جبرئيل قال اتيتك البارحة فلم يمنعنى ان اكون

دخلت الا انه كان على الباب تماثيل وكان في البيت كلبٌ فمر براسِ التماثيل التى على باب البيت فيقطع فيصير كهيئة الشجرة ومر بالستر فليقطع فليجعل وسادتين منبوذتين توطان ومر بالكلب فليخرج ففعل رسول الله صلى الله عليه وسلم وقال رسول الله صلى الله عليه وسلم يخرج عنق من النار يوم القيامة لها عينان تبصران واذنان تسمعان ولسانٌ ينطق يقول انى وكلت بثلا ثةٍ بكل جبارٍ عنيد وكل من دعا معُ الله الها آخر وبالمصورين :

> "Jibril came to me and said: I had come to you yesterday but could not enter your house due to pictures at the door, printed curtain and a dog inside your house and hence ask to remove these pictures except those of tree etc. and ask to tear the printed curtain into pillow covers and ask the dog to go off." Thus the Messenger did accordingly and added:
>
> "A long neck will come out of Hell on the Doomsday with two eyes looking, two ears hearing and a long tongue speaking, and will say that it is appointed on three persons: on every proud and arrogant person, on one who seeks partner to Allah and on the picture-makers."

This *hadith* shows that pictures of trees, those trampled upon under feet and those on pillow covers etc. which do not look prominent are permitted. But pictures for the purpose of decoration and taming of dogs will be caught in the Fire of Hell.

Bukhari and Muslim report from Ibn Umar (may Allah be pleased with him) that the Messenger of Allah (peace and blessings of Allah be upon him) said:

من جر ثوبه خيلاء لم ينظر الله اليه يوم القيامة :

> "One who hangs down his garment with pride will not have the look of Allah towards him on the Day of Judgment."

This *hadith* makes it clear that if one hangs his dress down the knees for the sake of style is prohibited and Allah will not look towards him on the Day of Resurrection.

Bukhari reports from Abu Hurairah (may Allah be pleased with him) that the Messenger of Allah (peace and blessings of Allah be upon him) said:

مال اسفل من الكعبين من الازار فى النار :

> "The trousers which hang down the knees will go to Hell."

Abu Dawud, Nasa'i and Ibn Majah report from Abdullah ibn Umar (may Allah be pleased with him) that the Messenger of Allah (peace and blessings of Allah be upon him) said:

الاسبال فى الازار والقميص والعمامة من جر منها
شيئاً خيلاءلم ينظر الله اليه يوم القيامة :

> "It is forbidden to lower down garments like trousers, shirt and turban and one who lowers them out of pride will lose the look of Allah towards him on the Day of Judgment."

Trousers, 'lungi' etc. up to half the shin, and above the ankle joint and the end of the turben up to half the back: lowering more of these garments is not acceptable to Allah.

Imam Ahmad, Abu Dawud and Ibn Majah report from Ibn Umar (may Allah be pleased with him) that the Messenger of Allah (peace and blessings of Allah be upon him) said:

من لبس ثوب شهرةٍ فى الدنيا البسه الله ثوب مذلةٍ يوم القيامة:

"One who wears dress for fame and distinction, Allah will make him wear dress of disgrace on the Day of Resurrection."

That is, one who wears a dress to achieve distinction; for instance, one wears green turban to be called 'Saiyyed', or black or green garments to be known as Haji, or shroud to be distinguished as 'fakir', are all prohibited.

Abu Dawud reports from Lady Aisha (may Allah be pleased with her):

> "Once Lady Asma'a (may Allah be pleased with her), the daughter of Hadrat Abu Bakr (may Allah be pleased with him) came to the Messenger of Allah (peace and blessings of Allah be upon him) wearing thin clothes. The Messenger turned his face from her and remarked:

يا اسمأ ان المرءة اذا بلغت المحيض لن يصلح ان يرى منها الا هذا و هذا واشار الى وجهه وكفيه :

> 'O' Asma'a when a girl attains her puberty, then it does not behove of her to show her body except her face and both the palms."

That is, a woman should refrain from wearing such a thin dress which makes her body visible save her face and hands up to the wrists. A woman, wearing thin dress, is, in fact, naked.

Imam Malik reports from Alqama bin Abi Alqama (may Allah be pleased with her) that she heard from her mother:

دخلت حفصة بنت عبد الرحمن على عائشة وعليها خمار رقيق فشقته عائشة وكستها خمارا كثيفا :

"Once Lady Hafsa, the daughter of Abdur Rahman came to Lady Aisha (may Allah be pleased with her) in thin *orhni*. The latter tore that off and gave her a thick one."

This *hadith* clarifies that a woman is not permitted to go in thin clothes even before other women what to speak of other relatives, particularly the relatives of the husband.

Muslim reports from Ibn Abbas (may Allah be pleased with him):

ان رسول الله صلى الله عليه وسلم رأى خاتما من ذهب فى يدِ رجل فنزعه فطرحه

"Once the Messenger of Allah (peace and blessings of Allah be upon him) saw a ring of gold in the finger of a person. He took it out of his finger and threw it away and remarked:

يعمد احدكم الى جمرة من نار فيجعلها فى يده

"One who wears it invites spark of fire towards him."

When the Messenger of Allah (peace and blessings of Allah be upon him) left, the person was asked to lift the ring and take some benefit from it.

Thereupon he said:

لا والله لا آخذه ابدا وقد طرحه رسول الله صلى الله عليه وسلم :

> "What has been thrown away by the Messenger of Allah (peace and blessings of Allah be upon him) will not be taken back by me."

As a perfect Muslim, he did not take back the ring which was once rejected and thrown away by the Messenger of Allah (peace and blessings of Allah be upon him) in spite of such an advice from the Companions.

Imam Ahmad, Abu Dawud and Nasa'i report from Ali (may Allah be pleased with him):

ان النبی صلی الله علیه وسلم اخذ حریرا فجعله فی یمینه واخذ ذهباً فجعله فی شماله

> "Once the Messenger of Allah (peace and blessings of Allah be upon him) took silk in his right hand and gold in the left and remarked:

ان هذین حرامٌ علی ذکور امتی :

> "Both of these are prohibited for the males of my *Ummah.*"

This *hadith* makes it clear that silk and gold are unlawful for the males, but these items may be taken in hand for some dealing.

Abu Dawud reports from Abu Hurairah (may Allah be pleased with him) that the Messenger of Islam (peace and blessings of Allah be upon him) said:

من احب ان یحلق حبیبه حلقةً من نار فلیحلقه حلقة من ذهب ومن احب ان یطوق حبیبه طوقاً من نار فلیطوقه طوقا من ذهب ومن احب ان یسور حبیبه سوارا من نار فیسوره سوارا من ذهب ولکن علیکم بالفضة فالعبوا بها :

> "One who makes his wife wear bangles of fire," he should make her wear bangles of gold; and one who wants to make his wife wear *hansli* (a collar worn round the neck as an ornament) of fire he should put into her neck collar of gold; and one who wants his wife to wear bracelets of fire should make his wife wear bracelets of gold; but, of course, silver is valid for you."

This *hadith* shows that wearing of earings, noserings, bangles, bracelets, collars of gold are unlawful for women. But other *ahadith* tell that ornaments of gold are valid for women, while the use of both gold and silver are prohibited for men. Hence, the above *hadith* is controversial.

Bukhari and Muslim report from Hudhaifa (may Allah be pleased with him):

نهانا رسول الله صلى
الله عليه وسلم ان نشرب فى آنية الفضة والذهب وان
نأكل فيها وعن لبس الحرير والديباح وان نجلس عليه :

> "The Messenger of Allah (peace and blessings of Allah be upon him) forbade us from eating and drinking in utensils of gold and silver and from wearing silk and 'diba' and from sitting on them."

'Diba' is a kind of silken cloth. Thus wearing of silken 'diba' and 'darai' clothes or making cushion from these cloths and eating and drinking in utensils of gold and silver are forbidden.

Darqutni reports from Ibn Umar (may Allah be pleased with him) that the Messenger of Allah (peace and blessings of Allah be upon him) said:

من شرب فى إناء ذهب او فضة او إناء فيه
شىء من ذالك فانما يجرجر فى بطنه نار جنهم : ،

"One who drinks from the utensils of gold or silver or utensils which have a portion of gold or silver, in fact, drinks the fire of Hell."

It is clear from this *hadith* that it is unlawful to eat and drink in the utensils of gold and silver or utensils have a portion thereof. Such persons will have to drink the fire of Hell.

Bukhari reports from Ibn Abbas (may Allah be pleased with him):

لعن النبى صلى الله

عليه وسلم المخنثين من الرجال والمترجلات من النسآء

"The Messenger of Allah (peace and blessings of Allah be upon him) cursed the males adopting the dress style of females and females that of males."

That is, the females who adopt the dressing style of males leaving their own and the males adopting that of females have been cursed by the Messenger of Allah (peace and blessings of Allah be upon him). In short, both men and women adopting each other's life style leaving their own are the accursed ones.

Bukhari reports from Ibn Abbas (may Allah be pleased with him) that the Messenger of Allah (peace and blessings of Allah be upon him) said:

لعن الله المتشبهين من الرجال بالنساء و

المتشبهات من النساء بالرجال :

"Allah has cursed the males adopting resemblance with the females and females with males."

That is, the males and females who resemble one another in dress, speech, walking and sitting have been cursed.

Abu Dawud reports Abu Hurairah (may Allah be pleased with

him):

اتـى النبـى صلـى الله عليه وسلم بمخنثٍ خضــب يديـه ورجليـه بالحنـاء فقـال رسول الله صلى الله عليه وسلم ما بال هذا قالوا يتشــبه بالنساء فامر به فنفى الى البقيع فقيل يـا رسـول الله الا تقتله فقال انى نهيت عن قتل المصلين :

> "They brought a eunuch before the Messenger of Islam (peace and blessings of Allah be upon him) who had coloured both his hands and feet with myrtle."

Thereupon, the Messenger of Allah (peace and blessings of Allah be upon him) remarked:

> "What type of person is he?"
>
> "He has coloured himself like women," they said.

Thereafter, the Messenger of Allah (peace and blessings of Allah be upon him) ordered to expel him and he was expelled towards Baqia. After that the people submitted:

> "Should we kill him?"
>
> "We have been forbidden to kill a person who says *salat* (prayer)", the Apostle remarked.

This *hadith* tells beyond doubt that the males should refrain from having least resemblance with the women. The eunuch had coloured his hands and feet with *henna* only but the Messenger of Allah (peace and blessings of Allah be upon him) asked his Companions to drive him out from the settlement.

Ibn Majah reports from Ali (may Allah be pleased with him):

كان بيدِ رسول الله صلى الله عليه وسلم قوس عربية فرأى رجلا بيده قوس فارسية قال ماهذا القها وعليكم بهذه واشباهها ورماح القنا فانها يؤيد الله لكم بها فى الدين ويمكن لكم فى البلاد :

> "The Messenger of Allah (peace and blessings of Allah be upon him) had an Arabic bow in his hand. Meanwhile, he saw a Persian bow in the hand of someone and asked him to throw that away and have one like that he had" and added, "Allah, the Almighty will help you in your religious matter and give peace in your country."

Persian bow is harder than the Arabian one. But the Messenger of Allah (peace and blessings of Allah be upon him) preferred the Arabic one and remarked that even that kind of bow would suffice by the Grace of Allah.

Abu Dawud reports from Abu Hurairah (may Allah be pleased with him) that the Messenger of Allah (peace and blessings of Allah be upon him) said:

تكون ابلٌ للشياطين اما ابلٌ فقد رأيتها يخرج احدكم بنجيباتٍ معه قد اسمنها فلا يعلوا بعيرا منها ويمر باخيه قد انقطع به فلا يحمله :

> "Some of the camels belong to Satan I have seen some persons going out with extra she-camels nourished especially for display without keeping them for riding purpose. They refrain from accommodating their tired brethren."

That is, those who breed camels for name and fame and take

them with themselves neither for riding nor allowing their Muslim brothers to ride even if they were terribly tired. Such camels, in fact, belong to Satans who become happy with such a display of haughtiness. The Muslim should desist from such a show which pleases Satans.

Muslim reports from Abu Hurairah (may Allah be pleased with him) that once the Messenger of Allah (peace and blessings of Allah be upon him) was asked about horses.

He said:

فالخيل ثلاثــة هــى لرجـل
وزر وهى لرجلِ ستر وهى لرجل اجر فاما التــى هــى لـه
وزر فرجل ربطها رياء وفخرا ونواء علــى اهـل الاسـلام
فهى له وزر واما التى هىله ستر فرجل ربطها فى سبيل
الله ثم لم ينس حق الله فى ظهورها ولا رقابها فهــى لـه
ستر و نا التى هى له اجـر فرجـل ربطهـا فـى سـبيل الله
لاهل الاسلام :

"Horses are of three types: One type of horses cover the defects and shortcomings; another type of horses carry reward for the keeper; and the third type carries lood of sins. That is, the first type assures others of the richness of the keeper; the second type is kept for fighting in the way of Allah; and the third type of horses are bred for show."

This *hadith* clarifies that it is unlawful to keep horses for pride and show. Keeping such a mount is an act of sin. However, keeping horse for fighting in the way of Allah is rewarding. These horses also provide proof of richness of the keeper.

Tirmidhi reports from Anas (may Allah be pleased with him) that the Messenger of Allah (peace and blessings of Allah be upon him) said:

النفقة كلها فى سبيل الله الا البنـاء ولا خـير فيه:

> "All that is spent on family with the intention of obtaining reward belongs to Allah except the construction of palatial house."

That is, if one spends on household affairs in order to fulfil the needs of his family members, servants and dependants he gets reward from Allah, the Almighty. However, to build house more spacious than what is needed carries no reward.

Abu Dawud reports from Anas (may Allah be pleased with him):

> "Once we accompained the Messenger of Allah (peace and blessings of Allah be upon him) to a place and in the way the Messenger saw a towering house and asked:
>
> "What is this?"
>
> "This house belongs to so and so from Ansar," the Companions replied. The Messenger kept silent. After some time the owner of the house came and saluted the Messenger, but he turned back his face from him. This exercise was repeated several times. At last the owner of the house read the expression of anger on the Messenger's face and communicated this to other Companions. The Companions informed him that the Messenger of Allah (peace and blessings of Allah be upon him) had gone out and seen your round house. The owner of the house rushed towards his house and razed it to the ground.
>
> After some days, the Messenger of Allah (peace and blessings of Allah be upon him) went out again and

passing by that house enquired:

"What happened to that round house?"

The Companions narrated to him all that happened. Thereupon the Messenger remarked:

ان كـل بنـاء وبـالٌ علـى صاحبـه الا مـا يغنيـه الا مالابد منه :

"Beware! Building big and round houses are sinful for the owner, but what is necessary."

That is, the house must be built according to needs. Thus, constructing bigger and more spacious houses than what are needed are quite displeasing to Allah and His Messenger. Hence, the Messenger of Allah (peace and blessings of Allah be upon him) turned his face from the person referred to above.

Abu Dawud reports from Abu Hurairah (may Allah be pleased with him) that the Messenger of Allah (peace and blessings of Allah be upon him) said:

تكـون بيـوت للشياطين قـال سـعيد لا اراهـا الا هــذه الاقفاص التى يستر الناس بالديباج :

"Some of the houses belong to Satans."

"I know not about such a house," Sa'eed submitted.

"Houses which are decorated with silken clothes."

Bukhari and Muslim report from Anas (may Allah be pleased with him):

نهى رسـول اللـه صلـى اللـه عليـه وسـلم ان يـتزعفر الرجل :

"The Messenger of Allah (peace and blessings of Allah be upon him) has forbidden males from applying saffron."

Tirmidhi and Nasa'i report from Yala bin Murrah (may Allah be pleased with him):

ان النبى صلى الله عليه وسلم رأى عليه خلوقا فقال
الك امرأةٌ قال لا قال اغلسه ثم اغسله ثم اغسله ثم لا
تعده :

"The Messenger of Allah (peace and blessings of Allah be upon him) saw me with *khluq* applied and said:

"It is perhaps from your wife's body."

I replied in the negative. Thereafter he asked me thrice to wash it, forbiding me to do it again.

Arab women used to apply perfumes made of certain elements. But it is not permitted to men. Hence the Messenger asked Yala thrice to wash it and asked not to repeat it in future.

Abu Dawud reports Abu Musa (may Allah be pleased with him) that the Messenger of Allah (peace and blessings of Allah be upon him) said:

لا يقبل الله صلوة رجلٍ فى جسده شىءٌ من خلوق

"Allah, the Almighty declines to accept *salat* (prayer) of one who applies *khluq* on his body."

Abu Dawud reports Ammar bin Yasser (may Allah be pleased with him) to have said:

قدمت على اهلى من سفر وقد تشققت يـذاى فخلقونـى بزعفران فغدوت على رسول الله صلـى الله عليـه وسلم فسلمت عليه فلم يرد على وقـال اذهـب فاغسـل هذا عنك :

"Once I came back home from journey with my hands injured. My family members applied *khluq* of saffron to my wounds. Next morning I appeared before the Messenger of Allah and said my Salam (salutation) to him. He responded and asked me to go and wash it."

Tirmidhi, Abu Dawud and Nasa'i report from Abu Hurairah (may Allah be pleased with him) that the Messenger of Allah (peace and blessings of Allah be upon him) said:

طيب الرجال ما ظهر ريحه وخفى لونه وطيب النساء ما ظهر لونه وخفى ريحه :

"The perfume of the males is one which has its smell open and colour hidden, while the perfume of females has its colour open and smell hidden"

That is, men are permitted to use such a perfume of which smell is felt but colour is not known, like *itr*; women should use such a perfume whose colour may be seen but not the smell, like saffron, sandal etc.

Muslim reports from Jabir (may Allah be pleased with him) that the Messenger of Allah (peace and blessings of Allah be upon him) said:

فـراش لـلـرجل وفـراش لامرأتـه والثـالث للضيـف والرابع للشيطان :

"One bed is for men, another for women, the third one is for the guest, but the fourth one is for Satan."

That is, one should have a bed for oneself, another for his wife, one more for the guest one may have beds according to the number of guests expected; and more than this belongs to Satan. It means extra beds kept for show and decoration belong to Satan.

Bukhari and Muslim report from Ibn Umar (may Allah be pleased with him) that the Holy Prophet (peace and blessings of Allah be upon him) said:

خالفوا المشركين اوفروا اللحى واحفوا الشوارب :

"Oppose the polytheists by keeping long beards and short moustaches."

Mostly Christians and Jews get their beards and moustaches shaved. Sikhs have beards and moustaches; while the Hindus shave their beards and keep moustaches. But the Muslims should desist from imitating the non-Muslims.

This *hadith* makes it clear that long beard is the symbol and sign of Islam. It is just like the uniform of a Muslim; and keeping beard less than one handful and growing moustache are symbols of unbelief.

Tirmidhi, Abu Dawud and Nasa'i report from Abdullah bin Mughaffal that :

نهى رسول الله صلى الله عليه وسلم عن الرجل الا غبا :

The Messenger of Allah (peace and blessings of Allah be upon him) forbade from combing hair but off and on.

That is, combing of hair daily by a male is not a necessity, it is just for the sake of adorement, hence it is forbidden. However, hair may be combed with the intervals of a day or two or in a week so that hair do not become unruly.

Abu Dawud reports from Amr bin Shu'aib (may Allah be pleased with him) that the Messenger of Allah (peace and blessings of Allah be upon him) said:

لا تنتفوا الشيب فانه نورا المسلم من شاب شيبة فى الاسلام كتب الله له بها حسنةٍ وكفر عنه بها خطيئةً ورفعه بها درجة :

> "Do not pull out white hair as they are 'light' of the Muslims. Anyone whose hair grows white in the state of Belief, has his virtue written, vice forgiven and class elevated by Allah, the Almighty."

It means white hair invites the Mercy of Allah. In case one hair of a Muslim grows white, he gets light from Allah; gets his forgiven and his position elevated.

Muslim reports from Ibn Umar (may Allah be pleased with him):

رأى صبيا قد حلق بعض راسه و ترك بعضه فنههم عن ذلك وقال احلقوا كله او اتركوا كله :

> "The Messenger of Allah (peace and blessings of Allah be upon him) saw a boy half-shaved. He forbade to do so and asked his guardians either to shave the whole head or not at all."

This *hadith* makes it clear that leaving some hair on head in any form or shape is a sinful act. Hence they should shave the head completely or leave it intact. It is more necessary for a grown-up Muslim.

Abu Dawud reports from Hajjaj bin Hesan that once he went to Anas bin Malik (may Allah be pleased with him) and transmitted from my sister Mughira:

"You were a boy those days and you had two locks of hair lying on the back. Anas (may Allah be pleased with him) caressed you with his hand on your head and uttered: 'May Allah bless you' and remarked:

احلقوا هذين او قصوهما فان هذا زى اليهود :

"Shave or cut both of them; because this is the style of the Jews."

This *hadith* clarifies that keeping locks of hair is the symbol of the Jews. Hence it is a duty entrusted to every Muslim to save his children from following the course of non-Muslims. And if one keeps such a type of hair out of ignorance, he must be corrected and his hair may either be shaved or cut.

Abu Dawud reports that a certain person among the Companions of the Messenger of Allah (peace and blessings of Allah be upon him) named Abi Hanzla narrates that the Messenger of Allah (peace and blessings of Allah be upon him) said:

نعم الرجل خريم الاسدى لولا طول جمته واسبال ازاره

"What a nice fellow is Khuraim Asadi save that his lock of hair and his trousers keep hanging."

When Khuraim heard about this remark he immediately took a knife and cut off his locks and raised his trousers up to shin.

That is, Khuraim Asadi, who was a Companion of the Messenger was declared a very nice fellow with two defects: he keeps long hair and hanging trousers. But as this remark was communicated to him, he put both right without loss of time.

Abu Dawud and Nasa'i report from Ibn Abbas (may Allah be pleased with him) that the Messenger of Allah (peace and blessings of Allah be upon him) said:

يكون قوما في آخر الزمان يخضبون بهذالسواد
كحواصل الحمام لايجدون رائحة الجنة :

> "At the end, there will be a community who will dye hair black shining like the breast of pigeon, but they will not have smell of Heaven."

This *hadith* clarifies that shining hair-dye must not be done because it is unlawful and one who does so will not even feel the smell of Heaven. One may, however, do it in order to look young while fighting in the way of Allah, the Almighty.

Bukhari and Muslim report from Ibn Umar (may Allah be pleased with him) that the Messenger of Allah (peace and blessings of Allah be upon him) said:

لعن الله الواصلة والمستوصلة والواشمة والمستوشمة

> "Allah cursed the woman who adds artificial hair to herself or to others; who tattoes herself and gets others tattood."

That is, Allah has cursed such a woman who adds artificial hair to her own and to others and get her own and that of other's body tattooed.

Bukhari and Muslim report from Hadrat Abdullah bin Mas'ud (may Allah be pleased with him) that the Messenger of Allah said:

لعن الله الواشمات والمستوشمات والمتنمصات
والمتفلجات للحسن المغيرات خلق الله :

> Allah has cursed the woman who gets her body tottooed, pull out hair of forehead for beautifying herself and make their teeth separate; these are the women who try to change the face created by Allah, the Almighty.

Some women have longer teeth so they file them to make them smaller and separate from each other for beauty's sake; others pull out the hair of their foreheads to make them wider; a few of them get themselves tattooed all these are accursed because they try to change the faces created by Allah, the Almighty.

Abu Dawud reports from Lady Aisha (may Allah be pleased with her)

لعن رسول الله صلى الله عليه وسلم الراجلة من النسآء

> The Messenger of Allah (peace and blessings of Allah be upon him) has cursed the woman who tries to become a man.

This *hadith* shows that the woman who dresses herself like a man, talks like him, and gives manly air is accursed.

وآخر دعوانا ان الحمد لله رب العالمين

الصلوة والسلام على رسوله محمد وآله وازواجه

واتباعه اجمعين

NINETY NINE NAMES OF ALLAH

Muhammad Iqbal Siddiqui

Brief notes on Asma-ul-Husna given in this book are aimed at explaining to the faithful the meaning and significance of individual attributes. This book on the subject is indeed a remarkable work in English.

Demy 8vo pp 178 3rd Edn. 1994

THE QUR'ANIC CONCEPT OF HISTORY

Mazharuddin Siddiqi

This book, the first of its kind on the subject in English, is an attempt to study the Qur'anic Concept of History.

It traces the reason for historical changes and the rise and fall of nations from the Islamic point of view. The author has drawn upon the views of the leading exegetes of the Qur'an to support his conclusions.

It also analyses the Quranic evaluation of the beliefs and moral values of other ancient peoples, like the Jews and the Christians, and comments on the modern philosophic concepts of Marx, Toynbee and Spengler.

Demy 8vo pp 246 1994
ISBN 81-7435-007-1

QUOTATIONS FROM THE HOLY BOOK

Obaid Qadri

The Holy Qur'an is the record of Divine revelations directly communicated to the Holy Prophet of Islam. The teachings of Islam are meant not for Muslims alone but for all mankind to follow. It is with this objective in view that this short collection of quotations has been prepared.

Demy 8vo pp vii+86 1994

ISLAMIC METHODOLOGY IN HISTORY

Fazlur Rahman

This book gives an outline of the historical evolution of the four basic principles of Islamic thought, namely the Qur'an, Sunnah, Ijtihad and Ijma. Its major value lies in the clarifications it has made on the meaning of the Sunnah. Far from the tendency to reject out of hand all that has happened since the original impulse of Islam in the life of the Prophet, it seeks to project what Muslims of various regions and times and sects, have made of that historical guidetime.

Demo8vo pp 218 1994
ISBN-7435-008-X

WOMEN IN ISLAM

M.Mazheruddin Siddiqi

In this book the author has ably tried to show how Islamic injunction in regard to the regulation of sex and family life can be adapted to modern conditions without departing from the principles underlying them.

Demy 8vo pp VIII + 160 3rd Edition 1993

ISLAM FORBIDS FREE MIXING OF MEN AND WOMEN

M.I. Siddiqi

In this book an attempt has been made to present the true position of the sexes in Islam and their mutual relationship and role in society. The concept of sex equality, the significance of purdah, the woman's role in the family, the modern woman's freedom movements and the problems created by promiscuous sex relations are fully treated in the light of the Holy Qur'an and Hadith.

Demy 8vo pp XII + 164 3rd Edition . 1992

ETIQUETTES OF ISLAMIC LIFE

Badr Azimabadi

Islam is not merely a faith but a way of life, a system ordering and organising human society. Islam is the natural and rational religion forall time to come. Its principles can and have met successfully challenges that may confront this world of ours. It is basically a religion of peace, equality and fratenity. It preaches love and brotherliness and way of life which is natural, simple and quite easy to follow. In fact the Islamic way of life alone can solve the world problems. This book sheds light on all these problems in their deatils.

Demo 8vo pp vii+172 1994

WHAT EVERY ONE SHOULD KNOW ABOUT ISLAM AND MUSLIM

Suzanne Haneef

Quite conforming to what the title declares this book by Suzanne Haneef, an American Muslim lady deals concisely but comprehensively with the fundementals of Islamic faith, beliefs and practices the rationale thereof. Written in confident style, flowing from the strength of conviction, in a fluent diction, it is a book which Muslims should give as present to their non-Muslim friends and earn *sawab*.

Demo8vo 1995

81-7435-030-6

LAWFUL EARNINGS IN ISLAM

S.M. Madani Abbasi

Corruption is rampant in every walk of life in the countries of the world. Consequently people are suffering from all sorts of maladies, ills, problems.

Crown 8vo pp. 52